Offenders and the Sexual Abu of Children

This book synthesizes the nascent but growing body of literature and research emerging on risk management and treatment of persons who sexually offend against children.

This volume demonstrates the need for change by placing current attitudes toward sexual offending in their sociocultural context and then discussing the impact of these attitudes. Rather than parse the needs of children who have been victimized from those who have offended, a model emerges that explains the interlocking dynamics of those who offend and those offended against. This book upends the convenient fiction that child sexual abuse can be reduced by locking away those who offend and then monitoring them upon release. Rather, the book addresses the need for ongoing interaction of the two populations; the reality that the two populations at times overlap; and the increasingly public question of how to manage those who acknowledge an attraction to children but deny an intent to act on that desire.

Providing alternative viewpoints, research avenues, and policy options that can accommodate a more realistic effort to reduce the risk of sexual abuse, it is a must read for all policymakers or professionals working with those who have offended or acknowledge attraction to children, alongside students and researchers from forensic psychology, clinical psychology, or criminology backgrounds.

James A. Cates is a board-certified clinical psychologist in northeast Indiana. He is adjunct faculty in the mental health counseling program at Purdue University—Fort Wayne, United States.

Offenders and the Sexual Abuse of Children

Interventions and Limitations

James A. Cates

Routledge
Taylor & Francis Group

NEW YORK AND LONDON

First published 2025
by Routledge
605 Third Avenue, New York, NY 10158

and by Routledge
4 Park Square, Milton Park, Abingdon, Oxon, OX14 4RN

Routledge is an imprint of the Taylor & Francis Group, an informa business

ISBN: 978-1-032-78415-1 (hbk)
ISBN: 978-1-032-78412-0 (pbk)
ISBN: 978-1-003-48775-3 (ebk)

DOI: 10.4324/9781003487753

Typeset in Optima
by Newgen Publishing UK

Contents

Contents

Preface

In this digital age, we are obsessed with numbers. That obsession is no surprise. We are bombarded with polls, scores, temperatures, distances—anything that can be calculated, someone will share online. Numbers provide a sense of order. A sense of precision in our lives when so much seems doubtful. Global warming. Nuclear proliferation. Fossil fuel depletion. These are amorphous, frightening concepts. But a number? A number can be understood. It offers security.

And perhaps that is why we are obsessed with counting those who sexually offend. At first, it may not seem like a counting obsession, but I encourage the reader to take a moment, go online, and review a sex offender registry. In that space, those who have been arrested and convicted of sexual crimes are listed. They are counted, and exposed to the community. Headshots, addresses, nature of the crime, and time on the registry are all there. At the click of a mouse, another miscreant signed, sealed, and delivered!

Unfortunately, as I will argue in this book, our sense of security is a false one. In reality, current efforts to contain the scourge of sexual offending do little to protect victims and potential victims, or to rehabilitate those who offend against them. Registries, incarceration, probation, and parole create a caste of pariahs, based on behavior. They do not, and cannot, stop the risk to children of sexual abuse.

Behind the numbers

My work with those who sexually offend, their victims, and survivors spans several decades. There are many tragic figures across that time. One stands out as I think of those whose stories compelled me to write this book.

He was incarcerated in a state prison, held in the mental health ward there. The "mental health ward" was reserved for those with serious mental illnesses, and those who were intellectually disabled (formerly called mentally retarded). My client fell in the latter category. I was retained to assess him and determine whether he had actually been competent to stand trial for his crime, a legal term that refers to whether he had actually been able to understand and participate in the court proceedings that led to his conviction. I met with him at the prison. Even if I rendered the opinion that he was not competent, such efforts to reverse court cases almost never succeed. These review processes are a rare and grudging opportunity to assure that justice was served.

For those who have never been in a prison, even the relatively low security facilities such as the one in which my client was held are cold and oppressive. Moving within them, staff and inmates alike may be pleasant, but emotions are superficial. The mood is cautious. Be wary of others. Friendships have limits. Trust is left to novitiates and fools.

I met with my client in a visitation room off the main dining area for his unit. In his early 60s, he appeared older. He had been convicted of sexual activity with a mid-adolescent female. He was friendly, open, and had little understanding of why he was imprisoned, or what he had done wrong. He explained, without hesitation and in detail, his relationship with the girl he loved. He had given the same, detailed explanation to the detective who investigated the complaint, waiving his rights to remain silent or have an attorney present. (When I questioned him about this, he failed to understand what these rights meant.) Psychological testing indicated his developmental level was close to the adolescent with whom he had been involved.

After completing my work with the client, I did a corroborative interview with a fellow prisoner who acted as his caretaker. In this prison, a reward system was in place for prisoners from the main facility. Those who were willing and qualified were allowed several hours a day during the week to provide one-to-one care to a prisoner in the mental health unit. My client's caretaker (a burglar serving a long-term sentence) had worked with him for almost a year. He described my client as a child in a man's body, who delighted in watching television and playing games, and had to be coerced into completing his expected chores. His greatest enjoyment was coloring pictures in coloring books. When he would complete one—and he was meticulous about doing so—he would tear it from the book and tape it on the wall of the dayroom. Doing so was a small ceremony, in that those inmates who happened to be nearby, as well as his caretaker, would stop, watch him hang his artwork, and applaud his latest effort. The attention never ceased to thrill him.

This was the sexual offender who placed the community at such risk he required remand to a prison. I did not find him competent, but the case was never returned to court for a hearing. A date had been scheduled, but before he could attend, the client died of a stroke.

This case is unusual, but not unique. He was a lost soul swept up in the rush to judgment. He would have required supervision in the community, but it is questionable whether his actions merited the pitiless barbed wire, cinderblock, cells, and fences that comprised his last home. And his story, and the stories of those like him, do not negate other stories of the horrific, callous sexual victimization of children. (Some of these cases are addressed in this book.) Global pronouncements about sexual offenses, however, capture any and all who engage in such behaviors, with no consideration for the range of circumstances that arise.

There is a wide breadth of accountability that those offending assume, from callous indifference to the deepest agony of remorse. Regardless of their response, the impact on their victims remains. Arguments for changes in the treatment of those who sexually offend cannot ignore the damage that sexual offending creates.

A voice for the victims

Some of those who read this book will prefer a narrative that argues for more effective ways to reduce the trauma of child sexual abuse. Other people will hope for advocacy for those who sexually offend—those they perceive as unjustly pilloried. And still others who read this book (or at least consider doing so) will be dismayed to find that those who sexually offend are not treated with contempt. Some readers may have been victimized themselves or may have experienced the victimization of a child, a close friend, or a family member. The pain inflicted is raw—a violation that continues to intrude. The wound is not easily, if ever, healed. So, frustration is a valid response.

Those who have been victimized by sexual abuse struggle to make sense of their experience. It is a part of the journey out of trauma, confusion, and pain. Too often, they see a choice between acknowledging the sheer helplessness of their situation or grasping some sense of control. Frequently they choose the latter, rationalizing that "if only" they had acted differently, the abuse would not have occurred. That desperate effort makes their plight even more painful. Rationalization is especially common if those who have been victimized and those perpetrating the abuse are members of the same family. It is easier to parse blame than to fault a parent, uncle or aunt, grandparent, cousin, or sibling for ripping apart the family. A mother must make the choice between blaming her much-loved brother and supporting her child. Parents face the reality that one sibling has sexually abused another. A daughter or son must confront the fact that their father has molested his grandchild. The turmoil a family faces is all too often known to the victims and reinforces the belief that they have contributed to this disruption. They become victimized not only by the abuse perpetrated against them, but also by the emotional chaos it leaves in its wake.

Unfortunately, they are not alone. Over the course of my career, I have seen and treated many clients who have been emotionally or physically violated. Not just those who were sexually abused, but children experiencing physical abuse and neglect; adults scarred by domestic violence, sexual assault, and violent attacks; and both children and adults ravaged by the trauma of war. But the process of healing includes finding a perspective for the tragic social and cultural events that were set in motion.

In stepping back and examining the sociocultural implications of the way we treat those who sexually offend, I do not dismiss the pain that has been inflicted. Nor do I suggest that such individuals should not be tasked with (or avoid) accountability. But I have seen cycles of abuse again and again. The recipients of physical abuse, which then leads to these victims becoming physical abusers. The impacts of drug and alcohol abuse, influencing those who later abuse drugs and alcohol. And the experience of sexual abuse creating those who sexually abuse or feel helpless in the face of intergenerational sexual abuse. This cycle does not explain all sexual abuse, but far too many of those who offend have been abused themselves. And the fallout of sexual abuse has created an inordinate amount of trauma across generational lines.

For those who are victims, those who offend, and for those who care deeply about both of them, hope is entangled with despair. How can they move forward from such tragic events? While this book speaks to the tangibles, the changes in mental health and the justice system that can make a difference, it seems important to understand the nature of despair, and the process of hope.

Hope and despair

Those who choose to work their way through the accompanying chapters have an investment in the topic that goes beyond a casual interest. As professionals, as students, as victims, as survivors, as those who struggle with the stigma, or as those who must come to terms with an offense in the family, the experience of despair strikes us all. How do we cling to hope?

In the past few years, I have been fortunate to supervise counselors as they complete their degrees, as they intern, and in the early stages of their professional lives as they work toward full licensure. Recently, I have been fortunate to work with a young counselor who is particularly dedicated and passionate as he moves forward in the field of mental health. In a supervision session, he struggled with a new client on his caseload. A female child, she faced a multitude of traumas in her brief life, including sexual abuse. And at this early age, she had learned the harsh lesson that sex could be power and could not be trusted with her younger siblings lest she wield that control. She readily acknowledged her own sexual acting out and seemed indifferent to the potential consequences.

This young counselor demands from himself hope for each client he sees, but in this unfeeling child, his expectations were challenged. Sitting with him and reviewing her case, sadness was etched on his face as he considered the grim prognosis. Outpatient counseling was the most viable option, but it might be too little, too late.

And yet, the next time we met and discussed her, his look was not sad, but determined. He recognized the difficulty of treating a child with such deep emotional wounds. He acknowledged the potential for failure. But he could not let the odds sway his commitment. He explained that, in his view, despair does not come from the tragedies that befall us. Despair comes because we had hoped otherwise. Hope strikes us down, and not the tragedy itself. He leaned closer, his eyes bright with the conviction of his beliefs, and said, "There is something absurd and foolish about hope. And yet, we can't help ourselves."

The views and the evidence shared in this book speak of the tragedies that befall us. We despair, because we had hoped otherwise. But as my protégé reminded me (flipping our roles, as I am thankful the young can so often do), we continue to hope. I would not have written this book if I did not have hope. Hope that we can protect children from the risk of sexual abuse. Hope that we can recognize the scope of the problem, and the need for courageous research. Hope that we can offer those who struggle against sexual acting out with children dignity, respect, and support as they become part of the effort to protect this vulnerable population. And hope that as a society, and as a culture, we can recognize that vilifying any group does nothing to create positive change, for them or for us.

Acknowledgments

There are so many people who were essential in the creation of this book, but given the topic they are best served remaining anonymous. Please know that even though their names do not appear, I am deeply grateful for the love and support that carried me through this project. Fortunately, I can thank several groups who contributed to this work, often without being aware.

All aspects of my career as a psychologist are satisfying, but working with students, interns, and early professionals never ceases to challenge and teach me. To those who have journeyed with me, thank you for sharing your time, your insights, and your excitement. Your curiosity and passion remind me that this effort is worth pursuing.

I have been incredibly fortunate with the mentors and professional peers who surround me. Their willingness to meet clients where they are, without judgment, has been modeled over and over again. To those who have walked with me and shown the need for respect and dignity for all, thank you.

I began working as a houseparent in a residential treatment center for emotionally disturbed children in 1977 and became a therapist in 1982. Across these years, the experience of serving others has been a gift. I learn as much from them as I am ever able to impart. To those whose lives have intersected with mine in the field of mental health, thank you for your shared time.

And there is a group of clients who make this book especially meaningful. For those I have met who sexually offended, so many of you have taught me more about integrity than you can possibly know. As I write these words, I hold five of you in particular esteem. Two are in prison. One is in jail, awaiting sentencing. One is home, recovering from the trauma of a prison sentence that should have been a psychiatric hospitalization. And yet another advocates zealously for the rights of those who struggle with the stigma of a sexual offense. Each of you has my humble appreciation. You have shown me what true courage is.

And I acknowledge a group that has been healing to me and so many millions of others. While I have never attended meetings, the principles of the 12 steps have been integral to my growth. Whether we struggle with an addiction or not, the recognition at some point that we are powerless, and the effort to change our lives to confront that truth is a formidable journey. To those who blazed that trail, my life is richer because of you.

1   Monsters under the bed

Postmodern culture and sexual offending

I am a psychologist, but mental health was not my original career path. I first attended college as a journalism major. A summer job, as houseparent in a treatment center for emotionally disturbed children, changed my focus. These were youth who had experienced horrendous neglect and abuse. I had found my calling and never turned back. In recent years, my service has included a role as a mental health expert in legal cases. I continue to encounter the outcomes of traumas, and it never ceases to be heartrending. I have worked with mothers who caused brain damage to their infants by shaking them. I have worked with fathers who beat their children, leaving ugly bruises and breaking bones. I have worked with parents who locked their children in bedrooms, closets, and basements for hours at a time, rather than take on their familial responsibilities. These are the next generations of the parents and caretakers of the children with whom I began my career.

Among these clients, no matter how many times I have engaged with the trauma of their lives, there are cases that have shocked, troubled, and unsettled me. I have drawn on years of professional development, a clinical perspective, and mindfulness to allow me to remain empathic, even in the face of blatant cruelty. Though it has not always been easy, I have found ways to remain compassionate, and to confront without demeaning. But the hardest cases? Those involve the sexual abuse of a child. These are the people with whom I find that my stores of empathy run low. Where I am tempted to ignore the reality that we are *all* capable of evil. Where I risk rejecting the client. Where I despair that healing is even remotely possible. My discomfort, at times, has been complicated by the pathos of knowing that the victimized son still loves his father. That the victimized sister still cares about her brother. And that they live in fear that their families will somehow dissolve because they had the courage to tell what happened to them.

We recoil at crimes of sexual abuse, with an almost instinctive response: separate the person offending from those they have hurt, imprison them, and register and monitor them upon their release. Yet the sexual abuse of children continues unabated. Much is missing from our understanding of risk and harm. And, as I explore the topic within these pages, this is because of our

DOI: 10.4324/9781003487753-1

stigmas and scruples about child sexual abuse. We need a different way of thinking about—and responding to—the sexual abuse of children. Our cultural narratives and interventions are insufficient to truly offer the protection we wish to provide.

A recent interaction reminded me that I am as susceptible to the culture in which I am immersed as those whom I am assessing. I was a court-appointed mental health professional, enjoined to render an opinion on the sanity of a defendant, a task I have undertaken hundreds of times throughout my career. The alleged crime occurred in a convenience store, and, in this age of video scrutiny, the violence had been captured from multiple angles. I made an arrangement with the prosecutor to view clips of what had transpired. Sitting in a conference room, we watched captured digital images as the defendant entered and glanced at items in the store. Then he pulled out a gun and shot three people. Two men, and one woman. No warning. No provocation. His marksmanship was impeccable. Despite a history of psychiatric hospitalizations, he had been allowed to own guns, and he regularly practiced shooting them. One victim dropped instantly, curled in a fetal position, dead. Four tightly spaced shots had pierced his back, one severing his aorta. The second victim was hit by four shots to the torso but began to slide away, pulling a terrified female with him. She was shot once in the arm. The gunman then ran from the store and fled in his car.

In my role as a psychologist, I could step back and consider the scene in an objective manner. Was this a man manifesting severe paranoia, meriting a legally sanctioned plea of insanity? Or was this a man who understood his intentions and could be found sane? I pondered the questions necessary for my next interview with the defendant as I drove away from that macabre display.

And then I began to consider the true horror that had played out. Those blood-spattered moments, taking place in a handful of time. A young man, doing nothing more ominous than reaching for a drink, died in a hail of bullets. Those who were wounded, and others who turned and watched in terror, were traumatized in a way that the glib use of this word cannot convey. And still, I could be detached and watch the events unfold, a professional observer caught up in the meaning behind the defendant's actions. My emotional response had been numbed by years of violence projected on the news, in video games, in movies, and on television.

Could I, my thoughts ran, be so detached and objective if this were a sexual offense? Could I sit with such calmness and watch a child be sexually abused? No. I would not have enough ingrained detachment to observe such an event without revulsion. Child sexual abuse remains a jarring and deeply disturbing emotional experience. And I am not alone in this opinion. Consider how the aftermath of this crime, versus the sexual abuse of a child, played out.

The defendant's actions in this case raise several social and legal issues. What is the role of civil (as opposed to criminal) commitment? The defendant had been hospitalized for psychiatric care numerous times. What role does gun legislation play? He was diagnosed with a severe mental illness but was never barred from owning a firearm. Where are boundaries in the broader issue of handgun ownership? Even if all the people in the store had carried weapons (none did), the attack was unprovoked, and it happened with such speed that no one had time for self-defensive measures. And after a defendant is incarcerated, either in jail or prison, what risk accrues to him? The defendant in this convenience store shooting poses a risk to others, yet he faces a lesser risk of being the recipient of physical harm than an inmate convicted of a sexual offense.[1]

The actions of the alleged gunman merited a media splash after the shootings, but no long-term outcry. The shootings did not become a prominent community issue. As a culture, we are often slow to respond to the threat of physical violence. But we retain a hair-trigger response to the threat of sexual violence against children.

Tracking the outcomes of sexual offenses

The act of sexually offending against children is sufficiently chilling to be considered more than just aberrant behavior. It has become a label for those who violate the rights of others: sex offender. The name conjures an overtly evil person—a monster—and a most vile crime. (I avoid the term "sex offender" in its pejorative sense in this book.) The public recoils in horror. Judicial and mental health systems respond in a concerted effort to both protect that same public and offer treatment to the offender. The protocol? Arrest and, frequently, incarcerate the offending party. Provide mandatory treatment, and then track that person's whereabouts on release (predominantly "his," although women and nonbinary individuals offend, too). The most common tracking tool is the online registry for those who sexually offend. In our determination to protect children from the risk of sexual abuse, we implement measures that reassure us the most.

But how effective is this system? Even with these broad measures in place, we still fear for the safety of our children and youth. Yet we stand watch at the wrong gates. Danger from an online stalker or a stranger in the streets is possible, but unlikely. Over 90 percent of those who perpetrate sexual abuse against children are family members or acquaintances. *Less than 10 percent are strangers.*[2] Children are coerced and cajoled into sexual activity by people who know them well, who have gained their trust and the trust of their caretakers.[3] When abuse comes to light, more often the horror is not only the reality that a child's security has been violated, but also the realization that a family member—often one who is loved and respected—has caused harm.

When child sexual abuse is reported, the person who has offended is charged and arrested, perhaps released on bond, and, if later convicted, receives probation or incarceration, depending on the severity of the offense. Treatment is normally required, either during a period of detention or under the watchful eye of the state while on probation or parole. For most, registration as a sex offender for a period of years, or even for life, is a further requirement. (Resolution of juvenile offenses varies by state or province.)

In tandem with an increased emphasis on treating those who offend, research into the sexual abuse of children has narrowed its focus. The concern has become how to best equip those attracted to minors with means to manage their desires.[4] Studies into the personality traits of those who sexually offend, or the sociocultural dynamics that lead to offenses, have been dead ends, and, except for an occasional esoteric inquiry, few professionals explore these areas. We have a wealth of information on where and how those who offend come into contact with victims, and which treatment approaches seem most efficacious to manage these behaviors. But we have a poor understanding of the *context* in which the sexual abuse of children occurs. This includes (1) insight into how that abuse is perceived by others who are significant in the victim's lives, (2) how differing subcultures or communities perceive sexual abuse, and (3) any demographic or cultural differences in perceptions vis-à-vis the interactions of those who offend with the community in which they live. Consequently, we are far better equipped to respond *reactively* to the trauma of sexual abuse of children than to respond *proactively*, with an understanding of the social, cultural, and dynamic variables that contribute to acting on one's sexual attraction to a child.

The sociocultural context of sexual offending

As one consequence of this lack of broader knowledge, research efforts have failed to follow social changes that contribute to sexual abuse as it arises in postmodern culture. Prior to the proliferation of social networking, "grooming behaviors" referred to face-to-face interactions or private telephone calls designed to lure a child into sexual activity. Today, children are groomed en masse, not as targeted victims, but by virtue of the ease with which they can obtain sexual information. The rising tide of sexual openness has led to an exponential increase in awareness and curiosity about sexuality at a younger age.[5] Amid the boons such a progressive mindset can offer, there are also downsides. "Dirty pictures" have given way to the dark web, and sexting among youngsters is a common pastime.[6] Agencies monitoring the use of child pornography or compliance with minimal age criteria on social media cannot follow every site and all users.[7] Children are sexualized at an early age with this easy access to diverse and explicit pornography. Parental controls are only as good as the controls on a friend's tablet or phone. Potential victims of sexual abuse are primed to be sexually curious through the knowledge imparted to them.[8] This online freedom speaks to the difficulty of implementing proactive protective efforts.

The increasing sexual freedom of postmodern society also confounds efforts to determine a lower age boundary for sexual consent. Twentieth-century US Supreme Court Justice Potter Stewart said, "I know it when I see it," but his reference to hard-core pornography does not translate to the sexual abuse of adolescents.[9] For example, some states have lowered the age of consent for sexual activity to 16, but federal statutes maintain that the distribution of sexually explicit photographs and videos of minors is illegal for anyone under the age of 18.[10] Therefore, in many states, a 21-year-old and a 16-year-old can legally engage in sexual activity, but they violate federal law if they exchange pictures of that same activity. They may also violate state law if they cross the border to a neighboring state where the age of consent is 17, or even 18, and engage in sexual activity. Even murkier is the age boundary between two younger children who engage in sexual play. The point at which play is coerced (and therefore abuse), or is simply curiosity (and therefore childhood exploration), can become an emotionally charged judgment call. As a hedge against prosecuting adolescents who are close in age, but with one of them above and the other below the age of consent, many states have enacted "Romeo and Juliet" laws that excuse these situations.[11] These laws again rely on judgment calls. Case-specific efforts serve better than a rigidly applied canon, but they cannot reliably resolve whether individuals who are close in age or in their developmental levels have engaged in an act of sexual abuse or in consensual sex.

A scientific study of the personalities and temperaments of individuals who act out sexually has largely been pushed aside, and there have been valid reasons to abandon this line of research. These can be seen as parallels to research on addiction. For many years, those working in the field of addictive behaviors struggled to unlock the secret of an "addictive personality." After amassing a wealth of inconclusive and contradictory data, experts concluded that no such personality exists. Just as there is no single personality type that reliably predicts who will or will not become dependent on a particular substance or behavior, no central set of traits or characteristics has been found that reliably predict those who sexually offend.[12] Addiction experts, however, turned to social, cultural, and genetic influences that impact dependency.[13] With the evidence gained from these efforts, addiction, mental health, and educational professionals have developed proactive efforts to address those at risk for addictions.

But studies of those who sexually offend against children have not made a significant attempt to pursue such a direction. Instead, research has focused on the presumably more beneficial area of treatment interventions. Unfortunately, that effort has demoted more than the search for a personality type—it has also dismissed or downgraded accompanying searches for comorbid conditions (those that exist simultaneously with and usually independently of another condition) that contribute to sexual offending. The impact of alcohol or drug use, manic episodes during a bipolar disorder, psychosis during a severe mental illness, or compulsive sexual acting out are therefore less thoroughly studied and contribute little to the treatment schemes that are deployed.[14] Instead, broad generic intervention models are more common.

These models focus on efficacy in reducing the specific behavior of sexually offending. Success is normally measured by a decreased rate of recidivism (the tendency to relapse into a previous mode of behavior) after those who have been arrested are released from incarceration. This is widely acknowledged as the best available choice in a limited pool of relevant criteria. As a measurement, it relies on the discovery, rearrest, and conviction of a previous offender for another crime. Studies vary in the length of their follow-ups (from a few months to several years), and whether they use the criteria of rearrest for a sexual offense only, or for any felony crime, to count as recidivism. Rarely do these models address efficacy with diverse subpopulations of those who offend, or with specific comorbid factors.

Research has done more to examine the stigma faced by those who sexually offend. Still, judicial and mental health systems acknowledge but rarely address society's imposition of a shameful status to those who offend. Some who perpetrate these offenses *do* deserve disdain. They are sociopathic, without a conscience. In one such case, a man with two prior convictions for sexual crimes against minors was charged with several new sexual offenses against children. His home was filled with toys, games, and stuffed animals. He procured these objects to entice children and then used them sexually. He would obtain promises of silence—with threats, if necessary. In my role as a mental health expert, I testified for the prosecution, arguing that his prior history, his lack of remorse, and his unsuccessful previous mental health interventions posed a further risk to the community if he was not incarcerated. His attorney made a vain effort to rehabilitate this client's reputation, but it was clear that the accused had no viable defense and would receive a maximum sentence.

The above example is also the type of case used to legitimize a frightening sociocultural perspective. For some members of the public, those who sexually offend have no right to live. But to play out that solution results in its own dark night of the soul. In another instance, an adolescent, coerced into a sexual relationship by an older man, eventually insisted that they stop. The older man refused. The boy handled this denial by shooting and killing his perpetrator. In his mid-teens, he was waived to adult, rather than juvenile, court and tried for murder. He served 15 years of a 30-year sentence. He has since been able to begin his life anew in his early 30s. But the ripple effects of the damage done, from the foreshortened life of the man who offended against him to his own truncated life outside prison, and the trauma created in the lives of so many involved in this drama, are powerful statements about the repercussions of the vigilante justice espoused by a vocal minority.

The subset of people who sexually offend without remorse does not represent the majority. These evildoers account for only a small portion of the sexual abuse that occurs. Instead, this book is about the overwhelming majority of those conflicted and anguished souls who, nonetheless, feel compelled to sexually offend. For example, consider a man who compulsively abused his daughter. In desperation, he told her, "If I do this again, tell

Mommy." He did, and she did, leading to his arrest and incarceration. He never strayed from accepting responsibility for his actions. Or the instance of a man who committed sexual abuse on a youngster from late childhood into the boy's teens. The sexual abuse this perpetrator had survived himself was never addressed, or even known, until long after his incarceration ended. He had been abused by his maternal uncle, but he waited until both his uncle and mother were deceased and could no longer be shamed by the revelations before acknowledging the years of humiliation he had endured. Or the case of an adolescent male who sexually abused a younger boy. The adolescent received treatment within the community where the offense occurred, only to be continuously harassed by his victim's father, who believed the consequences should have been much more severe. Haunted, life became too much. At the age of 25, a handful of pills ended his pain. These are people who sexually offended, but a full understanding of their behavior requires background information that the stark details of the offense itself do not reveal.

And there is still another population impacted by popular attitudes toward those who sexually offend against children. Coalescing under the descriptive identity of being "minor attracted," these are individuals who advocate for the safety and well-being of children while also acknowledging a romantic or sexual interest toward them. Some have never sexually offended. Others have offended but are determined never to do so again. They advocate for compassion and understanding. From their perspective, they have a sexual orientation they never desired and do not intend to fulfill, but they ask for acceptance of who they are. Their roles cannot begin to be explained or examined without understanding the social and cultural milieus in which they find themselves. At present, they have two options. They can bottle up their sexual orientation and live what are perceived as normal lives but deny their true selves. Or they can disclose their interest in children and find themselves humiliated and shamed, not for their actions, but for acknowledging their inclinations. Their interest in assuring the safety of children seems at odds with their sexual desires, a paradox about which many are skeptical. (I will return to these tensions in a later chapter.)

The dynamics of sexual offending

A clear understanding of the sociocultural context of those who sexually offend is essential for any type of effective treatment. But even if that context is better understood, it does not diminish the need to comprehend, at least in some rudimentary manner, the theorized psychological dynamics that contribute to an interest in children.

In our postmodern era, efforts to curtail sexual offending serve a primary purpose: protecting a child from unwanted and traumatizing sexual offenses. In the recent past, however, efforts to curtail sexual offending served a dual purpose: protecting a child from unwanted sexual advances and protecting a child from the distortion of that child's preexisting sexual proclivities. This

Freudian model held sway among the theories of child development, framing children as moving through, or resolving, a series of psychosexual stages.[15] Exposure to sexual activity by adults at too young an age risked prematurely teaching this nascent sexual being about such acts. (Postmodern exposure to sexually explicit material is not perceived with this same concern, a dynamic I address more fully in the next chapter.) While these Freudian developmental stages have been challenged and are far less commonly accepted nowadays, the essentialist versus constructionist debate in which psychoanalytic theory was grounded predominates, and it includes children's sexual awareness.[16] Experts continue to argue whether a predisposition exists toward sexual identity and orientation (the essentialist view) or whether sexual identity and orientation are primarily molded and developed through social interactions and cultural expectations (the constructionist view).

A logical fallout of this debate is the possible development of a sexual orientation toward children by adults, the minor attraction mentioned previously. Pedophilia (an attraction to prepubescent children) and hebephilia (an attraction to early pubescent children) have long been considered paraphilias. These are categorized with sexual behaviors such as partialism (attraction to body parts), exhibitionism (exposing one's genitals for sexual gratification), and voyeurism (viewing others' nude or partially nude bodies, usually without their knowledge, for sexual gratification). Paraphilias are usually assumed to be constructionist sexual quirks or disorders, developed through an interpersonal experience (or experiences) and modified, if required, through cognitive or cognitive-behavioral treatments, the current go-to approach for those who sexually offend. In this schema, an interest in children is a distortion of a healthy choice of a sexual object, leading to partialism (sexual gratification with someone other than a fully participating partner).[17]

Alternative models have long been on the periphery, but more recently, mainstream theorists have also been suggesting them. Is an attraction to children a sexual orientation, akin to heterosexuality or to a same-sex interest?[18] This is the essentialist viewpoint, arguing that a sexual and romantic attraction to children is innate in some individuals—a predisposition present from birth. The essentialist argument rests as much upon what has *not* been found as upon what has. The futility of efforts to find a personality disorder that leads to same-sex attraction was, in part, used to argue for the psychological and emotional well-being of those with that sexual orientation.[19] The same argument—a failed effort to find a common psychological or emotional disorder that leads to an attraction to children—can be applied here.

Still, both the constructionist and essentialist viewpoints create difficulties. For example, if an attraction to children is a paraphilia, then it is different from almost all other paraphilias. The attraction of an 18-year-old to a 13-year-old is a paraphilia (hebephilia). But the attraction of a 70-year-old to an 18-year-old, while it may raise eyebrows, raises no clinical flags. Creating clear definitions as to when—and how—this paraphilia manifests itself can be difficult. Or, if an attraction to children is essentialist, then the experience of those who are sexually abused and who, in turn, themselves engage in sexual abuse raises questions. Are they identifying with an aggressor?[20] Or are they merely acting on an innate preference? And, if the former, then do some of those who manifest other sexual orientations not demonstrate an *essential* orientation, but a *constructed* orientation by responding to trauma, despite the alleged debunking of such research? The model of a minor attraction as a sexual orientation poses scientifically, socially, and politically fraught questions.

What is an evidence-based and logical response to these contradictory expectations? Treatment is often ineffective, vigilante justice creates nightmare scenarios, and tracking those who have been convicted offers no reduction in the rate of reoffending. Too often, treatment providers—and the courts—act as if an offender is created with a specific set of traits, reacts to the act of offending in a predictable way, and will respond to a network of consequences in an equally predictable way. Those who sexually offend may choose victims online or in person. They range from the very few who express no guilt, no remorse, and who project blame on others, to the many who agonize over their behavior and accept responsibility for their actions. Friends and family may be aware of their aberrant behavior and choose to ignore it, or they may be genuinely shocked at what has occurred. This behavior may be calculated and cunning. It may happen during a mania, as part of a bipolar illness. Or it may take place compulsively, as a form of sexual addiction. In terms of timing, it may reflect years of acting out, or only a few isolated incidents. Despite these varied paths, the journey leads to a single, tragic outcome: harm to a child.

Sexual offending against children is an emotionally charged topic. But because of this baggage, academic books on the subject limit themselves. They focus either on victims or on those who offend, and they argue for advocacy and compassion, or for treatment and intervention. But, in actuality, the lives of those who sexually offend and those they harm are much more complex. Both are often inextricably bound together in family systems, friendships, and other social networks. Justice and mental health systems create programs that too often minimize the reality—namely, that the lives of those who offend are intertwined with family and social systems before their arrest, and these ties will continue during incarceration, after their release, and long after these two supposedly helpful systems have stepped back. To understand the dynamics of sexual offending also requires an understanding of the social and cultural contexts that surround it.

Those who sexually offend encounter a social stigma that renders them as two-dimensional characters, unwanted and unforgiven. This book examines the role of sexual abuse, and those responsible for it, in a larger context. We speak of "healing" those who sexually offend but offer little in the way of effective treatment. We speak of "reintegrating" these individuals into our communities but hold them at arm's length. And we speak of "safety" for the community but offer little that provides such protection. Meanwhile, sexual abuse is still rampant, and our prisons remain crowded, even while recidivism by those convicted of sexual offenses is at a low ebb. All of this suggests that these measures are ineffective in slowing—much less stopping—the rising tide of sexual abuse.[21] There is an urgent need for change, both in the means we use to protect potential victims and in the ways in which we treat those who sexually offend.

Over the course of my career, I have also seen distorted social and cultural beliefs about those who sexually offend lead to the creation of responses among the judiciary, mental health professionals, and the public that are ineffective, at best, and damaging, at worst. My hope is that exploring these systemic responses generated by our sociocultural perceptions will allow us to recognize the enigma. To do so is a necessary step in further reducing the trauma faced by children, adolescents, and adults affected by sexual abuse. Our current systemic response is failing—and failing badly—for all concerned.

Notes

1 Trammel & Chenault, 2009.
2 National Children's Advocacy Center, n.d.
3 Chenier, 2012.
4 Lösel & Schmucker, 2005.
5 Massey, Burns, & Franz, 2021.
6 Doyle, Douglas, & O'Reilly, 2021.
7 18 U.S.C. §2258A (2021).
8 Chassiaskos et al., 2016.
9 Jacobellis v. Ohio, 378 U.S. 184 (1964). It was in concurring with the majority that Justice Stewart made his now-famous statement, "I know it when I see it," in reference to pornography.
10 18 U.S.C. §2251, §2252, §2252A (2021).
11 Bierie & Budd, 2018.
12 Vandiver, Braithwaite, & Stafford, 2017.
13 Shaffer, 2012.
14 Langevin et al., 2008; McMurtrie, 2011; Mogavero, 2016.
15 Stevens, 2008.
16 Jackson & Scott, 2015.
17 Moser, 2001.
18 Seto, 2012.
19 Serovich et al., 2008.
20 Howell, 2014.
21 Horowitz, 2015.

2 Historical perspectives

Offending across cultures and time

Sexual abuse of children has occurred in every culture, throughout history.[1] Interpretations of abuse, however, have varied. One of the most famous licenses was the sexual and romantic involvement between men and boys, or pederasty, in ancient Greece, which was seen as a social norm.[2] The extent and tolerance of this phenomenon has been debated, and its historical significance relegated to a cultural cul-de-sac. Still, efforts to minimize the demonstrable tolerance of abuse do not change its prevalence. Flash forward a few millennia, and "Chester the Molester" was a recurring comic in *Hustler* magazine (published from 1974 to 1990).[3] Drawn by Dwain B. Tinsley, the protagonist assaulted women and girls with impunity. The cartoon drew scorn, as did the magazine, but it appealed to a male subculture. Such humor might have been panned then and would not be tolerated now, but in its timeframe the subject of minor attraction was far less taboo. As another example, the 1980 movie *Airplane* was wildly popular at its debut and continues to be lauded as a comedy masterpiece.[4] Among its recurring gags are the efforts of the pilot (played by veteran actor Peter Graves) to seduce a young boy named "Billy."

As these examples demonstrate, attitudes toward sexual offending have changed. Our current sociocultural stance would not tolerate dissemination of a cartoon depicting sexual offending as an amusing pastime. Nor would it tolerate a movie featuring a respected member of society attempting to seduce a child for laughs. Yet they continue to exist as mementos of recent history. So, the question still remains. What forces have shaped our perception of those who sexually offend from being merely objectionable to denigrated as the vicious social threat they are today?

"Heteronormative" is a term that refers to mainstream sexuality.[5] In slightly over 200 years, Western culture has transitioned from rigid class systems and two distinct developmental stages (childhood and adulthood) to fluid social rankings and a nuanced progression across the human lifespan. The rise of the middle class and the fluidity of social status have lessened the barriers that kept classes distinct and narrowly defined. The demand for further education has lengthened the period in which most young people assimilate the

DOI: 10.4324/9781003487753-2

tools needed to fully embrace adult responsibilities. Keeping pace with these changes, the rights of children and the perceptions of those who impinge on these rights have also evolved. It is only during the last 50 years that, in the sexual realm, these rights have been considered a matter of urgent concern, as what was viewed as humor in the 1970s demonstrates. Heteronormative has long been characterized by moral ambiguity, where sexual protection for children came at the expense of male authority. It was not until the feminist movement defied this stance, along with other codes, that change became an urgent concern.[6] Nonetheless, the question lingered. Why were abused children so easily dismissed?

There is no need to return to the era of Greek pederasty to discover a plausible answer. Across the nineteenth century, but particularly in the late nineteenth and into the twentieth centuries, changes in the global social and economic landscape, the devastating consequences of two world wars, and the gradual erosion of tightly controlled class systems were poised to push consequences for sexual offending to the forefront. Feminist politics created the impetus, but the overarching protections now in place represent a leap to the opposite end of the continuum from previous neglect.

Protecting the child: *Whose* child?

Sexual abuse in the nineteenth and early twentieth centuries

The first English laws to address child incest or abuse as a separate legal category appeared in the nineteenth century.[7] Previously, sexual crimes against children were prosecuted as assault. This proclivity to categorize child sexual abuse as assault, on a par with adult sexual violence, would continue through the early twentieth century. The interplay of gender, race, and class contributed as much as the age of the victim to a decision about whether a crime had been committed, and, if so, whether it was a crime that would be punished.

As the English stance toward the criminal process suggests, another barrier facing those in the past who weighed the evidence pertaining to child sexual abuse was its definition. Postmodern sensibilities have developed a reasonably clear set of criteria regarding child sexual abuse, although the gray areas that still exist suggest the difficulty of absolute definitions. In earlier times, such definitions were almost entirely lacking. Among nations that considered themselves Christian, the sole, universally accepted purpose for sexual behavior was procreation, occurring within the confines of marriage. For this reason, the act itself, more than the age of the victim, often became the focus of a criminal charge.[8] Such a distinction is maintained today among a few conservative religious groups, but even in these sects, non-procreational sex acts are usually seen as less heinous than the sexual abuse of a child. In our First World, postmodern age, it is more difficult to understand the overarching importance of procreation in prior eras and the evenhanded abhorrence toward *all* sin, regardless of the act, which contributed to a relative indifference to the traumatic consequences of such acts.

The question of consequences also appears to have been biased, based on gender.[9] In the late nineteenth century in South Africa, the scourge of sexually transmitted infections among young white females was assumed to be due to indirect contact with African household staff.[10] The potential for interracial sexual activity was not considered a route for infection, given the tightly controlled class structure of that time and place. A similar principle applied in France. Moral degeneracy was assumed to be class based, resulting from the cramped and filthy housing conditions of the poor. Social awareness of incest focused on the ill treatment of female children.[11] Physicians emerged as expert witnesses in court cases where defendants were accused of sexual assault or rape of a child, but often their statements did more harm than good. They frequently reported no physical evidence of assault or cast doubt on the veracity of the female victim's testimony.[12]

India may initially appear to be distinct from Western culture, but in the late nineteenth and early twentieth centuries, its status as a British colony stamped its society with both class and racial disparities that played out in the treatment of sexual assaults against children. Prior to colonial rule, the rights of Indian children were extremely limited. During times of famine, they could be sold into slavery or handed over for adoption to more financially stable relatives. Arranged marriages continued, even after British control of India.[13] A substantial age disparity remained common in marriages, with prepubescent females wed to adult males.

In 1889, a Hindu bride died while consummating her marriage on her wedding night. She was 10 years old, the age of consent in India. Her husband was 27. The outcry engendered by her death resulted, two years later, in the Age of Consent Act, which raised the age requirement to 12 years old.[14] In retrospect, it may seem like a hollow victory to have raised the age of consent by a mere two years, still leaving it well within the realm of childhood. Yet at the time, it was a major achievement, given Hindu cultural beliefs. It was not until the Child Marriage Restraint Act of 1929 that further legislation in India solidified the definition of a child.

In the early years of the twentieth century, Scottish folklore maintained that intercourse with a virgin would cure a man of a sexually transmitted infection.[15] Infecting a child was considered an aggravating factor for men charged with sexual assault, but physicians often attributed a vaginal discharge to a secondary infection (due to poor hygienic practices in the home) or a source other than sexual activity, particularly for females from the lower classes. Many cases were dismissed because of a lack of substantive evidence, a medical misdiagnosis for the victim, or both.

In England, maidservants had historically been treated as sexual chattel, to be used by the males in the homes where they worked.[16] By the end of the nineteenth century, there was an acknowledgment of a need for services for children who were sexually abused. In 1901, the Salvation Army opened

The Nest, a rescue house in London for such children, a home for girls and young women.[17] The era when governmental authority would intercede was still many years away. Well into the early twentieth century in Great Britain, the abuse of children by males in authority continued with alarming regularity.[18] In part this was due to the social acceptance of romance and marriage between young girls and much older men.[19] The intentions of older males who lavished their attentions on young females were rarely questioned if these men came from the appropriate upper class. The ongoing debate over the true nature of the relationship between Lewis Carroll and Alice Liddell, his youthful protégé who inspired *Alice in Wonderland*, is a prominent example of this type of relationship.

While boys were also known to be sexually abused (referenced legally as "carnally known and abused"), there was far less concern over their well-being, as well as over sexual abuse among the lower classes.[20] The trial of Oscar Wilde in April 1895 is probably the most infamous example of this double standard. His flamboyant affair with an aristocrat, Lord Alfred Douglas, resulted in Wilde facing criminal charges. While it was known that he engaged in sexual encounters with many young men, he preferred "rough trade" (lower-class boys). Because of their low social status, the well-being of these boys was not a concern. Therefore, they were not a target of investigation, beyond social disapproval of their gender.[21]

In the United States, similar cultural standards held sway. Child sexual abuse was reported more often for females, but a dismissive attitude toward its victims was common. The practice of slavery meant that sexual abuse was perpetrated with impunity toward those treated as property, a situation lasting well into the mid-nineteenth century.[22] Even after slavery was outlawed, the onus of minority status meant that virtually all forms of abuse perpetrated by the white majority against other racial groups could be carried out without fear of reprisal.

For much of the nineteenth century and the early part of the twentieth century, then, *whose* child was protected? Only a chosen few. Female children from the middle and upper classes were more likely to receive the benefit of concern for their well-being. But that benefit assumed they would prepare for adulthood at an early age—at least by their early teens. They were the more vulnerable gender and, as such, were readily handed off to more mature men as potential husbands. The developmental age at which sexual interactions would be tolerated was much younger than it is today, and this has only slowly increased. Younger males might be sexually abused, but this was less of a concern than the situation for their female counterparts. A greater concern was the potential to dabble in same-sex relationships, a moral outrage that often far outweighed a difference in ages. And given the shame conjured by such activity, it seems probable that reports of such incidents were extremely low.

And what of the lowest classes? Or persons of minority status? Child sexual abuse within these groups was recognized as a problem—sometimes attributed to poverty, and at other times to moral failure—but its importance was minimized. Since these people's worth to society was not the same as those having middle- and upper-class status, their children's well-being did not hold the same importance. Those who sexually offended youth from these lower categories were occasionally charged, tried, and convicted of sexual assault and rape, but this was not a primary concern. The Salvation Army or similar organizations might offer aid to those in need from the lower ranks, but most citizens preferred to keep their distance. And non-white children? They were often faced with the dual specters of lower-class status and racist ideology. They were easily victimized, since violence—including child sexual abuse within their own social group—was rarely a concern of the white majority, and violence perpetrated upon them by that same majority went unpunished.

Gradually, as the morality of the nineteenth century morphed into the twentieth century, changes occurred in views regarding child sexuality. These were erratic, at best, but they reflected movement toward greater awareness of the need to protect a child.

Evolving views of sexual abuse in the twentieth century

The repression of sexual discourse merely serves to heighten its power and influence—or so posited noted sexuality theorist Michel Foucault.[23] In one sense his premise seems validated. In 1886, German psychiatrist Richard von Krafft-Ebing wrote *Psychopathia Sexualis: Eine Klinisch-Forsensische Studie* [*Sexual Psychopathology: A Medico-Forensic Study*].[24] He had no intention of sensationalizing his work by writing for the lay public. To avoid popularizing his book, he used Latin references when discussing sex, but his efforts at obfuscation were unsuccessful. The book was a salacious bestseller through the remainder of the nineteenth century and well into the twentieth century, going through multiple editions. Krafft-Ebing was the first to clinically characterize an attraction to children. He referred to it as a "morbid predisposition" or "psychosexual perversion." By categorizing numerous aberrant sexual behaviors in this manner, he reframed them from criminal actions to clinical conditions, transforming their social meaning.

At about the same time, the age of consent was coming under scrutiny. As the Victorian era was ending, deviant sexual behavior was becoming hotly contested. One area that drew intense debate was the jurisdiction for handling inappropriate sexual activity with young people. Should this matter be a moral concern, to be treated through education and religious dogma? Or should it be adjudicated legally, with punishment administered by the courts?[25] As was true throughout most of these debates, the focus was on female children. Male children who might be sexually approached were of minor concern, if they were considered at all. Pressure from the public eventually led legislatures to adopt laws that addressed such sexual acting out. In the United Kingdom, a significant stumbling block remained throughout the late nineteenth century and into the early twentieth century. Children could not testify in court, since the question arose of whether a child could understand the obligatory oath. Their statements required corroboration.[26]

In the United States, meanwhile, as in other Western countries, the definition of a child was in flux. The very concept of "child" as an important construct was only emerging late in the Victorian age, so the idea of criminal prosecution for violating the age of consent, as opposed to criminal prosecution for violent sexual assault, was a novel concept.[27] While it was presumed, as a social convention, that children (often defined as those age 7 or under) were incapable of moral choices, codified prohibitions against sexual activity on that basis alone were rare. For example, in 1886 New York City raised the age of consent to 16 years old. Statutory rape, however, remained a secondary crime for many years. Prosecutors were familiar—and more comfortable— with a charge of rape as the primary offense, as had been the practice prior to raising the age of consent.[28] The choice was not capricious. Prosecutors feared that juries would fail to appreciate the *legal* similarity between a 5-year-old and a 15-year-old victim, paralleling concerns raised today. Indeed, despite more widespread prosecutions of adults engaged in sex with early adolescents, many states offer the partial shield of "Romeo and Juliet" laws. This type of legislation excuses sex with those below the age of consent if the offending party is close in age to the other person.[29] The nature, interpretation, and enforcement of these laws, however, differ from state to state. Just as the legal age of consent varies, so do the circumstances under which that age statute can be waived.

Educating children about sex was championed in the early twentieth century, but it was hardly the type of education we consider it to be now. Masturbation was often a topic of concern, with the understanding that it was a cause of moral and physical degradation.[30] The information passed on was more about health than sex and sexuality per se. It provided little that allowed children to understand their bodies or sexual development. And virtually nothing was mentioned about the risk of or responses to sexual abuse.

Media coverage also downplayed child sexual abuse. Rather than incurring a risk from including salacious elements, early twentieth–century newspaper articles reported the legal aspects of these crimes but skirted the details.[31] Stories continued to imply that female victims were complicit in their abuse, fostering the social narrative that no self-respecting female would allow herself to be placed in such a position. Changes in reporting evolved with alterations in the culture. World War II led to stories that filled in the graphic details of war, the realities of civil unrest, and a reshaping of social thought. As the public became accustomed to this grittier style of journalism, crime reporting was reshaped to include in-depth coverage, with details about the crimes themselves. Sexual abuses, along with other criminal enterprises, were recounted in far more vivid terms. By the 1970s, the scourge of pedophilia was openly discussed.

Reshaped social thought following World War II was reflected in the media but had been rooted in a collective social conscience. For many countries, their cultural view of sex crimes was evolving. Previously, such crimes had been considered offenses that violated the social order. They defied principles of morality, the family, honor, and chastity. In the context of a new global order, these same crimes were seen as offenses to liberty, self-determination, and physical integrity. They abrogated individual freedoms,[32] which increasingly included sexual licenses previously perceived as illicit.[33] As sexual freedoms expanded for those who chose to follow them, protection against sexual coercion and manipulation became an area of increasing concern. Even the United Nations became involved, since its members spent much of the 1950s debating an appropriate international minimum age for marriage.[34]

Psychological theory was also involved in the changing views on sexuality. When Victorians did focus on females as vulnerable, they had focused on their risk as victims likely to be seduced by lecherous males. The undercurrent of a female's active participation in a seduction might come into play, but the prim and proper role of womanhood was at odds with a blatant claim that youngsters could also be coy and flirtatious. As psychoanalytic thought began to dominate the realm of mental health, the role of a more problematic victim came to the fore.[35] The Freudian view of children as progressing through psychosexual stages opened new vistas in the panorama of childhood development. Children had a sexual identity, albeit one that needed to be shepherded by caretakers. Failure to adequately parent children and restrain childhood sexuality resulted in moral and psychological disturbances.

The period after World War II also saw several works by Alfred Kinsey, a famous sexologist. In 1948, Kinsey and fellow researchers published the first book-length study of male sexual behavior.[36] Their findings set off a firestorm of controversy, as they revealed the breadth of human sexual experience. In 1953, Kinsey and others followed this groundbreaking research with a study on female sexual behavior. His opinions on female child sexual abuse profoundly influenced the era's professional view of the topic.[37] Kinsey opined that approximately 80 percent of all children had been frightened by a sexual contact with adults, but, without cultural conditioning, these approaches would be no more disturbing than unexpected contact with an insect. He believed that the response of parents, police officers, and other adult authority figures was the impetus for trauma.

Armed conflicts and sexual abuse

The social disruption caused by widespread violence is well documented in multiple disciplines. The price it exacts on children—through all forms of abuse—is acknowledged but often glossed over as one of the many inevitable consequences of war. Despite efforts to look past its effects, we are left with stark images of moments of bleakest horror.

War and enemy occupation induce longstanding fears of sexual assault, with young girls often being a target of such depredations.[38] Citizens in New Orleans, Louisiana, expressed that fear during the occupation of their city during the American Civil War.[39] Britain used sexual violence against women as propaganda in encouraging support for the Great War, or World War I.[40] The savagery of the earlier fighting in their country meant that Russian troops invading Germany as World War II ground to a close were particularly intent on retribution.[41] That included assaults on civilians. It is easy to objectify females, rather than see them as human beings, particularly when racial disparities exist between combatants.[42] Often, sexual violence during armed conflicts has not been perceived as *assault*. Rather, it has been redefined as a *crime against honor*.[43]

Children have also been impacted by civil violence. The German bombing raids on London during World War II led to the evacuation of thousands of children from the metropolitan area, which was viewed as being essential. Nonetheless, survivors from that period described the abuse they experienced when sheltering in the homes of strangers who, themselves, were stressed to the breaking point.[44] In Russia, where the death toll during World War II was particularly heavy, orphanages were in chaos immediately after the war. Their overworked and overwhelmed staff often victimized their charges.[45] The most tragic stories, perhaps, come from Italy, where sexual tourism boomed following World War II. The level of poverty and starvation experienced there was so great that parents vied to sell their children as sexual objects for financial gain. And the awareness of this trade brought in those looking for a bargain.[46]

Into our time

What does this appalling history tell us? It reminds us that the best intentions still occur within the limitations of cultural perspectives, which are based on class and caste systems, patriarchal cultures, and indifference to the welfare of children. With these constraints in mind, we struggle to define what constitutes child sexual abuse. We have come to demand that it be seen as traumatizing, regardless of the nature of the perpetrated abuse.[47] And, in many cases, it *is* traumatic. The reporting of child sexual abuse continues to be based on race, ethnicity, and socioeconomic status.[48] Caribbean Island countries are popular tourist destinations, and sex tourism—race-based and inclusive of children—remains a concern.[49] Survivors of abuse among Native Americans recall the indifference with which their claims were treated.[50] The Catholic Church continues to struggle with the fallout from years of sheltering sexually abusive priests.[51]

The reality, however, is that child sexual abuse may not always be traumatic. A famous article published in 1998 created a furor. A meta-analysis of 59 research studies, based on samples from college populations, found that those victimized by sexual abuse were only slightly less well-adjusted than the control participants, with men less impacted than women.[52] Family environment played a significant role in their adjustment. Politics overrode the opportunity for further scientific exploration of these findings, however, as the article was censored by the US Senate.

The emergence of those who sexually offend as a categorical group is also a relatively recent phenomenon. Although Krafft-Ebing's "perversion" nomenclature would have allowed such a grouping to be created, it failed to coalesce until the judicial system established this category in the late twentieth century.[53] Those who offend are now pariahs, a status that serves them poorly. Mitigation efforts, such as offender registries, have virtually no impact on the safety of those they claim to protect. Instead, they have fostered vigilante attacks on those listed in them.[54]

But there have been changes that make a positive difference. With the responsibility for investigating and addressing child sexual abuse placed in the hands of governmental agencies, the tendency to overlook such abuse among socially and economically challenged segments of the population has decreased. Females are still recognized as facing a greater risk of sexual abuse, but the tendency to see them as culpable when victimized has greatly diminished. And the dismissal of males as potential victims of sexual abuse has all but disappeared.

Still, the historical record confronts our postmodern era with significant challenges. Heteronormative cultures across time indicate that those who sexually offend have, in part, been a creation of the culture, as much as the product of individual pathology or an ingrained orientation. Historical analyses of the sexual abuse of children are ongoing, and they highlight a failure to protect the child. But there is relatively little emphasis on the *context* of sexual offending, perhaps because (as the famous examples of Lewis Carroll and Oscar Wilde show) such efforts become a murky recognition of the social acceptance of questionable, if not blatantly damaging behaviors.

Other changes argue for the quixotic nature of social values. The use of offender registries that have no proven efficacy is one such example. The intractable argument that *all* sexual abuse is traumatic, regardless of empirical evidence to the contrary, is another. We can be certain that the safety and protection of children will become a secondary concern when widespread armed conflict erupts and needs are triaged, with sexual abuse becoming tertiary. And perhaps the most perplexing shift of all is the morphing age at which sexual offending against children begins. Hebephilia is a clinical condition that describes an attraction to early adolescents. Yet, for much of the previous two centuries, Western cultures encouraged a romantic attraction to early adolescent females. It was *social convention* that changed the age of attraction, rather than *clinical evidence*. Do we then assume that our recent ancestors were predominantly sexually attracted to minors? Or do we acknowledge that our definitions of what constitutes a sexual offense vary with social conventions? If we are to effectively address sexual offending, we must recognize the sociocultural contexts in which it occurs.

Notes

1 DeMause, 1998.
2 Holmen, 2010
3 Wikipedia, s.v. "Chester the Molester."
4 Wikipedia, s.v. *"Airplane."*
5 Thomas, 2009.
6 Smaal, 2013a.
7 Toulalan, 2014.
8 Smaal, 2013a.
9 Smaal, 2013b.
10 Hodes, 2015.
11 Giuliani, 2009.
12 Cage, 2019.
13 Anagol, 2020.
14 Pande, 2012.
15 Davidson, 2001.
16 Richardson, 2020.
17 Jackson, 2000.
18 Bingham et al., 2015.
19 Bulfin, 2021.
20 Bulfin, 2021.
21 McKenna, 2005.
22 Baptist, 2001.
23 Foucault, 1990.
24 Krafft-Ebing, 2011.
25 Stevenson, 2017.
26 Blewer, 2020.
27 Kincaid, 1992.
28 Robertson, 2002.
29 Bieri & Budd, 2018.
30 Gleason, 2017.
31 Bingham, 2019.
32 Frank, Camp, & Boutcher, 2010.
33 Bailey, 1989.
34 Tambe, 2020.
35 Devlin, 2005.
36 Kinsey, Pomeroy, & Martin, 1948.
37 Kinsey et al., 1953, pp.121–122.
38 Gaca, 2014.
39 Feimster, 2009.
40 Gullace, 1997.
41 Orlov, 2005.
42 Maxwell, 2009.
43 Heineman, 2008.
44 Akhtar, 2010.
45 Zezina, 2010.
46 Cleves, 2020.

47 Coviello, 2008.
48 Deer, 2009.
49 Sproul, 2021.
50 Million, 2009.
51 Formicola, 2020a, 2020b.
52 Rind, Tromovitch, & Bauserman, 1998.
53 Angelides, 2005.
54 Adelman, 2022.

3 Postmodern perspectives and diverse paths

The dynamics of sexual offending

The act of sexual offending is a behavior defined by national, state, and provincial legislatures. Once defined, its boundaries are spelled out by law enforcement and the courts. Law enforcement investigates, charges, and arrests those who are suspected of violating the sexual rights of victims. Legislators are tasked with defining violations and determining the appropriate punishment. The courts determine whether those charged with sexual offenses are guilty and sentence them accordingly. While this process is removed from the realm of mental health, the categories of those who offend, the impact of differing offenses, and the risk for reoffense rely heavily on the conclusions of this field.

Legislative efforts perceive sexual offending as a criminal behavior and generally codify these offenses based on the severity of injury to the victim. Mental health also focuses on behavior in order to categorize sexual offenses, but it sees them as manifestations of complex dynamics.[1] Efforts to classify those who sexually offend are based on emotional and psychological inputs, in addition to overt behaviors, thus creating a matrix of factors. These divide up those who offend, based on variables such as interest (regressed or fixated; focused either exclusively on children or on both adults and children), social competence, degree of fixation, and primary type of interaction desired with a child (from filial to friendship to romantic). These matrices are useful in understanding the intrapersonal dynamics of those who offend, but they fail to expand an understanding of the sociocultural variables that contribute to sexual offending. Nor do they incorporate related issues of mental health and clinical syndromes that can contribute to offending behavior.

Legislative classifications of sexual offenses have a place, but these need to coexist more closely with considerations of personality disorders and clinical syndromes. Doing so would create a three-dimensional image of the problem of sexual offending. Only then would we more fully grasp the treatment needs of those who sexually offend and more responsibly protect potential victims.

DOI: 10.4324/9781003487753-3

Typologies of sexual offending

Much like a parallel effort in an attempt to classify addictions, there appear to be too many variables that contribute to the ultimate behavior to reliably predict patterns of sexual offending. Nonetheless, long-standing categories are still referenced, and studies continue to search for similarities that can be woven into logical precursors to acting-out behaviors. One of the original typologies that retains a profound influence on both models of and treatment for sexual offending was developed by Groth and Birnbaum.[2] It hypothesized a bimodal model—either fixated or regressed—of those who offend.

Individuals defined as fixated are socially and sexually preoccupied with children. Their interest is assumed to be pathological, with an expressed egocentric purpose of meeting developmentally stunted needs. They are perpetrators who deliberately groom their victims, with the intention of engaging in sexual activity. Because of their developmental limitations, they are considered to be unable to find fully satisfying or meaningful intimate relationships with adults.

The other type of person who offends is defined as regressed. Although such individuals are capable of achieving satisfying and intimate relationships with adults, they offend against children when triggered by stressful life events. These perpetrators are opportunistic, targeting children who are easily accessible. Because their acting out is stress related, and because they maintain a potential for meaningful adult relationships, treatment is presumed to be more efficacious for those who are regressed, rather than those who are fixated.

Groth and Birnbaum's original model was clinically derived, but research supported its validity. Kenneth Lanning, a former agent with the FBI's Behavioral Sciences Unit, developed a refinement of the model that became a blueprint for law enforcement investigators.[3] He modified the terms fixated and regressed to *preferred* and *situational* pedophilia. The definitions of these terms were similar, but they broadened the circumstances under which each category could be applied. Lanning also emphasized that not all persons with pedophilia (a preferential interest in children) sexually offend, and not all persons who sexually offend with children demonstrate pedophilia.

As research progressed, Lanning shifted the emphasis of his model. The classifications were ranged along a continuum, rather than existing as discrete categories. He also identified those who offend situationally as being more likely to exhibit accompanying personality disorders (e.g., antisocial, narcissistic, or schizoid), while those who did so preferentially were more likely to exhibit other paraphilias, a term for aberrant sexual object choices such as voyeurism or sadism. Preferential offenders were also more likely to have repetitive patterns of sexual acting out with children, while situational ones were more likely to vary their sexual acting out. Lanning's goal was explicit. He did not intend to gain insight or understanding into why those who offended sexually with children did so, applying it for the purpose of treatment, but instead wanted to use this model to identify, arrest, and convict these offenders.

The concept of divvying up the types of people who sexually offend into those who are exclusively attracted to children and those who are attracted to both children and adults continues to be employed. Despite the tenacity of the bimodal model, its validity has been challenged by technology. The emerging and expanding options for social media in general, as well as for online pornography and child pornography as a subset of the broader pornographic field, blur the effort to categorize those who offend against children by basing it on a specific preference for this age group. At present, there seems to be a continuum of typologies online, too. At one extreme are the fantasy driven, whose interest is in communicating with or seeing videos of children, without desiring physical contact. At the other extreme are those who use online technology for the purpose of communicating and engaging with potential physical partners.[4] Between these poles are those who move from an interaction with videos to physical engagement; those who communicate via social media but do not engage in face-to-face contact; and those who use the anonymity of online engagement to develop fictitious personas, used to play out their own fantasies and, at times, to manipulate others. Hence the formulation of classifications lags behind explanations for the varieties of roles that those who sexually offend can utilize online.

An overlapping category includes those who distribute child pornography for profit. Many of these individuals also sexually offend. Some become distributors after initially downloading child pornography and realizing they could make money from selling it. Still others produce child pornography with a more overarching entrepreneurial goal, caring less about a network of like-minded persons than the profits to be reaped by selling a product that is in demand. While all of these people are sexually exploiting children, the degree to which they are attracted to the children they abuse versus the extent to which they recognize a commodity to be sold is often unknown.

Recent research has investigated the brain functions of those who sexually offend. Some would argue that, by virtue of an ability to become sexually aroused by a child, there is evidence of a neurological dysfunction, irrespective of finding physiological damage or a biochemical imbalance.[5] Disinhibition, related to a biochemical imbalance, may increase pedophilic sexual acting out.[6] More generally, there is evidence for biochemical influences in compulsive sexual behaviors.[7] In the latter cases, children become one of many potential sexual object choices.

Research is also proceeding on biomarkers in pedophilia. As would be anticipated, the clearest findings are those directly assessing a sexual interest in children (measuring visual attention and penile blood flow in response to child stimuli). Again, these indicate a tendency toward disinhibited behavior.[8] Physical abnormalities in the brain's frontal or temporal lobes can contribute to sexual offending, as can low or abnormal cerebral blood flow.[9] In one rare instance, the presence of a brain tumor resulted in a sexual interest in children, which disappeared after the tumor's removal.[10]

While these revelations are suggestive, they highlight the difficulties of research in this area. For instance, disinhibition is broadly studied throughout the field of criminology.[11] The discovery that those who sexually offend are disinhibited, compared with others, parallels findings among those who violate other social norms and laws. Whether this correlation holds promise in teasing out a particular pattern specific to those who sexually offend remains an open question.

There is still another category that is not considered in either clinical or criminal schemes but looms large on the sociocultural landscape. The influence of social power in sexual offending has been a public concern for over 40 years in the Catholic Church, and the role of priests in perpetrating sexual abuse has become a target of anger and angst.[12] While a decision to enter the priesthood is unlikely to precipitate a minor attraction, evidence indicates that strict morality in childhood and the expectations of the church often combine to create untenable demands on that person's sexuality.[13] Many other denominations are also finding that their clergy are capable of sexually offending.[14] More recently, the Boy Scouts have faced evidence of the abuse that occurs within their ranks.[15] These revelations of misconduct argue for the incorporation of a sociocultural explanation in current intrapersonal theories.[16] Presumptive models to explain such behavior return to the individual level and assume that these offenders are people drawn to positions of power from which they can act out their sexual desires. An equally valid, sociocultural interpretation would argue that positions of power exacerbate existing issues with intimacy and give rise to sexual offending.

A focus on classifying sexual offending continues. At the same time, pedophilia and hebephilia can be considered paraphilias. As such, there may be environmental conditions that create this arousal and, if explained, can assist in treatment for it. An emphasis on the individual, while essential, fails to adequately consider the broader potential for sexual abuse if it ignores these environmental factors.

The intersection of personality disorders and sexual offending

The majority of categories in this area focus on the sexual interests of the persons who offend. Personality types, if they are incorporated, are secondary to the criminal behaviors. In this classification system, the foreground contains elements of the sexual offense, and the background consists of items such as personality type and any clinical syndromes that contribute to a risk for offending.

Such typologies first addressed the finding that some persons who sexually offend identify children as their envisioned sexual objects (e.g., fixated or preferred), while others responded to children as sexual objects only under certain circumstances (e.g., regressed or situational). Beyond these rudimentary categories, a generalized lack of empathy can create an intent to sexually engage with children, not from a wish to interact emotionally, but from a desire to obtain sexual gratification via the route of least resistance. Such people display either an emerging personality disorder, such as a conduct disorder in adolescence, or a fully developed personality disorder (often an antisocial or narcissistic personality disorder) in adulthood. Some may also exhibit sociopathy, a more severe form of antisocial personality disorder (APD). In each of these disorders, sexual offending is indicative of a more pervasive lack of respect for the basic rights of others.

Conduct disorder, as described in the *Diagnostic and Statistical Manual of Mental Disorders*, 5th edition (DSM-5), includes an essential feature (Criterion A) in which there is a repetitive and consistent violation of the rights of others or of age-appropriate social norms and rules.[17] A diagnosis of conduct disorder is a required antecedent to a diagnosis of APD, in which these patterns of behavior have become an ingrained interpersonal style. For at least some adolescents, a conduct disorder will not only precede the development of an antisocial personality but will also lead to sociopathy, a more severe demonstration of antisocial traits.[18]

APD, as described in the DSM-5, includes the required feature of a pervasive disregard for the rights of others. This pattern begins in childhood or, at the latest, in early adolescence and continues into adulthood.[19] It is associated with childhood trauma, including childhood sexual abuse.[20] Persons with an APD engage far more often in criminal enterprises (such as theft, assault, and property damage) and are more likely to be involved in substance use and distribution. Persons exhibiting sociopathy are considered to have a more intense degree of antisocial personality, demonstrating criminal behavior, poor treatment outcomes, and a lack of conscience.[21] (Sociopathy is not included in the DSM-5.)

The essential feature of a narcissistic personality, as described in the DSM-5, includes patterns of grandiosity, a need for admiration, and an inability to empathize with others. These traits emerge by early adulthood and are present across interpersonal settings.[22] Although narcissism is considered less interpersonally disabling than APD, it can include a severe deficit in two basic traits—intimacy and empathy—and those affected by this disorder have trouble sustaining meaningful adult relationships.[23]

Persons exhibiting any of the above disorders can also become people who sexually offend. Those afflicted with narcissism or another personality disorder can demonstrate missing factors in their decision-making processes. But a sociopathic individual makes little distinction between burglarizing a store for easily fenced merchandise, manufacturing and selling methamphetamines for lucrative profits, and seducing a child, who is an easily procured sexual object. In each case, the purpose is immediate gratification, with little regard for its impact on others. The discomfort to others created by a burglary or the manufacture and sale of illegal drugs makes no difference to sociopaths, and any sense of disquiet generated by sexual activity with a child is overridden by the ease with which it can be accomplished.

In an age in which sexual offending, as a concept, has been inflamed into a moral panic, sexual acting out is what draws public attention.[24] Sexual offending is problematic, but it can be indicative of a more widespread impairment. In these cases the compelling issue is not treatment for the sexual offense, but treatment for a general lack of empathy and disregard for the rights of others.

At the crossroads of clinical syndromes and sexual offending

The DSM-5 recognizes numerous clinical syndromes, which it groups by category. Syndromes are considered to be complexes of symptoms that are indicative of a specific condition. Their causes, however, may not be directly understood.[25] Some sexual predilections that predispose an individual to sexual offending (e.g., pedophilia) are recognized as clinical syndromes by psychiatric organizations. Others (e.g., hebephilia/ephebophilia, or attractions to different age groups of adolescents) are not. Clinical syndromes are based on the type of symptoms they represent, so syndromes with similar clusters of symptoms are categorized together. There is no hierarchical ordering of syndromes, with one syndrome being quantitatively ranked as more severe than another, although syndromes do differ in their impact. For example, an intellectual disability has a much more profound and life-changing effect on an individual than an adjustment disorder. The former refers to limitations in intelligence and the ability to engage in activities of daily living. The latter refers to difficulties in response to an immediate life stressor.

There is no "sexual offending syndrome," per se. There are syndromes referencing paraphilias that can involve non-consensual sex (sexual behaviors with non-consenting adult partners or an attraction to child partners), but these do not address the legal consequences of such sexual desires. As discussed above, personality disorders can reflect a lack of empathy and violation of the rights of others, due to that disregard. There are other clinical syndromes that can also influence sexual offending against children. Among the most prominent are those that impair an individual's ability to rationally consider the results of acting out sexually with a child. Of these, substance use is a voluntary choice. Psychotic disorders (usually schizophrenia, schizoaffective disorder, and the manic phase of a bipolar disorder—all discussed below) and intellectual disabilities (in which the developmental age of the person who is sexually offending may be similar to that of the victim) are more likely to be circumstances in which a person's judgment is impaired.

Substance abuse

Substance abuse among those who sexually offend has been a less intense area of focus in recent years, but evidence indicates a strong correlation. Generally, sexually offensive acts are correlated with alcohol abuse.[26] The use of alcohol as a social lubricant is well documented and well understood. The potential for alcohol to lower inhibitions heightens the risk of sexual acting out.[27] And alcohol consumption, combined with deficits in emotional coping abilities, may predispose sexual acting out for those who offend against children.[28]

The use of other mood-altering substances, which also impair judgment, can play a role in these offenses.[29] An estimated 50 percent of all persons convicted of sexually offending have been diagnosed with a chronic substance abuse disorder.[30] Substance use other than alcohol, however, has been more difficult to determine. A reluctance to report illicit drug use, variability in the quality and mixture of substances, and unknown substances included in some street drugs make accurate reports of their impact more difficult. But drug use of some type (often marijuana) has been found to be common in those who sexually offend.[31] As marijuana legalization expands, its use as a drug of choice among those who offend will probably increase.

What research cannot discern is whether substance abuse leads to sexual offending, or whether shame and guilt over minor attraction leads to substance abuse, increasing the risk for acting out these sexual feelings. When factoring in childhood trauma, a family/genetic history of substance abuse, or unrelated stressors that impinge on daily functioning, the potential for cause and effect between substance abuse and sexual offending becomes even more difficult to sort out. Despite the unresolved question of which appeared first, the correlation remains. Substance abuse is often a factor in child sexual abuse.

Psychotic disorders

Psychosis as a correlate of sexual offenses is less common but still present. Psychosis refers to distortions in the perception of reality, and its hallmark is hallucinations, usually auditory ones. These "voices" give directions or offer commentary—at times comforting, and at other times malevolent or frightening—all of which are based on the words of people who are not present. Visual hallucinations can also occur, although less frequently. And delusions, or irrational belief systems, also arise. Common delusions are a fear that one is being poisoned, a conviction that a loved one is unfaithful, or the belief that a person has a divine mission.

There are several clinical syndromes in the DSM-5 that include this cluster of symptoms, among others, but three manifest themselves most frequently. Schizophrenia spectrum disorders are characterized by abnormalities that may include delusions (irrational beliefs); hallucinations (either auditory or visual); disorganized thoughts (often demonstrated by illogical speech); and/or grossly disorganized or abnormal motor-function behaviors (varying from agitation or restlessness to an inability to move).[32] The "negative symptoms" of schizophrenia can include social and emotional distancing from others, and apparent emotional apathy.

Bipolar disorders include severe mood swings. In considering the impact of mood swings on sexual offending, mania predominates as the one most likely to impair judgment. Mania is defined as an expansive mood. Its symptoms include excessive optimism, or grandiosity. People who are in a manic state can engage in reckless activities (including sexual indiscretions), despite the potential for catastrophic consequences, due to their impaired judgment. They lack insight and rarely recognize that they are ill or in need of help. Consequently, they often resist treatment or hospitalization and are frequently arrested.[33]

Schizoaffective disorder refers to a combination of schizophrenia and bipolar symptoms. In this disorder, impaired thinking, mania, or both can disrupt appropriate decision making and contribute to sexual offending.

Research suggests that persons with a serious mental illness (such as schizophrenia, bipolar disorders, or schizoaffective disorder) often have an accompanying diagnosis of a substance use disorder.[34] Such individuals are also found to be more apt to offend against strangers, rather than family members, and to offend while experiencing delusions of persecution or auditory hallucinations, or while in a manic state. Sexual acting out during these psychotic episodes may relate to disinhibition. Normal sociocultural restraints on behavior give way as cognitive processes deteriorate. The urge to act on sexual impulses also becomes disorganized.[35] Even diabetes can have an impact on cognitive functioning, creating psychosis or symptoms mimicking mania.[36] Diabetes with accompanying psychological symptoms has been found to be more prevalent among those who sexually offend against children than in the general population.

The disorganizing influence of psychosis can be overwhelming. In one case, the FBI served an adult in his 40s with a warrant for possession of child pornography with intent to distribute. He had been observed online downloading thousands of files over a period of several days. What law enforcement could not know was that he was in the throes of a severe manic episode. He had remained awake and at his computer for at least 72 hours, downloading virtually non-stop, in an obsessive attempt to find videos of a single adolescent female. When the warrant was served, he panicked, threatened that he had a gun (he did not), locked himself in his bedroom, and attempted suicide with an overdose of his medication. A SWAT team eventually entered the home and transported him to a hospital, where he was placed on a ventilator in an intensive care unit. After his recovery, he was placed in jail. Charges were eventually reduced to simple possession, and he served five years in a federal prison. While his actions were driven by his illness, that fact was given no consideration during his prosecution.

Intellectual disabilities

Another population that offers a significant challenge consists of those with intellectual disabilities (formerly described as mental retardation). Ironically, victims who fall into this category often find themselves being sexually offended at the hands of other persons with intellectual disabilities, so the roles of perpetrator and victim remain blurred when assigning responsibility.[37] Staff who work with these individuals in residential care are more likely to recognize their reasoning and decision-making deficits and remain less judgmental about sexual offending than the general public.[38] That distinction does not always apply in law. For example, research has established that people demonstrating intellectual deficits due to fetal alcohol syndrome are treated with greater care when they are victims of sexual crimes. In contrast, for those perpetrating sexual crimes, the developmental delays created by fetal alcohol syndrome are generally ignored.[39] Treatment is often ineffective for this population, with the most successful results limited to those who are higher functioning.[40] Many have difficulty conceptualizing their behavior as sexual offending. Even if they can understand what they have done, their competence to stand trial—a requisite of the criminal justice system—is often lacking and incapable of being restored.[41] They are therefore ineligible to be adjudicated through the criminal courts.

In another example, an intellectually disabled young woman, recently out of her teens, was charged with child molesting. She had engaged in sexual intercourse with two males, each of them in early adolescence. The boys were willing participants, but because of their ages, they were considered to be legally unable to consent, while she was deemed an adult. Although she had completed high school by attending special education courses, psychological testing found that she functioned in the "mildly intellectually disabled" range, and her academic skills were at the second-grade level. Measurement of her adaptive behavior indicated her activities of daily living were approximately at the level of a 10-year-old. Charges were dropped when it was determined that not only would she not be competent to stand trial, but also that, based on that state's insanity statute, she was unable to comprehend the wrongfulness of her actions (having sex with a minor) at the time they occurred.

Another population that often overlaps with the intellectually disabled are those who experience autism. Individuals with this diagnosis can act in such a way that investigators find them cold, aloof, and remorseless. More accurately, they display an inability to access emotion or empathize, which is symptomatic of this syndrome.[42] Their inability to relate effectively to others can also predispose an involvement with child pornography.[43]

Cyberspace: The anonymous, distant offense

As a global reliance on online services expands, so has pornography. It provides a sexual release, and it also offers secondary emotional gains. Approximately 4 percent of online sites are now porn related, and over 90 percent of men and 60 percent of women report having watched porn in the last month.[44] Child pornography is primarily found on the dark web (areas of the web requiring specific software, configurations, or authorizations for access). This anonymous and secure arena is assumed to have kept pace with an increasing demand, although its extent and the frequency of its use are difficult to determine.[45] The clinical and legal disparities in sexual offending are particularly important here. While many states maintain an age of consent at 16 years old, the federal government continues to consider the dissemination of visual materials of a sexual nature featuring persons under the age of 18 as child pornography. Therefore, an individual may not sexually offend by having sex with a minor aged 16 or 17 but may be tarred by the same brush for distributing or even possessing nude videos of that minor.

The obvious purpose in viewing child pornography is sexual gratification. Another goal may be an interest in exploring sexual taboos.[46] Child pornography also serves as an outlet in coping with general stressors, such as negative emotions and an inability to establish or maintain interpersonal relationships. Regardless of the reasons for initially viewing child pornography, the ongoing use of such materials seems predicated on an attraction to the attributes of children or the thrill of viewing explicit and forbidden materials.[47]

A history of sexual victimization in childhood may be more probable for persons who view child pornography than for those who sexually abuse a child bodily, although this is a tentative finding.[48] In general, though, those who initiate their sexual acting out by physically offending with children are more likely to expand into child pornography. Those who begin by sexually offending with child pornography are less likely to expand into physical sexual abuse.[49]

The widespread use of all types of pornography, difficulty in tracking the use of child pornography, and the uncertain distinction between licit and criminal pornography fog the windows of evidence regarding the frequency, duration, risk, and overall predictive power of child pornography as a precursor for physical sexual offending.

The puzzle within a postmodern perspective

From the 1970s on, there has been a sustained effort to categorize those who sexually offend. This trend has nestled uneasily alongside psychiatric diagnoses, for its purpose was not to embed offending into the existing traits and behaviors that define personality disorders or clinical syndromes. Instead, the intent was to create a legal typology of offenders—at best, a bridge between judicial and clinical definitions. The most parsimonious classifications treated sexual offending as a discrete behavior. Their purpose was to signal distinct actors in the field, who could then be identified, characterized, and neatly thumbnailed for reference.

The logical classification that held up against scrutiny (although it was given various names) argued that the impetus for those who sexually offended was based on an enduring interest in children. Ironically, this category has merit, but for the wrong reasons, as it contains two distinct groups. Having an enduring interest in children is now being considered a possible sexual orientation: those who are minor attracted. The other group is viewed as acting in response to acute cues (i.e., those with a rapid onset and a relatively short duration): stressors, disinhibitions, or impulses. Its members' interest in children may not have been constant but arose instead in response to specific triggers. This latter group has reluctantly been recognized as often exhibiting comorbid diagnoses.

The current chapter has addressed this latter group. Although demonstrating many symptoms, the spotlight is often on their sexual acting out. Socioculturally, it is the most alarming of the behaviors in which they engage. But it is often not the one of greatest concern. Those diagnosed with an APD exhibit a more general disregard for the rights and well-being of others. Treatment for their sexual acting out targets one small area within their overall dysfunction. People with a substance abuse disorder may significantly reduce their use of alcohol or drugs while incarcerated. Hence treatment for their sexual acting out may minimize the potential for this behavior, but it ignores a more general tendency toward disinhibition. And those who are actively psychotic—either exhibiting delusions, thought disorders, or mania—while engaging in sexual acting out achieve little benefit if they do not receive support to sustain the positive aspects of their daily lives in the face of a mental illness.

Those who sexually offend are a diverse group, and we would do better if we consider sexual offending in the context of more complex issues. There is much greater diversity in the problems to be addressed, and they require more than simply monitoring the sexual behavior of those who are apprehended.

Notes

1 Groth & Birnbaum, 1978.
2 Groth & Birnbaum, 1978.
3 Lanning, 2010.
4 Lim et al., 2021.
5 Nitescu, Ramba, & Nitescu, 2020.
6 Ristow et al., 2018.
7 Chatzitoffis et al., 2022.
8 Jordan et al., 2020.
9 Stinson, Sales, & Becker, 2008.
10 Choi, 2002.
11 Venables et al., 2018.
12 Formicola, 2020a.
13 Anderson, 2015.
14 Denney, Kerley, & Gross, 2018.
15 Dockterman, 2020.
16 Dagmang, 2012.
17 American Psychiatric Association, 2022.
18 López-Romero et al., 2022.
19 American Psychiatric Association, 2022.

20 DeLisi, Drury, & Elbert, 2019.
21 Larsen, Jalava, & Griffiths, 2020.
22 American Psychiatric Association, 2022.
23 Schalkwijk et al., 2021.
24 Fox, 2013.
25 American Psychiatric Association, 2022.
26 Monson et al., 1998.
27 Abracen, Looman, & Ferguson, 2017.
28 Looman et al., 2004.
29 Peugh & Belenko, 2001.
30 Kraanen & Emmelkamp, 2011.
31 Langevin & Lang, 1990.
32 American Psychiatric Association, 2022.
33 American Psychiatric Association, 2022.
34 Lam, Penney, & Alexander, 2022.
35 Craisatti & Hodes, 1992.
36 Langevin et al., 2008.
37 Martinello, 2015.
38 Steans & Simon, 2018.
39 McMurtrie, 2011.
40 Marotta, 2017.
41 U.S. Reports, Dusky v. United States, 362 U.S. 402.
42 Mogavero, 2016.
43 Allely, 2020.
44 Graveris, 2024.
45 Kuhle et al., 2017.
46 Knack, Holmes, & Federoff, 2020.
47 Steely et al., 2018.
48 Elbert, Drury, & DeLisi, 2022.
49 Ly, Dwyer, & Fedoroff.

4   The myth of community safety

Assurance but not deterrence

I was asked to testify in a sentencing hearing for a defendant in his mid-20s. He was charged with having sexual intercourse with an 11-year-old female. The child had initiated contact, engaging with him via social media, and was now pleading with the court not to incarcerate him. The prosecutor asked that I testify regarding the potential reasons for the victim's illogical advocacy and the trauma that could later develop, even if she did not feel victimized now. The prosecutor recommended a sentence of 25 years, followed by probation when the perpetrator returned to the community. The defense countered with a sentence of 15 years, followed by community-based probation. The judge heard my testimony, as well as testimony from the families of the victim and the defendant. He chose to ignore the recommendations of both attorneys. Instead, he imposed a sentence of 35 years in prison. Due to the nature of the felony, the defendant was limited by a "credit time restriction," which meant that he would serve most of that sentence without potential reductions in the time served.

One week later, I was required to interview a young adolescent female. She was seeing a counselor-in-training I supervised, who questioned whether a physical altercation between the teen and her father warranted alerting the relevant authorities under mandatory reporting laws. The client was forthcoming in our interview. In the midst of an argument, her father shoved her against a wall. Her father and his current "girlfriend" (her word) often screamed at each other during arguments, but nothing was thrown, and there were no physical assaults. Likewise, while her father often raised his voice and was demeaning in the way he spoke to his daughter, he did not call her names and had not previously struck her or her siblings. She liked her father's girlfriend but did not trust herself to become close to the woman. This was the fifth romantic partner with whom her father had cohabitated in the past two years. The daughter had learned that becoming close to her father's various partners only meant that she would be hurt when a final argument occurred, and he forced his girlfriend to leave. The shove did not leave bruises, and no other physical altercations had occurred.

DOI: 10.4324/9781003487753-4

While this information was deeply distressing, in the state in which I practice, none of it qualified as grounds to contact the authorities. The custodial parent—her father—was meeting the basic requirements required by the law to maintain independent and unsupervised parenting rights. If he chose to bring his daughter to counseling, they could voluntarily work on these issues, but there was no legitimate reason to involve an outside agency to investigate child physical abuse.

In sum, a man who traumatized a child by engaging with her sexually on two occasions will be punished by spending most of his adult life in prison, a financial burden to the citizens of the state. Yet a father who traumatizes his daughter by demonstrating horrendous parenting skills across the course of her childhood will probably continue, unabated, to make her life a living hell.

Is the community at large safer with a man who sexually offended being locked away for decades? Will it remain safer, given his status as a probationer and someone listed on a registry once he is released? Or has the state incurred a massive financial debt for his care, with a marginal increase in safety for the community, to placate a self-serving panic among voters while ignoring the plight of a child traumatized day after day as she remains with her parent? If these were isolated incidents, they might be reluctantly acknowledged as fallout from an imperfect system. But they are not. They are common occurrences in every state.

Who makes the news?

There are routine stories about those who have sexually offended. They may have fondled a relative or coerced a neighbor's child into sexual activity. For the media, these acts are no more newsworthy than the distress a family experiences returning home from a vacation to find that their home has been burglarized and irreplaceable possessions have been lost. The stories of sexual offenses against children that command headlines—whether local, national, or international—are the sensational ones. The most common among these is a child brutally raped and murdered, dumped in a forlorn woods, and the body later found mutilated or partially decomposed. Such incidents capture the imagination with their horror. As they should. Subsequently, law enforcement across multiple jurisdictions mobilizes to find the perpetrator, and regular media updates include recaps of previous information. Even the exceptions prove the rule. Two of the most notable were a long-running series of articles, beginning in 2002, in the *Boston Globe* investigating sexual abuse in the Catholic Church and various media reports on the Penn State University case involving the serial child sexual abuse by Jerry Sandusky.[1] Does this type of reporting skew the public's perception of sexual offending?

Traditional journalistic outlets and social media have both been identified as contributors to the moral panic toward sexual offending.[2] Over time, these media outlets have expanded their investigations into the topic and focused on the unintended consequences of laws and legislation. In doing so, news outlets utilized statistics to bolster the findings they were reporting. The veracity of these statistics, however, varied. At times, they were culled from individual research studies, using small samples. At other times, they were based on figures provided by governmental agencies, but these data remained dated, poorly referenced, or were open to multiple interpretations. At its best, sound journalism encourages balanced reporting, editorial fairness, and factual accuracy. At its worst, it provides hyperfocused stories, easily cooked statistics, and a bully pulpit for law-and-order legislation. The closer journalism comes to the latter description, the greater its potential to feed a moral panic.[3] This is particularly the case when media outlets address sensational crimes, which intensify the risk of sacrificing the truth for a larger audience share.[4]

Members of the public who follow informational media are more likely to assume that sexual offending is on the rise and, in turn, desire more punitive consequences for those who sexually offend.[5] The emotional impact of media stories exacerbates this tendency.[6] This is true even with regard to specific practices, such as residency restrictions for offenders.[7] These beliefs remain entrenched, despite evidence that repeat sexual offending by those who have been convicted and released is not appreciably different than for matched peers who have never been convicted of a sexual offense.[8] Ironically, an egalitarian attitude toward gender seems to have hardened public opinion toward females who sexually offend. The impact of female sexual offending was previously minimized—and in some cases even romanticized—but the public is increasingly developing a stance that is equally as harsh toward women as their male counterparts.[9]

But the basic question remains unanswered, whether it makes the news or not. What is the risk of recidivism for those who sexually offend? Nothing even approaching a definitive response exists. Emily Horowitz, an advocate for the rights of those who sexually offend, has argued that the myth of high rates of recidivism has been responsible for the devastating legal opinions handed down by some of the highest courts.[10]

We do know that sexual violence against children and adolescents continues to be problematic. In the 2021 Youth Risk Behavior Survey among high school students, conducted by the Centers for Disease Control and Prevention (CDC), 13.5 percent of females and 3.6 percent of males reported a past experience of forced sexual intercourse.[11] And 17.9 percent of females and 4.6 percent of males indicated that they had been subjected to sexual violence within the 12 months prior to the survey. Statistics on victims are easier to compile than data on those who offend, however. The CDC figures came from anonymous participants in online surveys. Victims who are asked to step forward and make criminal charges are often less forthcoming. In addition, variations in the way researchers operationally define recidivism, fluctuations in the length of follow-up periods, and differences in the populations under investigation make comparisons difficult.[12] One of the largest studies to date found a reconviction rate of 3.5 percent for those charged with any type of sexual offense.[13] Evidence is also mounting that the frequency of recidivism declines with age.[14]

Vigilante justice

It should come as no surprise that those who sexually offend are the targets of vigilante justice. Vigilantes are romanticized figures in American culture. We value the strong, independent, (usually) man of action who dares to right wrongs that the justice system either dismisses or handles at ponderous speed. Yet an outcry arises when a vigilante comes for *us*, in the form of a road-raging motorist, a neighbor who refuses to compromise, or the parent of another child who firmly believes that it is *their* child—not ours—who has been wronged. The following are three of many possible examples, but they describe vigilante justice in the national media, as an online presence, and at the local level, and the damage that each can do.

The television series *To Catch a Predator* made its debut in 2004.[15] The producers filmed sting operations. In each segment, an adult male responded to someone online (identified as underage) and engaged that individual to the point of requesting a physical meeting. Arriving at the rendezvous, instead of meeting a child, the adult met Chris Hansen, the show's host, who attempted to interview the potential predator about his intentions. Waiting law enforcement agents would then arrest the anticipated assailant as he left. Controversy about the ethics of the show's format boiled over, starting with the first episode. Questions of entrapment (segments never displayed the full online interactions that led the alleged perpetrator to the potential victim) and the drama of the confrontations with and subsequent arrests of those who, legally, should be presumed innocent until proven guilty raised concerns for many. Despite these troubling aspects, the series made for gripping reality television, and ratings trumped ethics.

The show ran through 2008, when it was taken off the air following the suicide of a suspect as the police attempted to serve a warrant. Despite its cancellation, episodes still appear, and segments are available on YouTube. Based on the most popular of these YouTube clips, the greatest viewer fascination comes from the confrontation between Hansen and the alleged perpetrator. At first, Hansen plays a naïve interloper, wondering why that person is in the home, and eventually drops the pretense of puzzlement and familiarity to confront the awful truth.

To Catch a Predator began its run in parallel with a group identifying themselves as "Perverted Justice," which was formed in 2003.[16] Its members worked as an active decoy operation online, with the avowed purpose of snaring those seeking underage youth. The group's website listed 623 convictions due to their efforts before suspending operations in 2019 due to the changing nature of online social media. With the advent of social networking, their primary task—infiltrating the sources where those attempting to ensnare children trolled—became overwhelming, in light of the group's limited resources.

These are vigilante efforts writ large, with each extolling their efforts nationwide. There are also similar efforts, albeit on a smaller scale. One of them, Bikers Against Predators, is located in Goshen, Indiana.[17] It is registered as a nonprofit organization with the IRS, and its members have used tactics similar to Perverted Justice at the local level. Upon finding those they consider predators, they contact law enforcement. If they do not feel there is enough evidence to justify police action, they use intimidation to force suspected individuals into seeking mental health services.

The publicity these efforts receive varies widely, ranging from international and national attention and a lingering presence on YouTube to local awareness. But for individuals whose lives are impacted by these sting operations, the trauma remains. Would they have been seeking young people if they had not been attracted to this behavior by the vigilantes? Perhaps. It is the old—and often unanswerable—question, which is why entrapment is such a slippery slope. What if I saw someone drop a $1 bill? Would I call out to them and give it back? What if it was a $5 bill? Or a $10 bill? Or a $100 bill? At what point is morality overwhelmed by selfish desire? In the same way, will creating an opportunity to offend stop the inevitable, or will it initiate a situation that would otherwise not exist?

Management in practice

Juveniles

Mental health professionals, law enforcement members, and legislators all agree that juveniles who sexually offend should not be held to the same standard as adults. Their lack of appreciation for the impact of their actions and their failure to exhibit fully developed impulse control, as well as the expectation that their behavior will be supervised, all contribute to a mindset that argues for a *rehabilitative* model rather than a *punitive* one. That does not change the fact that these juveniles have committed sexual offenses and generated a moral panic similar to that of their adult counterparts. In creating a model that offers treatment while assuaging community fears, a question still remains. If juveniles who sexually offend are to be effectively managed, exactly who are they?

A dysfunctional family is common among many youths who act out sexually.[18] A large proportion of these juveniles have also been exposed to some form of physical violence within the home.[19] Studies of their intelligence levels and academic performance have generated mixed results. In a comparison of samples matched for the intellectual functioning of juveniles who had offended and those who had not, cognitive impairments were more pronounced among the former.[20] This indicates that limitations in development or cognitive maturity probably contribute to sexual acting out at an early age. Juveniles who sexually offend are also more likely than their non-offending peers to be diagnosed with a clinical syndrome—often depression, an attention deficit/hyperactivity disorder, or a conduct disorder.[21]

These findings are logical. Juveniles who lack stability in their homes, display cognitive or developmental delays and limitations, and are diagnosed with a mental disorder are generally more likely to demonstrate poor handling of their emerging sexual drive. Treatment options include interventions in the community, treatment in a residential facility, or, for juveniles committing more violent sexual assaults or sexual acting out in combination with other criminal acts, incarceration in state correctional facilities. Of these options, community intervention or residential treatment for several months is used most often. Evidence for the efficacy of treatment within the community versus residential care is not strong, since recidivism following either form of treatment is approximately 5 percent.[22]

The question of what should be the appropriate management for juveniles who offend is answered on a state-by-state basis. For example, sexting is ubiquitous among young people. Even though federal law considers it to be trafficking in child pornography, state-level responses to this behavior are mixed. Should adolescents who are convicted of felony sex crimes be expected to register as sexual offenders? Again, state legislation varies, and some states make decisions on a case-by-case basis. Which governmental agency should serve as a watchdog when a juvenile offends? In some cases, juvenile courts and probation officers take the lead. In others, a state's social service agency, responsible for the well-being of families and children, is primarily responsible. In general, however, there is greater tolerance for juveniles who sexually offend, as well as an assumption that these behaviors lack the predatory nature ascribed to adults.

An often-unrecognized struggle for the family of a juvenile who sexually offends is the magnitude of its ripple effect. Any family faces trauma and chaos when a father and husband, or even an uncle or cousin, is arrested for a sexual offense against one of its members. But the revelation that a sibling has sexually abused another sibling can create a heartrending dilemma for parents. At 15, "Brian" was the oldest of three siblings, with two younger sisters. Over time, Brian fondled first one and then the other, extracting promises that they would not tell their parents. The abuse had stopped for several months before the youngest chose to share this information with an aunt. The police were called in, a detective investigated the situation, and Brian was moved to his grandparents' home, where he lived for the next two years. His parents were cooperative with their son's community-based treatment and complied with all probationary expectations. But his mother described the devastation she experienced over her son's behavior, and the distrust she felt toward him. That experience is now 10 years behind them. Brian recently celebrated the birth of his first child, a son. Shortly thereafter, I saw his mother in a local store and chatted with her briefly. In a whispered aside, she told me, "I feel bad saying this, but I was so thankful it wasn't a girl." Love may trump trauma, but trauma leaves its scars.

Probation, parole, and location

Those convicted of a sexual offense may remain in the community while serving out their sentence or be released into the community following incarceration. If they remain in the community, they often do so under the terms of a period of supervision, or probation. Being set free after incarceration usually triggers one of two options. They can be on parole, which means that they continue to serve their sentence, but do so within the community, adhering to specific expectations. Or they can be released after having completed the incarceration portion of their sentence, although they still must follow the terms of their probation.

The rules of probation or parole vary by jurisdiction (federal, state, or county), but they have broad parameters that are usually similar for any probationer/parolee. (Hereafter, I will simply use the term probationer.) Travel outside the state or a circumscribed area is prohibited unless first given permission to do so. Possession of alcohol, illicit drugs, or weapons (such as guns or knives), even if they belong to other members of the household in which the probationer lives, is usually forbidden. Screening for the use of drugs or alcohol is routine. And probationers either call on their assigned probation officer or are visited on a routine (and, at times, a surprise) basis to assess their status.

Those who have sexually offended often face additional, unique prohibitions. Common requirements include no online access or online access that is monitored or limited by probation supervisors, particularly for those who have previously engaged in child pornography. Pornography of any kind is routinely prohibited. Their housemates or roommates must not have committed a sexual offense, even if that offense was a misdemeanor rather than a felony. If a probationer who sexually offended intends to engage in a romantic or dating relationship, the probation officer must be informed. Polygraph examinations may be routinely conducted to determine the veracity of information provided to the probation officer and assure the officer that no prohibited contact with minors has occurred. When present, these rules are rigidly applied, with few opportunities to flaunt them without being incarcerated. Incarceration can be a brief period in jail (for probationers who have committed a less significant lapse) or a return to prison to complete a full sentence (for probationers who have committed serious infractions).

Release into or maintenance within the community has also engendered legislation to protect children by geographically restricting the living opportunities for those who sexually offend. This effort continues, despite evidence that less than 10 percent of children who are sexually abused are approached by a stranger.[23] Residency restrictions have been upheld by state courts, and the US Supreme Court has declined to rule on this issue. These restrictions set a boundary around schools, parks, or other gathering places for children within which those convicted of sexual offenses cannot reside. This places a further burden on those already forced to acknowledge a felony conviction in their search for housing. In periods of or areas where there is limited supply and peak demand, landlords can afford to be selective, and those who have sexually offended often find themselves at a serious disadvantage when seeking shelter as best they can. This practice still exists, despite a lack of evidence that residency restrictions protect the youth they intend to shield or mitigate factors leading to rearrest for those who have offended.[24]

A remarkable demonstration of the rigid application of this law occurred several years ago in a small Indiana town. "Edward" had been released from prison and remained on probation. He found a second-floor apartment that doubtless violated fire codes, since it had one exit—a narrow stairway, descending onto the sidewalk directly across from the local police station. He remained in his cramped but utilitarian quarters for two years, until one of the town's churches decided to renovate a storefront one block away and create a youth bistro for area adolescents. Once the bistro plans began, they put Edward in violation of residency rules requiring him to be at least 1,000 feet from any location in which youth might congregate, and his probation officer insisted that he move. This objection was met with a letter from the town's police chief, who countered that it was to their benefit to have a registered sex offender living *across from the police station*, with the only entrance to his apartment visible from the station's windows. That letter made no difference. Rules were rules. And, in perhaps the ultimate irony, Edward found an apartment 1,050 feet from a local elementary school.

The offender registry and civil commitment

Registration of those who sexually offend began in earnest in the United States in 1994 with congressional passage of the Jacob Wetterling Crimes Against Children and Sexually Violent Offender Registration Act. Although this initial legislation required those who had sexually offended to register with the appropriate authorities (usually the police), public notification was not a part of it. That requirement would be enacted with Megan's Law, passed two years later. The Pam Lychner Sex Offender Tracking and Identification Act was passed that same year, and it required the formation of a national sex offender registry. In 2006, the Adam Walsh Act was passed, also known as the Sex Offender Registration and Notification Act (SORNA). These and subsequent legislative efforts were designed to inform the public about the nature of sexual offenses and increase public awareness of the presence of those who had sexually offended.

The general public continues to support SORNA, placing access to the names and locations of those who have sexually offended over questions of rights to privacy and concerns about the discriminatory treatment these acts create. A recent, exhaustive study by the Federal Research Division of the Library of Congress determined that the efficacy of SORNA could not be demonstrated.[25] This should not be surprising. The initial act creating a registry and subsequent legislation moving it forward are all named after the young victims of horrific sexual assaults. The well-intended efforts by the parents of each of these victims were designed to create a system in which no other child would be lost in such an unspeakable manner. But their logic is flawed. The assumption is that knowing about those who have offended and being aware of their residence in a specific area makes it less probable that an abduction will occur, but this has not been proven by any source. In addition, the flood of offenders that now fill the registry makes the possibility of recognizing someone on that list highly improbable. As an example, I searched for such persons on my state's registry. There are 718 names in my midsize city alone. The potential to later recognize one of their faces is negligible, and the probability of being able to identify that individual as harboring malfeasance toward a child is even lower.

Studies have also found that sexual offender registries are often inaccurate.[26] They fail to offer the protection they allegedly provide, since they include the names of those who have died, those who have been reincarcerated (often due to non-sexual crimes), and those who have neglected to report a move. And people listed on these registries report discrimination in regard to employment, housing, and educational opportunities.[27]

Civil commitment laws (for court-ordered, compulsory admission to a psychiatric facility) have a long history in the United States, but only recently have they been widely applied to cases of sexual offenses. At the state (rather than the federal) level, civil commitment assumes that there is imminent danger on the part of a person with a mental illness. This danger can be either to self or to others, requiring the state to assume responsibility for that person's well-being.[28]

Civil commitment for those who sexually offend has an oddly linear history.[29] In 1955, Leroy Hicks perpetrated the first sexual offense for which he was arrested. A pattern of incarceration, release for time served, and rearrest for sexual offenses continued until he was scheduled to be discharged from a Kansas prison in 1994. The Kansas state legislature had enacted a Sexually Violent Predator Act that permitted persons identified as such to be civilly committed following the completion of their sentence. Under the Kansas statute, a multidisciplinary team reviewed Hicks's case and recommended that a petition for civil commitment be filed. The prosecutor did so, the petition was granted, and Hicks was transferred from prison to a secure psychiatric facility.

Hicks's case proceeded on appeal to the US Supreme Court. There, the justices established that civil commitment for those who were deemed sexually violent predators was constitutional. Kansas's legal actions met the dual burdens of respecting due process under the law and avoiding double jeopardy (being tried twice on the same charge). The use of civil commitment for sexual offenses is now considered a broad, viable option. As of 2020, 6,300 persons were detained in the 20 states that have civil commitment laws for those who sexually offend.[30]

The silent statistic: Offender suicide

In efforts to protect the community, the prevailing attitude is almost always "us" against "them." But those who have offended are part of the community, too, and sometimes they are more integrally involved than comfort allows us to acknowledge.[31] Their attempts at reintegration—and, at times, the struggle to confront their demons—can become too much.

Those who have sexually offended often receive mandatory mental health services.[32] The risk of self-harm theoretically could be reduced through ongoing contact with a mental health professional, but this is generally not the case. Those who offend are often reluctant to communicate their fears and their fantasies to a third party, since they are aware that records can be shared with probation and parole officers. These mandatory clients remain vigilant toward the risk of being returned to jail or prison. Misunderstandings by therapists regarding mandatory reporting laws—often erring on the side of unnecessarily reporting behaviors or even thoughts—further erode the trust of those who have sexually offended and seek professional help.[33]

Viable statistics are difficult to determine for those charged with a sexual offense who then commit suicide. Gathering such data is difficult due to unknown or unclear causes of death, failure to link a suicide victim with a charge of a sexual offense, or suicide committed after a person completes probation. One study suggests the sobering reality: Those who had committed a sex offense against a child were 183 times more likely than the general population to die by their own hand.[34] The effect of a charge of sexual offending already has a significant impact on those close to the perpetrator. Suicide complicates an already difficult situation.[35]

The most tragic victim of suicide, unquestionably, is the person who dies. Regardless of our beliefs about human dignity and the right to choose life or death, an individual who has weighed the options and chosen death delivers one of the most forceful statements that can be made. The ripple effect of suicide, however, means that the tragedy does not stop with a single lost life. The power of that deadly statement reverberates through family, friends, and the victims of sexual abuse who are left behind, all of whom are faced with a mixture of horror, grief, and anger. The suicide of a person who has sexually offended means that we have failed the *entire* community.

The reality: Recidivism and risk

The struggle, for those who have sexually offended and remain in or return to the community, is one for which there is no clear answer. It is a constructionist versus essentialist question.[36] Are those who sexually offend driven by distortions in their thinking? This constructionist view is one that most of those who offer treatment believe in. Are these individuals capable of changing their distorted patterns of thinking and developing a more empathic, logical, and appropriate set of expectations toward others? Or, from an essentialist viewpoint, are they innately corrupt and incapable of changing their interpersonal perceptions? Do they pose a risk, no matter how much time and effort goes into their rehabilitation? Or are they (as is probably always the case in response to complex questions about the human condition) spread across a continuum, in which a few are easily treated, a few are intractable, and the majority fall somewhere in between?

Who is at risk for recidivism? And what proportion of the people who have sexually offended are likely to reoffend? These percentages vary dramatically and are difficult to determine. The differences are based on several factors. First (and most obvious) is the length of time that a group of people who have sexually offended is studied. The longer the period of observation, the greater the likelihood that repeat sexual offenses will be found. Longitudinal studies of those who have sexually offended are now following them for a period of 25 years or more. Still, these investigations are fraught with their own difficulties. Persons who have sexually offended are not a discrete population. Some are arrested for multiple offenses, of which a sexual offense is only one. Over time, they may be reincarcerated for non-sexual offenses. Such arrests are not necessarily reported or followed for over a quarter century, and they may skew the dataset since those individuals had a limited ability to reoffend while in jail or prison. Moreover, changes in the circumstances of a person's life can be dramatic, and these cannot always be assessed nor can they ever be controlled. Therefore, taking a single variable such as "sexual reoffense" and using it as a standard against which to determine risk, treatment success, or any other variable is fraught with its own pitfalls.

Longitudinal studies also cannot account for changes in legislation over time. Revisions in what constitutes a sexual crime, plea agreements that dismiss some counts but not others, and varying levels of charges in different jurisdictions all impact the meaning of a sexual offense as it applies to recidivism. Such information is not readily available in long-term studies.

The risk of sexual offending against minors versus the risk of *all* forms of sexual offending, is also not always separated out in longitudinal studies. While it may be of interest, at an overall level, to know the risk for a sexual reoffense among all persons so charged, for purposes of community safety, it is better to understand the risk of reoffense for, among others, (1) those who perpetrated this crime against very young children, (2) those who carried it out against adolescents near the age of consent, and (3) those who committed violent sexual assaults against adults. These breakdowns in the data give a clearer picture of who presents the greatest risk, but such distinctions are often unavailable in the studies.

In sum, we understand very little. We do not know how to best protect our children. We do not know how best to treat those who sexually offend. And we certainly do not know how best to manage those who sexually offend once they return to the community.

Notes

1　Zatkin, Sitney, & Kaufman, 2022.
2　Cucolo & Perlin, 2013.
3　Fox, 2013.
4　Haney, 2009.
5　Zatkin, Sitney, & Kaufman, 2022.
6　Malinen, Willis, & Johnston, 2014.
7　Simeone, 2018.
8　Kahn et al., 2017.
9　Christensen, 2018.
10　Horowitz, 2023.
11　Centers for Disease Control and Prevention, n.d.
12　Przybylski, 2015.
13　US Department of Justice, Bureau of Justice Statistics, 2003.
14　Smethurst, Bamford, & Tully, 2021.
15　Wikipedia, s.v. "To Catch a Predator."
16　Perverted Justice, n.d.
17　Bikers Against Predators, n.d.
18　Righthand & Welch, 2004.
19　Hunter et al., 2003.
20　Miyaguchi & Shirataki, 2014.
21　Vandiver, Brathwaite, & Stafford, 2017.
22　Howey, Lundahl, & Assadollahi, 2022.
23　Gallagher, Bradford, & Pease, 2008.
24　Levenson, Zgoba, & Tewksbury, 2007.
25　Federal Research Division, Library of Congress, 2022.
26　Thompson, 8/25/2020.
27　Bonnar-Kidd, 2010.
28　Testa & West, 2010.
29　Vandiver, Brathwaite, & Stafford, 2017, pp. 321–323.
30　Williams Institute, 2020.
31　Thomas, 2014.
32　Byrne Lurigio, & Pimentel, 2009.
33　Walker, Butters, & Nichols, 2022.
34　Pritchard & King, 2005.
35　Hoffer et al., 2010.
36　Waldram, 2009.

5 Postmodern interventions

The evolution of treatment models

The current generation of treatment models for those who sexually offend—and, more generally, for those who are incarcerated for any crime—can be said to have begun with what has come to be called the Martinson report on recidivism, made public in 1975.[1] That investigation has a checkered past. In 1966, the New York State Governor's Special Committee on Criminal Offenders commissioned a research inquiry into effective means of rehabilitation. A review of over 200 studies from 1945 to 1967 found that treatment had no appreciable effect on recidivism. One of its coauthors, Robert Martinson, questioned the viability of the survey, and the state prohibited its publication. Only after a copy of the study was subpoenaed for a 1972 court case was it made available to the public. Following that disclosure, Martinson published a summary of the 1,400-page document, titled "What Works? Questions and Answers about Prison Reform." The publicity it generated placed its findings somewhere between empirical evidence and shock journalism.

In a subsequent publication five years later, Martinson did back off from the most pessimistic, "nothing works" pronouncements in the report and acknowledged the efficacy of some rehabilitation efforts.[2] Others argued that while its findings were dire, the study opened a path to improve the effectiveness of treatment.[3] Nevertheless, the report's original arguments had a chilling effect on rehabilitation, as federal and state governments used these findings to scale back treatment efforts.[4] Ironically, this pessimistic view of the effectiveness of treatment for those incarcerated, particularly for sexual offenses, paralleled an argument—made for far different purposes—by the nascent sexual minority movement. Aversion therapy—which attempts to create negative associations by pairing uncomfortable stimuli with a patient's deviant sexual arousal—had long been the treatment for paraphilias, including same-sex interests.[5] (This effort is discussed in Chapter 6.) The argument that these treatments were cruel, unnecessary, and ineffective was gaining momentum at the exact moment that the use of treatment for incarcerated individuals, including those charged with sexual offenses, was deemed ineffective. Mental health interventions for those who sexually offended were rapidly losing favor to the idea of removing these people from society.

DOI: 10.4324/9781003487753-5

A return to treatment program models was difficult, but it eventually succeeded. Financial considerations played a key role. Unless those who sexually offended were to be given life sentences, with the accompanying exorbitant costs of prison stays, they would return to their communities. And if, when going back to these communities, they were not provided with an adequate level of oversight, which was equally cost prohibitive, there would need to be some means of trusting them with limited supervision. Treatment models, whatever their weaknesses, were the logical choice. Over the past half century, models that emphasize risk assessment for recidivism, treatment options to reduce that risk, and the implementation of cognitive and cognitive-behavioral treatment interventions have emerged as the evidence-based standard. Nonetheless, the debate rages over their efficacy. Meta-analyses generally support positive results obtained through treatment, but they vary according to the type of treatment, client base, duration of post-treatment measurement, and definition of recidivism (e.g., definitions of sexual recidivism and of sexual versus other types of offenses).

This chapter analyzes current treatment models for those incarcerated for sexual offending. Prior chapters have highlighted the difficulty of incorporating sociocultural expectations in definitions of child sexual abuse, particularly when the victims are adolescents; the manifestation of child sexual abuse as a symptom of other mental health issues; and the essentialist versus constructionist debate (nature versus nurture) regarding the origins of a sexual attraction to children. Technology now allows anonymous and virtual offending via cyberspace. Thus, the demand for treatment models becomes complex indeed. Although subpopulations and aggravating factors are recognized more frequently, models are rarely tailored to accommodate these concerns. At their best, then, how effective can treatment models be? Meta-analyses provide some answers but are hardly exhaustive. A brief history will explain the steps that led to the current approaches.

The cost of sexual liberation

As the 1970s ended, a perfect storm had formed for those who sexually offended. Interventions had (apparently) been debunked.[6] Nascent support for their sexual rights had been withdrawn. A backlash, demonstrating a desire to return to traditional conservative values, was almost inevitable, given the sociopolitical climate.[7] Social equilibrium could be restored by ensuring that children, at least, would be safe from the rampant immorality pouring into the streets—or so the most fearful logic went.

Despite an increasing demand for legislation to incarcerate those who offended, research supported ongoing efforts in and the effectiveness of treatment.[8] And the general public was less punitive than many of their elected representatives assumed.[9] In retrospect, this uptick in advocacy for the protection of children was linked to high-profile cases.[10] Studies had found that those who sexually offended served proportionally greater sentences than those charged with other crimes that were considered to be of equal severity.[11] The 1981 murder of 6-year-old Adam Walsh in Florida created a staunch and highly visible advocate in his father, John Walsh. International attention given to the serial killer John Wayne Gacy, who targeted boys and young men, incited further panic. But at any point in history, journalists have sought and publicized high-profile cases, and, as the adage goes, sex sells. The groundswell of enmity against a population that lacked support and could almost universally be condemned gained increased force from rapidly shifting social values.

The attitudes of policymakers and criminal justice practitioners were in flux as they tried to read public opinion. There was widespread recognition that policy and legislation were ineffective, both as protection for children and as a deterrent to reoffending. There was equally little trust, however, in treatment being effective.[12] Legislators were influenced to protect their own demographics. A study at the time argued that politicians created laws designed to protect white, female children assaulted by strangers—a very small percentage of those victimized but representative of their own families.[13]

The federal government weighed in on the controversy, beginning in 1994, with what would become the first of several initiatives addressing sexual offending. The Jacob Wetterling Crimes Against Children and Sexually Violent Offender Registration Act established several baseline expectations for states: (1) registry standards; (2) an increased-risk offender class, termed "sexually violent predators"; (3) mandatory address verification annually for all registrants and every 90 days for those classified as sexually violent; (4) mandatory minimum 10-year registration for all and lifetime registration for those classified as sexually violent; and (5) discretionary public notification as a measure of protection.[14] Ten more major federal efforts have since been enacted, all with the purpose of providing further protection for children, and each of them tightening the monitoring of those convicted of a sexual crime. A study of eight states considered the most conscientious in their legislative efforts to charge, convict, monitor, and treat those who sexually offend found no consistent pattern of effectiveness in the application of these laws.[15] In addition, the impact of registration is significant, but only in the detrimental effect it has for reintegrating those who sexually offend back into the community. It limits their options for housing, increases stigma, and demonstrates no consistent impact on reoffending or the protection of children.[16]

The legislation crafted in the latter decades of the twentieth century could not begin to prepare for the next assault on children: the internet. It vastly expanded the reach of child pornography and, in doing so, magnified a problem that remains unresolved to this day.

Sexual offending and the dark web

Online experiences, as anyone with access knows, offer a cornucopia of delights from the comfort of one's own home. From hopeful chefs to ambitious gardeners, from tomorrow's musical genius to today's get-rich-quick impresarios, the components to plan or to dream are all easily accessible. These same elements are available for romance and sex. From dating sites for religious singles, to sites that promote casual sexual encounters, to pornography in every imaginable permutation, sexual fulfillment (of a sort) is a click away. These latter sites, for those so inclined, include children, particularly in areas online noted for containing illicit information, commonly called the dark web.

How are images of children determined to be obscene? The US Supreme Court created a landmark case in 1973 in *Miller v. California*.[17] In this ruling, the Court defined unprotected obscenity—that is, not covered by the First Amendment's freedom of expression guarantee—by creating what has since been called the Miller Test, or the three-prong obscenity test. Three criteria are used to determine obscenity:

1 Whether the average person, applying contemporary community standards, would find that the work, taken as a whole, appeals to prurient interests (i.e., sexual matters)
2 Whether the work depicts or describes, in a patently offensive way, sexual conduct specifically defined by the applicable state law
3 Whether the work, taken as a whole, lacks serious literary, artistic, political, or scientific value

Federal legislation limits child pornography distributed via interstate or international commerce, as well as the production and distribution of images online in this country. Viewing and possessing child pornography is also restricted, for two reasons. First, this practice exploits the children used to create the images. Second, but of equal importance, it is believed to act as a stepping stone for physical child sexual abuse, although this is less common than popularly believed.[18] There are persons who sexually offend against children who also view child pornography, but the pattern is reversed.[19] The overwhelming majority of these individuals first engage in hands-on sexual child abuse. Only after being charged with a hands-on offense against a child do they turn to child pornography. There are relatively few viewers who also create child pornography. The majority use and distribute existing child pornography materials but do not produce the images themselves.[20] Federal laws to prohibit the production and dissemination of child pornography acknowledge but fail to address the problem of children and adolescents who generate and circulate such pornography among themselves, usually by sexting. States vary in how vigorously they pursue the prosecution of minors who offend in this way.[21]

Those engaging in child pornography offer several justifications for its use.[22] Consistent with adult pornography, child pornography is a means of sexual gratification. The illicit or "taboo" nature of child pornography is a further incentive for some, particularly as they become satiated with mainstream pornographic sources. While a preexisting sexual interest in children is a driving force for certain individuals, not all participants start there. Boredom and a motivation to expand sexual horizons can create paraphilias, including an interest in children. Among those with a romantic interest in children, termed a minor attraction, some justify the use of images as a less harmful form of engagement than physical sexual contact. Many also identify this as a coping mechanism for their negative emotions.

In parallel with a subset of those who routinely view adult pornography, some who watch child pornography report an addiction to it.[23] These individuals describe a progression in which the need to expand their sexual horizons becomes hyperfocused on viewing child pornography. As they do so, many of the behavioral and emotional correlates of an addiction come into play (i.e., desensitization to the materials; increased tolerance, requiring greater stimulation for arousal; inability to resist the urge; greater acceptance of risky behaviors; and social isolation). These echo the reasons for other compulsive/addictive behaviors, so this finding is not unexpected.

One of the paradoxes of child pornography is the distance between a victim and the person who is offending. A child actor in pornographic materials may have been victimized decades ago in a country far removed from that of the individual now viewing the offending images. The concept of restitution has traditionally been employed in legal proceedings to prevent a criminal's enrichment at the expense of a victim. This was traditionally defined as instances when the criminal was the primary cause of harm to the victim or the victim's property. A 2008 court case changed that.[24] The attorney for a victim of child pornography asked for damages from a defendant who had downloaded her images. By 2014, the US Supreme Court, in *Paroline v. United States*, affirmed mandatory restitution for child pornography victims.[25]

The intention behind this decision and the subsequent federal law (commonly called the Amy, Vicky, and Andy Act of 2018) was noble. Those convicted of viewing child pornography were to pay restitution to identifiable victims. What this legislation could not anticipate, however, was the industry it spawned. Law firms, contracting with their clients for a percentage of any fees obtained, troll for cases to enrich themselves in the quest for restitution. An unresolved question is whether the victims receive fair compensation or are victimized once again. Another dilemma is, how can we protect and offer restitution to the victims if the children themselves create the images? These are difficult questions to resolve.

"Lock 'em up!": And then?

Keeping those who sexually offended off the streets was an appealing proposition, but long-term incarceration was not the answer. By the 1980s, limitations in our understanding of this situation were being touted in the research literature.[26] In 1989, an exhaustive review concluded that treatment for those who sexually offend was largely ineffective, although the authors cited a lack of adequate follow-up data, rather than unsuccessful treatment per se, as the primary difficulty.[27] That finding was vigorously challenged, but changes in treatment since its publication offer testimony to its validity.[28] Even so, research into interventions largely reports on group therapy programs for sexual offenders in correctional facilities.[29] Outpatient and other forms of treatment receive less scrutiny.

The ethics associated with treatment for those who sexually offend require a delicate balance. While retaining respect for and appreciating the dignity of the person who offends, optimal treatment targets the safety of potential victims and the community to which that person is returning.[30] Accordingly, ethics must consider risk management, program design, the focus of interventions, community protection, therapists' values, and standards of care. These are not easy elements to balance. They often need to be applied within incarcerated communities, where those who offend are at risk of physical violence from other inmates, who justify that violence as a means of promoting cultural norms against child abuse.[31] Once an offender is released into the community, these ethical difficulties often occur within mandated treatment settings, monitored by probation requirements. In an aptly titled article—"It's Just You and Satan, Hanging Out at a Pre-School"—a psychologist has analyzed the stigma that treatment must overcome if there is to be effective rehabilitation.[32] The question of whether treatment-as-management strategies violate the fundamental rights of those who are convicted of sexual offenses also remains in play.[33] For now, mental health providers who agree to treat those who have sexually offended also agree to put aside ethical concerns about violating the rights of these involuntary clients, in order to provide a service to both the client and the community.

By the early 1990s, predictors for the successful completion of residential treatment programs (including for the incarcerated) were recognized as being of paramount importance. Social competence seemed to be one key, with those demonstrating improved social skills being more likely to succeed.[34] In addition, the principles that would drive treatment models into their present form were coming into focus, as was their primary purpose. A reduction in repeat offending was the target of any intervention model. To accomplish this goal, treatment would need to focus on risk, need, and responsivity.[35] *Risk* mandated higher levels of service for those with a greater likelihood of reoffending. *Need* targeted services to match the type of offense. And *responsivity* paired the mode of service with the learning styles and abilities of those being treated.

The risk–need–responsivity (RNR) model and its modifications continue to dominate treatment today. But the limitations of a model that applies only to those who already have offended are now coming into focus, and the need for a treatment model for persons who are minor attracted but have not acted on their desires has received increasing scrutiny.[36] Despite this awareness, the fundamental emphasis remains on being reactive—that is, only treating those who have been charged with a sexual offense.

Implementation and evolution of risk–need–responsivity and related models

How well does RNR work? The precepts of the original RNR model have evolved based on emerging legislation, empirical study, and the changing needs of those who offend. This evolution has encompassed an overarching concept—principles of effective intervention (PEI)—which encompasses a wide range of factors that are deemed essential for effective treatment.[37] With this shift, the developers of RNR continue to espouse its efficacy. They assert that its principles are the fundamentals necessary for effective treatment.[38] And research continues to bear at least some of these assertions out.[39]

The first principle of RNR, risk, is an essential consideration. Communities have long expressed concern about the presence of those who sexually offend in their midst, so any treatment must allay the fear of offenders returning among the general public. A desire to contain risk also fits in well with a fundamental principle of prisons. Given the nature of their populations, they, too, focus on risk, albeit of a more immediate and physical type.[40] The second principle of the model, need, addresses criminal behaviors that are likely to continue. Sexual offending is a primary focus, but the model's parameters also emphasize other antisocial behaviors. The third principle, responsivity, centers on providing treatment *to* the person offending *as a client*, in the most efficacious manner possible. This tenet argues that treatment should be tailored to individual needs, whenever possible.

The inclusion of RNR in the PEI model endeavors to broaden the former's emphasis from its three primary components and create a more humanistic approach. Despite these efforts, particularly when treatment is offered in prisons, the system of choice often remains the stand-alone RNR model.[41] Nonetheless, an alternative has emerged that attempts to enhance the capabilities of those who offend. Rather than emphasizing relapse prevention, which is the focus of RNR (even within PEI), the aim of the good lives model (GLM) is to improve an offender's quality of life by stressing its positive (i.e., "good") aspects, thereby reducing the chances of recidivism upon release.[42] Instead of attempting to eliminate negative behaviors, which is the goal of RNR, GLM capitalizes on strengths.

GLM's "goods" are fundamental: life (including health), knowledge, the ability to excel in both work and play, agency (autonomy and self-direction), self-directed reassurance (inner peace), friendships, a sense of community, spirituality, happiness, and creativity.[43] The principles of GLM parallel the basic concepts of therapeutic community (a group-based treatment program for those who are incarcerated).[44]

GLM's implementation has faced strong criticism.[45] Its short-term efficacy, ability to put its fundamental principles into operation, and long-term success are challenged by proponents of RNR. Another concern is how to monitor therapists' fidelity to such a complex model.[46] The idealism underlying GLM's principles has been challenged as either untenable or paternalistic. Others debate whether those who are incarcerated or are living under close supervision in the community prefer risk management techniques, provided by the RNR model, rather than GLM's goals for personal well-being.[47]

Despite this wariness, GLM has gained a foothold. Components of both models are interwoven, so pure RNR and GLM programs are less common, at least in name. Those using RNR often incorporate GLM principles into their interventions.[48] GLM encourages buy-in from those who have offended, and participants experience a sense of ownership and investment that is not present if the program is structured in such a way that all interventions are imposed rather than mutually considered.[49] As the use of GLM proliferates, opportunities to assess its effectiveness versus standard relapse programs increase. Using GLM has not been shown to result in greater improvements, but neither has it been less successful than other programs.[50]

Studies do indicate the importance of planning for reintegration within the community upon release as a factor in avoiding recidivism using GLM.[51] Additional research has analyzed those facing legal consequences who are not yet convicted. For these individuals, participation in group therapy using a GLM framework initially motivated them externally through pressure to demonstrate compliance with its precepts. Over time, the majority experienced a shift to internal motivation as they hoped for better lives.[52] The potential for an integration of GLM and restorative justice (where those who have offended and their victims meet and reach resolution) has also been posited as a step in expanding GLM.[53] One of the obstacles to GLM, however, is the pursuit of the "goods" that it assumes are fundamental for those either released into the community or who remain there as they undergo treatment. Much of this is tied to offender registration and the housing obstacles created by laws in the United States.[54] If these goods are unattainable, the efficacy of the model is weakened.

The evidence: What do treatment models actually do?

Treatment models, once in place, leave two nagging questions. First, are they effective? And, if so, how can this be measured? Second, regardless of their effectiveness, how much freedom should those who sexually offend have?

Mental health treatment in the twenty-first century is predicated on evidence that it works, although the "evidence" behind evidence-based treatment models creates its own problem.[55] Dilemmas immediately arise in applying RNR and its modifications if a participant's needs cannot be adequately assessed. Criminal charges are the most obvious starting point in determining risk. But within the justice system, these are as much bargaining chips as they are reflections of criminal activity. The frequent use of plea bargains means that the original charges may be dismissed or reduced to lower ones in exchange for a guilty plea. Do the allegations on which the defendant is later convicted reflect the severity of the crime? Or are they a compromise between prosecution and defense? In some cases, a behavior might have been sexually motivated, but a plea bargain was struck, so the indictment reflected a minimal sexual element.[56] By what criteria, then, does RNR determine risk?

GLM constructs are even more difficult to measure than RNR ones. The fundamental question here is whether improving an offender's quality of life or offering risk management techniques is more essential in reducing recidivism. The practical answer has been to create hybrid programs that incorporate elements of both models, since research suggests that one is not more efficacious than the other. It seems probable that mental health providers offering services to those who sexually offend hope for potentiation—that is, using the two models in combination to create greater efficacy than using them in isolation. To date, however, no research supports this possibility.

Are treatment models for those who sexually offend effective? Several meta-analyses indicate that they are—within limits. Meta-analysis is a statistical process that incorporates the findings of multiple individual studies. In this case, it provides a powerful lens to examine the efficacy of treatment models for those who have sexually offended.

An early study, published in 1990, found that the risk of recidivism correlated strongly with the extent to which treatment programs appropriately met the principles of RNR.[57] Another article ascertained that recidivism among those who sexually offend was already low, but effective treatment reduced the risk of sexual as well as more general criminal offending.[58] As meta-analyses continued, it became clear that not all interventions reduce recidivism. Programs that adhere to the RNR model's components are more likely to demonstrate efficacy.[59] A meta-analysis specifically examining the effectiveness of treatment for those who sexually offend against children, however, was unable to demonstrate consistent results.[60] Nor did there appear to have been improvements after studies on this topic began in 1980.[61]

Regardless of how well treatment may work, both federal and state legislation is now grounded in the premise that post-conviction regulation of those who have sexually offended is permissible.[62] Many states require that adolescents (or, at a minimum, older adolescents) be listed on an offender register once convicted of a sexual offense. Whether adolescents have the developmental capability to understand and appreciate—and therefore respond to—the supposed deterrence of a registry is unknown.[63] And a longitudinal study over several decades indicates that their recidivism is less than that of peers who were adjudicated for non-sexual crimes.[64] Empirical support for the need—or efficacy—of such regulation does not exist, but the belief that it serves as a deterrent overrides logic. Offender registries are often counterproductive. They only marginally change the behavior of those included in them.[65] Instead, registers are more likely to negatively impact those members of the general public who are already fearful of crime and frustrated by the potential for repeat criminal behavior. Registry laws do little to raise awareness of the need to supervise children or to offer community safeguards. Their purpose is to give voters the impression that their legislators are serving them.

A more effective treatment for offenders upon their release has been the implementation of Circles of Support and Accountability.[66] This program originated in Canada as a volunteer service designed to ease the reintegration of those who had sexually offended into their communities. It reduced their isolation and provided reassurance for neighbors concerned about their presence. Studies have found this program to be both an effective support for offenders and a means of reducing recidivism.[67]

The short answer? Treatment *does* work. But that answer is based on the single measure most often used to determine its efficacy: recidivism. There are many more considerations that should be examined in the matrix of what constitutes treatment effectiveness, but these have been too often laid aside to obtain a convenient measure. As a result, we have virtually no understanding of the nuances of treatment, the potential impact of differing programs, or the sociocultural influences that contribute to the risk for recidivism. The emphasis has been on an easily measured construct—protection of the community from recidivism, an already low risk—not on the quality of life for those who have been victims and their families, or for those who offend.

Notes

 1 Lipton, Martinson, & Wilks, 1975.
 2 Martinson, 1979.
 3 Glaser, 1974.
 4 Ross & Hilborn, 2008.
 5 Feldman, 1966.
 6 Denno, 1998.
 7 Alter & Zürn, 2020.
 8 Gendreau & Ross, 1987.
 9 Cullen, Cullen, & Wozniak, 1988.
10 Calleja, 2016
11 Walsh, 1984.
12 Meloy, Boatwright, & Curtis, 2013.
13 Meloy, Curtis, & Boatwright, 2013.
14 Office of Sex Offender Sentencing, Monitoring, Apprehending, Registering, and Tracking [SMART], n.d.
15 Meloy, Saleh, & Wolff, 2007.
16 Socia & Stamatel, 2010.
17 U.S. Reports, Miller v. California, 413 US 19
18 Horowitz, 2015.
19 Ly, Dwyer, & Federoff, 2018.
20 Lim et al., 2021.
21 Thompson, 2014.
22 Knack, Holmes, & Federoff, 2020.
23 Rimer & Holt, 2023.
24 Lollar, 2013.

25 U.S. Reports, Paroline v. United States, 572, US 434.
26 Earls & Quinsey, 1985.
27 Furby, Weinrott, & Blackshaw, 1989.
28 Marshall & Pithers, 1994.
29 Borzecki & Wormith, 1987.
30 Ward & Salmon, 2011.
31 Trammel & Chenault, 2009.
32 Waldram, 2009.
33 Birgden & Cucolo, 2011.
34 Gully et al., 1990.
35 Andrews, Bonta, & Hoge, 1990.
36 Lievesley et al., 2022.
37 Latessa, Johnson, & Koetzle, 2020.
38 Bonta & Andrews, 2017.
39 Olver et al., 2018.
40 Parker, 2022
41 Wormith & Zidenberg, 2018.
42 Ward, 2002.
43 Ward & Stewart, 2003.
44 Ware, Frost, & Hoy, 2010.
45 Andrews, Bonta, & Wormith, 2011.
46 Prescott, Willis, & Ward, 2022.
47 Glaser, 2011.
48 Willis, Ward, & Levenson, 2014.
49 Willis et al., 2012.
50 Barnett, Manderville-Norden, & Rakestrow, 2014; Harkins et al. 2012.
51 Willis & Grace, 2008.
52 Ryan, McCauley, & Walsh, 2019.
53 Walgrave, Ward, & Zinsstag, 2021.
54 Harris, Pedneault, & Willis, 2019.
55 Deming & Jennings, 2020; Shedler, 2018.
56 Rice et al., 2006.
57 Andrews et al., 1990.
58 Lösel & Schmucker, 2005.
59 Hanson et al., 2009.
60 Grønnerød, Grønnerød, & Grøndahl, 2015.
61 Hanson et al., 2002.
62 Calkins et al., 2014.
63 Najdowski et al., 2016.
64 Caldwell & Caldwell, 2022.
65 Caputo & Brodsky, 2004; Gesser, 2021.
66 Fox, 2017.
67 Clarke, Brown, & Völlm, 2017; Wilson, Cortoni, & McWhinnie, 2009.

6 Postmodern treatment modalities
Advances and limitations

The previous chapter analyzed current, overarching treatment models for those who sexually offend against children. But efforts to manage and treat this population long predate those comprehensive efforts.[1] With the rise of psychoanalytic theory, by the late nineteenth and early twentieth centuries, sexual deviations were considered mental abnormalities that could be addressed in therapy and, at times, cured.[2] By the 1960s, sexual choices outside the mainstream, including same-sex interests or an interest in children, were treated as similar paraphilias—a distortion of healthy sexuality—due to the selection of a sexual object other than an intimate relationship with an opposite-gender adult. For those who could not afford or disdained psychoanalysis, the treatment of choice was behavioral, primarily relying on aversive conditioning.[3] This included the introduction of a noxious stimulus, administered while the patient conjured up sexual fantasies of the behaviors to be suppressed.

Despite their popularity, these methods were soon found to be ineffective. And they were discredited because a funny thing happened on the way to the 1970s. Gay rights became a social firestorm, and the use of aversion techniques to create a change in sexual orientation was vilified. Empirical evidence supported this social outrage, and over the course of the next half century, the techniques used to alter a minority sexual orientation were also stigmatized. But not the use of virtually these same techniques for those who sexually offended.

This chapter examines the enduring legacy of these sexual orientation change efforts (now known by the acronym SOCE).[4] The few practitioners continuing to implement SOCE with sexual minorities have modified their techniques over the years, recognizing the potential harm of aversive interventions and the need for more empowering approaches, despite evidence that even these modifications remain ineffective. And SOCE-based principles remain embedded as a form of treatment in models applied to sexual offenses, including the risk–need–responsivity (RNR) and good lives model (GLM). (See Chapter 5 for a discussion of RNR and GLM). This chapter examines the nature of these techniques, their status as a discredited

DOI: 10.4324/9781003487753-6

intervention for sexual minorities, and the social and political demand for the continued use of these principles with those who sexually offend.

Suppressing perversion?

Freud's outsized influence on theories of sexual development extended to those areas he perceived of as aberrations.[5] He considered mature adult sexuality to be penile–vaginal intercourse. (Oral and anal activity were acceptable as foreplay but were more often recognized as expressions of childhood sexual acting out.) Sexual interests that diverged from this norm could be explained as a failure to successfully resolve the psychosexual stages of childhood, or as a response to trauma that caused regression.[6] In either case, this diversion from a normal sexual interest could be treated, helping a patient reach a more acceptable level of psychosexual development.

By the 1960s, behavioral techniques vied with psychodynamic approaches for prominence as the treatment of choice for sexual aberrations. The latter, which probed into the psyche looking for a psychological cause and effect, was giving way to behavioral work, pioneered in the 1950s.[7] These techniques identified a problem behavior and attempted to eliminate it, dismissing concern for its underlying cause. In comparison with the talk therapies of the time, behavioral approaches were fast, economical, and effective in reducing symptoms. Particularly for patients struggling with the embarrassment—or even the shame—of a sexual disorder, the potential for relief was a strong draw toward this form of treatment.

More radical methods were in use for those thought to present the greatest risk to society. Castration and neurosurgery were dramatic procedures for those considered to be dangerous sexual deviates.[8] These drastic solutions were rarely employed, however, and rapidly fell out of favor. For a time during the 1970s, chemical treatment for persons who sexually offended was touted as promising.[9] Benperidol, an antipsychotic found to be useful in cases of hypersexuality, was proposed as a psychopharmaceutical intervention for those at risk for offending.[10] Other antipsychotics that suppressed sexual drive were also explored, with marginal success.[11] More effective, but still unreliable, was the use of estrogen and estrogen-mimicking drugs to reduce testosterone levels in males who sexually offended.[12] Antiandrogen became a frequently used chemical intervention, as it was better at blocking the production of testosterone than estrogen.[13] Such pharmaceutical approaches later fell from favor, due to problematic side effects and poor consistency in reducing sexual drive.

Social change was also in the air. The 1969 Stonewall Rebellion had become a rallying cry for gay rights. In those fomenting early years, boundaries were still in play, so the subgroup of men attracted to younger males could—and did—align themselves with the burgeoning gay movement.[14] The initial overlap was significant. David Thorstad, a president of both New York's Gay Activists Alliance and the Coalition for Lesbian and Gay Rights, left those organizations to found the North American Man/Boy Love Association (NAMBLA), advocating for the legalization of sex between adults and children.[15] As efforts to advance the rights of sexual minorities coalesced, the social and political risks of including the pederast agenda crystalized. The gay rights movement distanced itself, identifying different agendas and populations. By the mid-1990s, the gay rights campaign was firmly entrenched as a separate and distinct social movement from NAMBLA.[16]

While the pederast agenda spun its wheels, the gay rights agenda gained traction. In 1973 the American Psychiatric Association voted to remove homosexuality as a diagnosis, a signal victory for the fledgling movement.[17] This decision also fueled social unrest, as established efforts to change people's sexual orientation came under fire. Such approaches—often labeled sexual aversion techniques, and sometimes called reparative or conversion therapies—are now identified as SOCE. They purport to change an individual's sexual behavior, identity, or orientation to conform to the Heteronormative. As the LGBTQIA+ community consolidated its social and political gains across the past half century and expanded to include those who identify as nonbinary and transgender, sexual minorities now routinely enter the broader conversation. That push has led to increased acceptance of sexual minority status as a psychologically healthy and moral choice. As a corollary, it has also led to intensified scrutiny of SOCE, generating further research that indicates these practices are ineffective at best, and harmful at worst. Offering such treatments is now considered to be unethical by virtually all professional organizations for mental health practitioners. Few clinicians still engage in such efforts, recognizing the risk these interventions create.[18]

Challenges to SOCE led to legal protections, particularly for those at risk for coercive treatment. At least 36 states have legislated prohibitions against the use of change efforts with minor clients.[19] These policies were not instituted without dissent, and they apply primarily to licensed and/or license-eligible mental health providers.[20] They exempt religious practitioners,[21] as well as those who treat adults.[22] The grassroots movement of the sexual minorities who oppose SOCE curtailed their use as a standard treatment intervention. But how closely do the treatments now reviled as an intervention with sexual minorities dovetail with the treatments used for those who sexually offend?

Treatment via SOCE

The overwhelming majority of those who have sexually offended against children and the broader, overlapping population of those who are minor attracted do not advocate for the right to engage in sexual and romantic liaisons with minors. Their willingness to submit to treatments that protect a vulnerable population is a fundamental reason why methods utilizing SOCE principles are so readily applied to these groups. There has been no outcry that such interventions are inappropriate. Nor has the social or emotional impact of this mode of therapy been questioned.

Despite the lack of clamor, doubts about the efficacy of SOCE-based interventions apply directly to the use of their counterparts with those who sexually offend against children. SOCE advocates—mental health professionals and clients who desperately want to change—have poured years of effort and determination into these treatments, only to have study after study demonstrate their failure.[23] Longitudinal analyses of their effectiveness are particularly disappointing.[24] Treatment could not move the sexual orientation needle in another direction for almost any client who submitted to the procedures.

In fairness, there are scattered empirical studies that argue for the efficacy of SOCE.[25] But they have been challenged as being poorly designed and statistically weak.[26] SOCE research is inevitably hampered by a lack of field studies, samples of convenience (from close-at-hand populations), change criteria based on the researcher's operational definitions, and post-intervention follow-up for as long as is feasible, but often lasting no more than a few months. (These same arguments toward SOCE research are leveled against studies of treatment for those who sexually offend.) Valid criticisms though they are, these inherent methodological flaws in SOCE studies cannot stem the overwhelming tide of data that argue against the effectiveness of these techniques.

Another rebuttal to these change efforts has asserted their continued lack of effectiveness in the face of more than half a century of modifications. As discussed above, they began with what is now seen as rudimentary aversive conditioning. Working in sessions tailored to the needs of the patient, therapists determined the sexual deviation to be suppressed (or "extinguished," in behavioral psychology terms). Sometimes actual props were used (e.g., if the patient's heightened sexual reactivity was to women's shoes or an opportunity to dress in women's clothing). As the patient fantasized about the deviant activity, he, and occasionally she (never "they" at this decidedly binary period in history!), was subjected to an aversive stimulus. This stimulus could be an electric shock, an uncomfortable noise, a noxious smell, an emetic, or any device that produced immediate discomfort without long-term harm. Thus, the rewarding but deviant sexual arousal became linked with a negative sensation. The therapeutic goal was that by pairing an unpleasant stimulus with the patient's deviant sexual arousal, pain would override pleasure, and the arousal would no longer be positively reinforced. Instead, it would be associated with discomfort and thus avoided.[27]

Patients needed determination and a strong stomach (unless their paraphilia included masochism) to tolerate multiple sessions with repeated pairings of noxious stimuli and sexually arousing thoughts. This procedure was also used to suppress same-sex interests. As gay liberation made inroads into the mental health community, these treatments came under scrutiny,[28] as did psychoanalytic efforts to treat same-sex sexual attraction.[29]

By the turn of the twenty-first century, SOCE included modifications recognizing that those struggling with sexual minority status were unlikely to make dramatic changes in their orientation. Cognitive and cognitive-behavioral approaches were incorporated, attempting to shift thought patterns associated with same-sex interests. SOCE advocates began to add social and spiritual values to their interventions.[30] Rather than directly confronting the goal of realigning the patient's sexual orientation or identity, treatments incorporated either mindfulness[31] or narrative therapy, the latter designed to encourage a better understanding of one's identity.[32] The emphasis for SOCE was expanding from a narrow focus on changing a person's sexual behavior to an understanding of sexual behavior being embedded within the broader context of identity, social environment, and culture.

This broadened emphasis is doubtless reassuring for those in our postmodern culture who continue to question a minority sexual orientation or identity and seek to change it. Unfortunately, the empirical evidence still suggests that treatment using SOCE is ineffective. It serves more as a support for those who feel trapped by sexual thoughts and feelings that they neither desire nor wish to act upon, usually due to their moral or spiritual beliefs.[33]

SOCE-based treatment and sexual offenses

These were the findings when these procedures were applied to changes in *sexual orientation*. *Sexual offense* change efforts not only proceeded unabated but also continued to be assessed and refined from the 1970s into the 1990s. The use of hormone-suppressing drugs was still under consideration in the late 1980s and early 1990s.[34] (While current studies still explore the biochemical makeup of those who sexually offend, they have moved away from attempts to suppress sexual drive.)[35] But what did *not* work—and what was not known—was rapidly becoming apparent. Sociocultural perspectives had shifted. Sexual behaviors outside the Heteronormative, previously grouped into a single negative category, were now being parsed. Sexual minorities primarily identifying as gay, lesbian, and bisexual were gaining acceptance in both the broader culture and the mental health arena. They would later be joined by those who are nonbinary and transgender. Advocates from their communities were in the mental health field, both as practitioners and as researchers. They were well positioned to target SOCE as the handiwork of those peddling prejudice and fear.

Not so for the treatment of those who sexually offended. They were neither a cause nor a movement. Instead, they were seen as needing treatment in addition to punishment.[36] But treatment remained mired in approaches using SOCE-based principles. These approaches had evolved, but that evolution was a desperate effort by those committed to changing a person's sexual orientation, in hopes of finding palatable alternatives to the behavioral failures of the 1960s. And not all practitioners were willing to retreat from these early behavioral efforts.

The intransigence of treatment programs was indicated by a survey of 34 US and Canadian programs for people identified as sexually offending, completed between 1983 and 1985.[37] Theoretical orientations varied among the programs surveyed. These included behavioral, psychodynamic, and humanistic approaches. Some emphasized the importance of the therapeutic community. Others touted the use of a multidisciplinary approach. But the majority of these programs, regardless of their theoretical orientation, viewed sexual acting out as a learned behavior. Many used arousal conditioning to reduce the frequency of a pleasurable paraphilic response, a modification of the ineffective introduction of unpleasant stimuli attempted in the 1960s. And a plurality continued to use noxious stimuli (primarily electroshock and offensive odors) as props in aversive conditioning. Most of these programs also assessed their patients as lacking heterosexual and more general social skills. Accordingly, they offered sex education and cognitive retraining, such as heterosocial and life skills in areas where deficits had been determined. Some programs also continued to offer antiandrogen treatment.

These interventions paralleled the SOCE treatment principles decried as inefficacious in changing sexual orientation and sexual identity for gay, lesbian, and bisexual individuals. Empirical research suggested that little or no substantive change could be brought about in an individual's sexual-object choice or self-view with these approaches. But there was no acknowledgment by those treating sexual offending that parallel sexual orientation efforts were being challenged. The arguments made on both sides of the sexual minority debate are worth considering.

The sexual minority community avers that a same-sex interest is an orientation. Because it is ingrained, akin to personality traits or a genetic predisposition, change is impossible. The best that SOCE can hope to accomplish, then, is not the sexual *orientation* change that is promised, but a sexual *behavior* change, with the latter prone to regress to its pretreatment inclination, based on internalized, essentialist (i.e., "nature" in the nature-versus-nurture controversy) patterns. But SOCE practitioners argue that sexual orientation is learned and, therefore, is behaviorally based. Thus, what has been learned can be unlearned. Or, if there is an essentialist element to sexual orientation, then the power of behavioral learning can override these natural tendencies and allow a heterosexual orientation to dominate. These are the externalized, constructionist (i.e., "nurture" in the nature-versus-nurture controversy) patterns.

Interventions that rely on SOCE-like principles therefore assume that deviant sexual behavior (such as sexual acting out with minors, or an attraction to children) is either learned and can be unlearned, or its essentialist basis can be superseded by alternative learning. No application of this type of intervention, however, explains differences in its use with (1) a sexual attraction to children, (2) sexual acting out with children, (3) a sexual attraction to one's own gender, or (4) sexual acting out with one's own gender. The *function* of the intervention, if the theory underlying the principle is valid, should be the same. But, if so, it remains to be explained why the intervention would be efficacious with one sexual paraphilia/orientation but not another.

One of the more ambitious studies of these early postmodern intervention efforts compared people treated for sexual offenses and those who sexually offended but did not receive treatment.[38] The investigators studied the risk of recidivism as the most common measure of success. As is true in most field studies, they commented on the difficulty of operational definitions (e.g., ways of defining types of offenses when legal charges vary, specific components of programs when their application varies, etc.) that allowed an accurate comparison of one program with another. Despite these obstacles, the authors found no discernible difference in recidivism rates between those who were treated and those who did not receive treatment. Their finding was not isolated. It has been replicated many times.[39] These repeated assessments indicate that behavioral adjustments were not due to an intervention, and they suggest that this change effort (as is true with SOCE for sexual minorities) is often ineffective. It has existed and thrived for as long as it has because there has been no social or political mandate for its reform.

The legislators and judicial and mental health personnel responsible for these offenders have not deliberately clung to an ineffective intervention. Their purpose has been—quite genuinely—to advocate for the successful treatment of people who sexually offend. With that goal in mind, the emphasis turned from an ineffective treatment method to what was hoped to be a comprehensive model with greater impact, and a greater potential for behavioral change.

SOCE principles and the risk–need–responsivity (RNR) model

As the sociocultural perception of sexual minorities was evolving in the early 1970s, so, too, was an understanding of how best to deal with those who committed criminal offenses. At the time, three schools of thought predominated. One advocated for *justice* and emphasized punishment as the fundamental and appropriate response to those who violated the law. The potential for recidivism was a negligible concern.[40] The other two stood in stark contrast to this punishment approach. *Labeling* advocated for as little involvement as possible with the criminal justice system. This school argued that the more entangled individuals were with the courts, incarceration, probation, and parole, the more stigmatized they became, and the fewer the opportunities for them to resume a normal life in mainstream society.[41] *Deterrence* advocated for a larger investment by the judicial system in the lives of those who criminally offended. Without such involvement, the argument ran, criminals lacked the external supports necessary to make significant positive changes in their lives. The greater their fear of punishment and consequences, the greater their suppression of criminal behavior.[42]

Regardless of whatever logic was followed, an emphasis on treatment during incarceration was mounting. Evidence for the effectiveness of treatment approaches was still in flux, but the inefficacy of incarceration without some form of intervention was clear, since any change that did occur was often for the worse.

Social scientists focused on what became known as *criminogenic needs*. These were identifiable mental processes that included personal attitudes, values, and thinking styles that favored violation of the law.[43] Criminogenic needs could manifest themselves in various ways. The most obvious were violations of the rights of others, such as theft, aggression, or damage to persons or property. But they could also be disclosed through inappropriate, awkward, or limited social behavior; inadequate empathy; rationalization; or distorted thinking to justify acting out. Criminogenic needs were also perceived as being dynamic or fluid, changing across time and through various situations. For example, social weaknesses might be less pronounced while a person is incarcerated. There, a prisoner's daily routine is highly regimented and the required social repertoire is limited, compared with settings offering greater freedom. On the other hand, inadequate empathy might become more pronounced for these same individuals as they negotiate life in a distrustful environment.

Identification of criminogenic needs is central to determining *risk* factors to be addressed in treating criminal behavior—the first step in the RNR model. The principle underlying this step is a careful analysis of the *needs* of the person who has criminally offended. Based on this analysis, the intensity of service is paired with the level of risk: more intense for those at higher levels of risk, and less intense for those at lower levels.[44] *Responsivity* refers to the selection of interventions most appropriate for the person who has criminally offended, or, in the case of groups, the class of people who have done so. Interventions are matched with target behaviors to be changed and the learning style of the individual or group.

The RNR model was becoming a standard practice for those who had *criminally* offended. The leap to those who had *sexually* offended was a puddle jump, at best. RNR fit the program to the needs of the person involved. Higher risk individuals received more intense services. Needs were determined, and responses were tailored to these needs. But the mechanics of the program— the interventions themselves—were drawn from SOCE principles. Suggested interventions included behavioral and social learning and cognitive change. Specific techniques included modeling, graduated practice, rehearsal, role playing, reinforcement, and resource provision.[45] The playbook for these intervention methods could have been lifted directly from efforts to work with sexual minorities as they attempted to suppress their sexual orientation. Sexual offenders were clients who would have been even more motivated to express change than the sexual minority clients originally treated via SOCE. The stakes here were much higher.

The good lives model (GLM) and SOCE

By the turn of the century, the limitations of RNR were being scrutinized, and options were appearing in the literature. The GLM took a place of prominence.[46] Ironically, the transition to GLM parallels therapeutic changes among SOCE practitioners.

GLM emerges from positive psychology and the humanistic tradition. It advocates an approach that enhances capabilities and improves the quality of life for those who have offended. By doing so, this model hypothesizes a reduction in recidivism. It argues that the RNR model, in contrast, focuses on risk management, emphasizing the safety of the community, rather than the quality of life for the person who criminally offends. GLM proponents argue that the RNR model has limited motivational success.[47] Its focus on criminogenic needs takes attention away from the entirety of an individual as a treatment entity. Instead, it addresses targeted but overly specific areas. RNR emphasizes *eliminating* negative attitudes, *reducing* cognitive distortions, *extinguishing* deviant sexual interests, and *avoiding* relapse. While these are essential goals, they are not balanced by approach goals—positive behaviors that people who sexually offended are attempting to incorporate into their repertoire. This oversight occurs because the RNR model fails to address personal identity, the role of personal agency, non-criminogenic needs (e.g., anxiety, low self-esteem, or other types of psychological distress), and social and cultural contexts. By focusing on these attributes, GLM balances RNR with a strength-based approach—actualizing a person's potential.

GLM also reframes the purpose of acting-out behavior. This behavior becomes problematic when, for example, those who sexually offend use an inappropriate or illegal means to secure a positive in their own lives, such as sexual acting out with a child. Placing their need for immediate gratification ahead of the potential distress they create for a child lacks scope. Sexual offenders may also have conflicting goals for a positive that they seek. Their desire to engage romantically with a mid-adolescent may overwhelm the recognition that the child is not sufficiently emotionally mature to handle that type of relationship.

These goals parallel the changes in SOCE, which have likewise evolved to focus on the overall person and emphasize the positive. The goal continues to be movement away from a minority sexual identity or orientation, but reaching this state occurs through a more holistic approach, in which the entire person is seen as being in need of treatment. Emphases on mindfulness,[48] narrative therapy,[49] and acceptance rather than the struggle involved in learning to manage one's identity are often key concepts in SOCE today. Unfortunately, evidence continues to suggest that these approaches remain inefficacious.[50] Since GLM or a GLM/RNR combination both continue to rely heavily on SOCE-like techniques, it is questionable whether they can achieve long-term success.

SOCE, RNR, GLM, and a glimmer of hope

The trajectory of treatment interventions within the predominant models for those who sexually offend has shifted in parallel with changes in SOCE. The difference has been in the effort to shut down SOCE, while SOCE-based principles in RNR, GLM, and hybrids of these models remain in use. Still, the parallels between SOCE and these other models, and the lack of innovation in all these treatments for sexual offenses, are troubling. Proponents modified SOCE as they responded to empirical and social pressures. The initial behavioral, cognitive, social, and spiritual techniques that isolated sexual behaviors and attempted to change them were ineffective and thus were challenged. As SOCE transitioned to a more humanistic approach, addressing the whole person, the efforts of those treating sexual offenses also shifted. Research findings on the efficacy of SOCE are poor, and legislation has limited the use of SOCE. The results of studies on the efficacy of RNR, GLM, and their hybrids (as well as other treatments for persons who sexually offend) varied—and continue to vary—but the social and political climate has supported the continued use of these models.

A major dilemma is the choice to view research on *sexual orientation change efforts* and research on *sexual offense treatment* separately. If their interventions were disparate, then a choice to combine investigations on them would be fallacious. Instead, not only do their approaches utilize the same principles and techniques, but they also target a similar behavior. At least some people who sexually *offend* are beginning to identify their sexual *orientation*. In addition, an attraction to adolescents is a concept that has always remained a murky disorder, with its definition more often dictated by legislative mandate than clinical findings, particularly for those in mid-adolescence. The choice to categorize one population as exhibiting normal behavior (whose attraction begins with older adolescents) and another population as exhibiting a clinical syndrome (whose attraction begins with mid-adolescents) is untenable. SOCE-like interventions are being applied to change what may be a normal heterosexual orientation at the lower end of the age continuum.

It seems time to restart the investigation of differing types of persons who sexually offend, as well as those who are attracted to children but have not offended. What subcategories exist? What are the treatment approaches that best serve these various categories? And, perhaps most importantly, what novel and efficacious treatments can be developed that cast aside the disproved and harmful treatments of the past?

Research does suggest a glimmer of hope. While treatment efforts to forcibly change one's sexual orientation may be inefficacious and even harmful, evidence is mounting that sexual orientation is dynamic across a person's development and lifespan.[51] Such changes are particularly pronounced among sexual minority adolescents.[52] While the finding is particularly true for sexual minorities, those who are minor attracted have not been included in this research.[53] Still, it does indicate a possibility for creating modifications in sexual attraction. The theory of sexual fluidity in one's sexual orientation may be a corollary to such transitions. Research indicates that those who believe sexuality is fluid are more likely to experience it.[54]

Recent genetic research has also shed light on certain implications for sexual minorities. One genome project indicates genetic proclivities for the likelihood and frequency of same-sex involvement.[55] Whether similar findings can be applied in a broader context is unknown at this time, but their implications for treatment of those who sexually offend against children could be significant. A frequency/intensity predisposition toward minor attraction could be a useful marker in terms of tailoring effective treatments and interventions, enhancing the utility of existing programs, or even suggesting a diversity of new programs.

Notes

1 Bulfin, 2021.
2 Kincaid, 1992.
3 Barlow, Leitenberg, & Agras, 1969; Feldman, 1966.
4 American Psychological Association, 2009.
5 Carr, 1987.
6 Freud, 2016.
7 Skinner, 1953; Wolpe, 1958.
8 Field & Williams, 1970.
9 Field & Williams, 1970.
10 Field, 1973.
11 Field, 1973.
12 Bradford, 1983.
13 Bradford, 1990.
14 Thorstad, 1991.
15 North American Man/Boy Love Association [NAMBLA], n.d.
16 Weir, 1994.
17 Anderson & Holland, 2015.
18 Green et al., 2020.
19 Movement Advancement Project, 2023.
20 Clucas, 2017.
21 Mallory, Brown, & Conron, 2018.
22 Drescher et al., 2016.
23 See, for example, Ashley, 2019; Freeman-Coppadge & Home, 2019; Ryan et al., 2020; Serovich et al., 2008; and Suprina et al., 2019.
24 Spitzer, 2003, 2012.
25 Nicolosi, Byrd, & Potts, 2000; Jones & Yarhouse, 2011.
26 Sullins, Rosik, & Santero, 2021.
27 Feldman, 1966.
28 Ford, 2001.
29 Drescher, 2016.
30 Rosik & Popper, 2014; Yarhouse, 2001; Yarhouse & Tan, 2005.
31 Tan & Yarhouse, 2010.
32 Yarhouse, 2008.
33 Wilkinson & Johnson, 2020.
34 Bradford, 1990.
35 Chatzitoffis et al., 2022; Risto et al., 2018.
36 Cullen & Gendreau, 2000.
37 Borzecki & Wormith, 1987.

38 Furby, Weinrott, & Blackshaw, 1989.
39 Hanson, Lee, & Thornton, 2022.
40 Cullen, Cullen, & Wozniak, 1988.
41 Andrews & Wormith, 1989.
42 Gendreau & Ross, 1987.
43 Andrews, Bonta, & Hogue, 1990, p. 33.
44 Glaser, 1974.
45 Andrews et al., 1990.
46 Ward, 2002.
47 Ward & Stewart, 2003.
48 Tan & Yarhouse, 2010.
49 Yarhouse, 2008.
50 Wilkinson & Johnson, 2020.
51 Katz-Wise & Todd, 2022.
52 Katz-Wise et al., 2023.
53 Mock & Eibach, 2012; Katz-Wise et al., 2016.
54 Katz-Wise, 2015.
55 Diamond, 2021.

7   The family system
The broad impact of sexual offending

When sexual abuse is first exposed, the story that grabs attention centers on the perpetrator of the offense. If they have a high enough profile, or if the offense is heinous enough, a mug shot from the arrest makes the rounds. The story may even include video footage of the perp walk following an arrest. This intensive focus on the individual charged with the crime serves two purposes. From a psychological standpoint, it reinforces a perception that the community is now safe from predatory behavior. From a practical standpoint, victims maintain their privacy and avoid intrusive public scrutiny.

This limited focus also brushes aside difficult truths that accompany these arrests and convictions. I worked with a mother and her children following her husband's arrest for the sexual abuse of their 8-year-old son. The family had limited financial means, so the father could not pay the bail bond required for his release and was held in jail. He was eventually convicted and served a lengthy prison sentence.

While poor, the couple had maintained a stable living situation for their children. The father's employment had provided medical insurance, and they had been proud of their self-reliance. As the mother applied for government support, she found that until she burned through their meager family savings, they were ineligible for some assistance programs, while the measured tread of bureaucracy meant that other services for which they were eligible would only slowly become available. The mother's family offered her financial support, but they were impoverished, too. Wages for any work available to her would have been absorbed by the cost of childcare. She was eventually evicted from their apartment. During the first summer months when I saw her and the children, they lived in a camper behind her sister's home. A garden hose supplied drinking water. They used the bathroom and laundry facilities in her sister's house.

The son, first abused and now raised by a stressed single parent, was angry and distrustful. His reaction to the family's altered situation continued to deteriorate. He gravitated toward delinquent peers in the neighborhood, and by early adolescence he was remanded twice to a residential program after committing violent crimes. At that point I lost contact with him.

DOI: 10.4324/9781003487753-7

This story, which is not unique, highlights the domino effect of sexual offending. Most defendants charged with such crimes against minors are male. When sentenced to extended periods of incarceration, they are not only removed from the victims they have molested but also leave behind families who must generate new sources of emotional and financial support.

Readers may well say, "They are better off without him." The alternative is the risk of allowing a known perpetrator of sexual abuse to remain in the community. But professionals who work in the fields of mental health and social service know a gritty reality about the bigger picture of guarding the welfare of children. Daily—hourly—a significant question hangs in the balance as a new report of child abuse is investigated. How much abuse is *too* much abuse? These agencies constantly make decisions about the severity of *physical* abuse, and whether it rises to a level requiring intervention. Does spanking with a belt that leaves red marks, but not welts or bruises, need to be addressed? Does the degree of acting out for which this punitive consequence is being administered make a difference? Has the caretaker been investigated before? And in what state or locality does the punishment occur? All of these factors have weight in deciding whether an incident will result in an agency's intervention.

Agency personnel are empowered to make judgments about how much physical abuse is too much. And many children are left in the hands of the perpetrators of this physical abuse, either because there were no marks; the stories were inconsistent; or, on balance, the disruption of placing the children in foster care was considered more traumatic than leaving them in their home. Despite this, we prefer to draw a deep line in the sand when it comes to *any* form of *sexual* abuse. Physical abuse may require a remediation plan, but the person perpetrating this abuse may be left in the home. All too often, sexual abuse results not only in removal of the perpetrator, but also in their incarceration.

This chapter examines the broad impact of sexual abuse on the family system—that is, a family seen as a unit, where something affecting one member affects them all. Its effect on the victim—whether instigated by a loved and trusted adult or a stranger via contact through a computer—can be traumatic. Once it becomes known, the need to stop that abuse, quickly and permanently, is an unequivocal mandate. But efforts to do so shape long-term consequences that are too often ignored. Fallout from efforts to isolate the risk and punish the person who did the offending results in the victim being revictimized, and others in the family becoming secondary victims. The assumption that removing the party who committed the offense will resolve the issue is astonishing in its naivete.

"Family bashing": Are dysfunctional families prone to sexual abuse?

An extensive body of research has examined risk factors for sexual abuse within families. But very few of these studies are longitudinal or cross-sectional, following families from the birth of the first child onward (or, even better, from the union of the two parents onward), thus being able to assess family dynamics across an extended time span. Instead, data are collected from families in which sexual abuse has been reported and compared with families who have presumably not experienced abuse. Nothing acts as a control for the possibility that the latter families (1) had abuse in their family system but did not know it; (2) experienced abuse, are aware that it occurred, but failed to report it; or (3) will experience abuse in the future. Also, factors that predispose families to sexual abuse, versus the extent to which the trauma of sexual abuse is responsible for the reactions that then are observed, are difficult to determine. With these caveats in mind, the following are some of the more consistent findings.

Children in two-parent homes, regardless of whether these parents are biological or adoptive, are less likely to be victimized. This includes physical abuse, neglect, property crimes, or exposure to community violence, as well as sexual abuse. Families defined as being less stable are more likely to run the risk of having a victimized child,[1] while blatantly dysfunctional families are more likely to face the peril of a sexually abused child.[2]

Studies of sexual abuse within families find a correlation with maternal sexual abuse and dysfunction. Some estimate that as many as 50 percent of sexually abused children had mothers who were sexually abused themselves.[3] Such mothers are also more likely to have experienced concurrent physical and emotional abuse and neglect.[4] These same women report more frequent histories of substance abuse, panic disorder, and depression than mothers who have not been abused. In addition, their children are more likely to act out.

A maternal history of interpersonal violence contributes to a mother's distress when confronted with the sexual abuse of her child.[5] That experience, no matter how distant it may now be, impedes a mother's ability to aid her daughter in recovering from the trauma of sexual abuse. A correlation also exists between a maternal history of interpersonal violence and the risk for child sexual abuse by a parent. Mothers in homes in which father–daughter incest occurred are more likely to be emotionally and physically detached from the victimized daughter, at times ignoring signs that the sexual abuse is occurring.[6] Females with an intellectual disability have a higher probability of being violently sexually abused.[7] They are also less liable to report that abuse and more apt to be assaulted by acquaintances and non-family members than their non-intellectually disabled peers.

Yet what these studies often fail to take into account is that females are sexually abused (or report sexual abuse) with much greater frequency than males. Mothers are more likely than fathers to experience emotional and psychological symptoms stemming from sexual abuse, because the former are a population at greater risk. Are these negative correlations solely a reflection of the impact of sexual abuse on mothers? Or are they equally an indication of sociocultural fallout, since females have a higher risk of being sexually abused? If sociocultural factors play an important part, then what appear to be correlations between maternal maladjustment and sexual abuse may more accurately be conceptualized in a broader social context, with male significant others playing a crucial role in the way that the effects of female sexual abuse play out across the lifespan.

Sexual experimentation is common between siblings when they are minors, but such behavior can also become sexually abusive. Research suggests that three attitudes predominate among parents when sexual abuse between their children is discovered.[8] Some deny the abuse could have occurred. Others acknowledge sexual contact but reframe it as age-appropriate experimentation, refusing to believe the behavior moved beyond childlike exploration. And still others embrace the reality of abuse but may weave it into the fabric of a tragic family history, where it becomes further evidence of the dysfunction that plagues their family's fortunes. This dysfunction, however—including the tendency for a child to take on the role of an adult (parentification)—does not necessarily correlate with child sexual abuse.[9]

Determining that child sexual abuse has occurred is predicated on discovery of the abuse. That information often comes from mandatory reporters, usually professionals who are in contact with the children.[10] Still, a child's home life, or the perceived family environment, often determines whether a report is made.[11] Recurrent reports of abuse are less likely when the situation involves children of color, families who receive social services after an initial complaint, a victim with a disability, or families with financial need.

Emotional impact and the family

Familial dysfunction is a logical precursor to child sexual abuse. As the above discussion indicates, field research cannot determine cause and effect, but there is evidence that sexual abuse has an intergenerational effect, as well as an emotional impact on the entire family once child sexual abuse is discovered.[12] Everyone is traumatized, particularly when the perpetrator is tightly woven into the family system.

Mothers of sexually abused children can experience a range of reactions.[13] Common initial responses include denial, followed by anger, either toward the offender or toward themselves, for failing to be aware of the abuse. Concurrent emotions often include depression and anxiety. While some family members seek social and emotional support, others prefer avoidance and distraction. Still others become hypervigilant in supervising the abused child or other children in the family, overcompensating as a means of assuaging their self-blame. Fathers often acknowledge shame and a sense of powerlessness.[14]

Mothers can also feel ill equipped to respond to a child's emotional distress once sexual abuse has been disclosed.[15] Strategies employed to counter this helplessness include greater emotional and behavioral engagement. Moreover, the impact of sexual abuse on siblings is one that is often overlooked.[16] A revelation of abuse can trigger intense emotional responses between children in the family, with variable outcomes.[17] Relationships can become strained and disconnected, or even polarized. At their best, however, these revelations can heal and intensify the bonds between siblings.

Attitudes about child sexual abuse within a family system can vary. Participants in one study were presented with a hypothetical case involving a 14-year-old female.[18] Denial and blaming the victim were viewed as equally harmful responses to that child's disclosure of sexual abuse. But perceptions of the severity of the assault were mitigated by the type of contact that occurred. Instances involving vaginal penetration were deemed to be more serious than provocative suggestions, non-contact exhibitionism, or genital fondling. Males believed there was a less traumatic impact on the victim from any of these sexual abuse scenarios than females did. Males also assigned less culpability to the person perpetrating non-penetration offenses.

Females who hide their abuse may do so based on three contingencies: (1) the individual perpetrating the abuse, (2) their family, and (3) their culture.[19] The abuser may demand silence, employing psychological tactics to identify potential victims and then secure their cooperation. A family system's hierarchy and the victim's role within that hierarchy can be structured so that cooperation between all members is assured. And in some cultures, disclosure is associated with shame and a fear of rejection. Wives who choose to remain with husbands who sexually offend describe a disenfranchised grief, in which they lack support for the emotional losses they have suffered.[20]

A study from the 1980s explored the impact of an incestual father—that is, a man who engaged in sexual activity with a close family member—on a family system.[21] Prior to disclosure of the sexual abuse, victims would maximize the positive aspects of their father–child relationship and minimize its negative aspects. This defensive adaptation preserved paternal approval. Once the abuse was disclosed, the victim's defense strategy expanded into displaced anger and hostility toward the authorities who were now intruding into the family's life. This projection of blame thus sidestepped the violation of trust that had occurred. If this scapegoating was generalized and became an established defense within the family, its members could then covertly resist efforts to establish a more functional system.

The use of sex offender registries also impacts families.[22] Those in a registrant's family system can become victims of harassment, threats, and even violence because of their close association with the offender. When this occurs, family members are faced with a difficult and limited choice: either distancing themselves from the registrant or acquiescing to the discrimination that accompanies the label.

Necessary post-revelation adjustments for the family become interlocking traumas. Psychological and emotional bonds have been strained and broken by a betrayal of trust, but this situation does not negate the existence of the person perpetrating the act or that individual's role within the family system. Negotiating a journey toward healing is an arduous task, made more difficult by the tendency for those in the community to use a broad brush in applying the stigma of offending to the entire family.

Victims, survivors, and family dynamics

Adults who experienced sexual abuse in childhood often display psychological distress and poor sexual adjustment, but these characteristics correlate with *all* aspects of familial dysfunction, rather than only with sexual abuse.[23] Symptoms include low self-esteem, poor body image, and negative sexual attitudes. Even when a victim is supported by non-offending caregivers after the abuse has been disclosed, this change has a marginal impact on improving that person's social and emotional adjustment.[24] It also appears that for both adults and children, the accompanying shame and self-blame are significant ancillary factors in the relationship between sexual abuse and its resultant emotional distress. Adolescent females who have been sexually abused blame themselves if conflicts increase between their adult caregivers.[25] These victims also blame themselves if more general, interpersonal conflicts occur within their family.

The journey from victim to survivor is neither straightforward nor well defined. Logically, there will be brief periods when those who have overcome their status as victims of childhood sexual abuse will regress to this victimized role in the face of other trauma or unexpected stress. While ongoing contact between survivors and those who perpetrated the abuse has been investigated, the results are equivocal. For some victims, such contact is damaging, furthering their trauma. For others, contact is a more complex phenomenon, with both positive and negative emotional and psychological impacts emerging from this experience. Females who are able to maintain positive ongoing interactions with the person who abused them can also effectively isolate that individual's role in their lives.[26] To do so, these survivors become adept at compartmentalizing the abuse. They separate it from their identity and, in so doing, diminish the influence of the person who perpetrated the offense.

The multiple aspects of grief following the death of a person with whom there has been a complicated relationship are well recognized,[27] although an extended discussion is beyond the scope of this chapter. Some individuals who have been abused as children and are now adults describe having a polarized emotional relationship, simultaneously hating and loving a significant figure in their lives who violated their trust but still offered them love. They experience relief from releasing the memories of abusive interactions and knowing that others are safe. Yet they also feel a sense of loss, since an important relationship is gone. For others, the potential for confrontation and then closure has disappeared. Some victims describe feeling burdened because their significant others project their expectations onto them, anticipating how this loss *should* feel. Other survivors describe a reconfiguration of their own sense of identity or experience a deepening in their process of forgiveness. The death of a sexual offender also opens the potential to reconfigure relationships between the survivor and that person's remaining family system.[28] A closely aligned, but even less well-explored, dynamic occurs when a parent is dying, and sibling sexual abuse once again emerges as an issue to be addressed.[29]

Another group of victims who struggle to resolve their trauma are child pornography survivors.[30] Pornographic images of children may have broad, illegal distribution, but in many cases they were first produced by family members or acquaintances. As children, the victims experience shame and guilt. As adults, they continue to have these feelings, fearing that those who view these images of them believe they were consensually obtained, even if the survivors, when innocent children, were coerced into participation. Some find comfort in the knowledge that, as children, they did not fully understand what was happening. Others need to seek self-forgiveness for what they perceive as their complicity in the acts.

For many, a bond between the victim and the person who offended— whether it is negative, positive, or ambiguous—continues until death. Often, interconnections within the family system mean that this link also persists for others. Relationships are, by their very nature, dynamic. Those who offend, as well as their victims, will struggle to find resolution from pain. Family members who remain close to both the victim and the person who offended must also find a way to resolve this ongoing, but often unspoken, relationship.

The financial and emotional impact of incarceration

Mainstream literature rarely studies the ripple effect on the families of those incarcerated for sexual offending, but a robust number of studies exist on the impact of incarcerating parents, as well as the researchers' concurrence on a need for change.[31] They also agree that incarcerating parents or other family members has a detrimental impact on the remaining family system.

Incarceration is based on the principles of punishment for those who offend and protection for their victims. While imprisonment may indeed serve as punishment, fallout from an attempt to provide protection suggests that the latter falls short of its intent. Peripheral outcomes from confinement for offenders include placing the family's non-abused children at risk for increased stress, poor social and academic functioning, and a potential lack of supervision, since the remaining parent usually works longer hours to fill the family's financial gap.[32] An unexpected finding, however, is that the impact of incarceration may be far wider than has been assumed. It is well known that academic achievement declines for children of incarcerated parents.[33] But even children of the imprisoned person's extended family members are less likely to graduate from high school and have longer educational absences.[34] Hypotheses for this finding include financial and emotional disruptions occurring across the entire family system.

One excellent source of data on the outcome of incarceration of a parent has been the Future of Families and Child Wellbeing Study (FFCWS). This longitudinal investigation, formerly known as the Fragile Families and Child Wellbeing Study, initially followed a cohort of new, largely unmarried parents from 20 American cities, beginning with 5,000 interviews between February 1998 and September 2000.[35] Economically advantaged women were more likely to work extended hours after the incarceration of their partner than economically disadvantaged women.[36] The longer the incarceration, however, the greater the probability that even better-off women would reduce the number of hours they worked, adjusting their lifestyle to their reduced income.

Research using the FFCWS found that the destabilizing influence of incarceration was more acute among couples experiencing a first-time incarceration.[37] Imprisonment creates "relationship churning"—a pattern of separation and reunification that intensifies dysfunction within a family. This pattern remains robust, regardless of whether a male or female partner was confined. Another investigation using the FFCWS found that paternal incarceration was associated with increased physical aggression in male children.[38]

Parental imprisonment also increases the risk for family members to become the victims of other crimes, and for children remaining in the home to become delinquent.[39] Again using data from the FFCWS, research found that sons of fathers who were incarcerated were more likely to violate rules, experience disciplinary problems in school, demonstrate poor academic achievement, and be more prone to later criminal involvements than peers whose fathers had not been imprisoned.[40]

The above studies suggest the ripple effect of a family member's incarceration for *any* crime, not just sexual offending. They also indicate the negative pattern that occurs when a parent or relative is removed from the home, in order to safeguard the children remaining there. This effort at protection comes at an unanticipated cost.

The decision to hide sexual offending

A prominent storyline in the media involves decisions to hide the occurrence of sexual offending. Continuing scandals in the Catholic Church and a tendency for the Amish to hide such behavior have become a staple in news reports. The practice of hiding sexual abuse also remains common among some cultures. For example, Native American,[41] Appalachian,[42] and Hispanic[43] cultures all contain subgroups of individuals who prefer to ignore sexual offenses.

Among some Hispanic subcultures, undisclosed child sexual abuse is the norm.[44] Intergenerational abuse is common enough for children to be encouraged to avoid disclosing their own abuse, given that older generations survived without revealing what had happened to them. "Keeping the secret" also maintains the integrity of male figures. Machismo, an essential element in traditional Hispanic culture, preserves the concept of males as protectors of females under their care. In addition, maintaining secrecy about sexual abuse may allow females to sustain the pretense that they are virgins when they marry.

In many cultures shame inhibits the disclosure of sexual abuse.[45] Shame can be attached to religious beliefs, perceptions by family members or the community at large, the risks associated with involving authorities, or a combination of these and other factors. In cultures that prize masculinity, sexual abuse of a male is easily hidden.[46] Accusing boys of same-sex interest if they are abused by a man, or allowing boys to rework the script in order to give themselves a dominant role if they are abused by a female, ensures their complicity in maintaining the secret.

Males are more likely than females to experience perpetration by same-gender individuals. In this case, those perpetrating sexual offenses are less likely to be family members and more likely to meet their victims within the community, such as coaching or assisting with sports teams, serving as church leaders, or working in schools.[47] Compared with females, males delay reporting abuse, possibly due to perceived negative stereotypes or the heightened publicity that accompanies a community figure being accused of a sexual offense.

The choice to hide sexual abuse can also occur for other reasons. Children may know that disclosing abuse could mean dire consequences for the adult who is involved, thus harming someone they love.[48] Children may also have been cajoled—or even threatened with physical harm to themselves, family members, or pets—if they report what occurred. For others, a slow escalation of the abuse may have normalized this behavior and perhaps even made it enjoyable.[49] Many believe that complicity is empowering and more comfortable than feeling victimized, although the tradeoff is shame at having been involved in sexual abuse.

The investigation of a man who sexually abused 17 children in Stockholm, Sweden, offers insight into some of the reasons why these incidents are underreported.[50] The male perpetrating the abuse assaulted each child only once. These assaults were well documented, as he either kept a photographic record of the events, later confessed to them, or both. When eight of the children, who ranged from 3 to 10 years old, were interviewed, they gave clear descriptions of non-sexual details of their encounters. But they were more reluctant to recount sexual details, despite being told that they were being interviewed because of the sexual abuse they experienced. The investigators noted that some rationales, such as loyalty to the person perpetrating the abuse and fear of negative consequences, did not seem to be prominent factors in explaining the children's reticence. More likely explanations included fear and subsequent trauma, or feelings of shame.

Less frequently discussed in the literature are children who report abuse but are not believed. There can also be circumstances in which allegations of child sexual abuse are weaponized. For example, in child custody disputes, desperate parents may either fabricate such allegations or distort and magnify their children's comments, based on their own fears and suppositions.

More often, however, in situations where a report is suspect, the alleged per-petrator of the abuse is confronted, denies the abuse, and, if the report is deemed to not be credible, the child is either punished or the allegations are dismissed.[51] At times, children will report abuse and then recant. In these situ-ations, the validity of the sexual abuse claim is questionable, and a criminal justice system that relies on reasonable doubt is reluctant to move forward with charges. Nonetheless, a shadow of doubt often remains within the family and creates unresolved tension as its members silently choose sides, despite the fact that no action was taken.

Reconsidering sexual offending management in the interest of the family

Responses to sexual abuse have gone in two directions. One path advocates for the needs of those victimized by abuse. Here, a wealth of research studies has examined the psychological, emotional, and social impacts of the experi-ence, as well as possible interventions. The other path promotes the needs of and management for those perpetrating the abuse. Multiple investigations in this area have studied the most effective treatments to reduce recidivism, as well as social mechanisms (e.g., offender registration) that provide a sense of safety—however illusory—to the community.

While these two research avenues fail to meet, the paths of those who are being studied do. These individuals are often members of the same family. And the literature suggests that the process of identification, isolation, and incarceration of those who sexually offend often causes harm to the family system, including the victims. This effect is recognized, but it is minimized as being necessary collateral damage. Children who have been sexually abused are revictimized when their families are destabilized by the removal of a significant family figure. Parents already stressed by the discovery or revela-tion that one family member is sexually abusing another now face the added burdens of coping with shame, guilt, and financial loss.

Those who advocate for the incarceration of all those who sexually offend presume that this will safeguard their community, as well as the abuser's family members who are at risk. They believe that, through a process of pun-ishment, shaming, or treatment—or a combination of these factors—when the person who offended is reintegrated into the family and the community at large, that individual will no longer be a danger. External safeguards will be enough. This, at least, is the presumption of the *justice system*.

But impacts on the *family system* are not considered in efforts to protect child victims or proactively safeguard future victims. As a consequence—and by default—the family is left to struggle, not only with the shock and trauma of the sexual abuse itself, but with the financial, emotional, and psychological realignments that must take place as one of its key members is removed. Failure to consider the widespread effects on the broader family system, and indifference to those impacts, even when they are acknowledged, are key considerations in the changes that need to occur in the treatment of those who sexually offend.

Notes

1 Turner et al., 2013.
2 McCloskey & Bailey, 2000.
3 Lewin & Bergin, 2001.
4 Baril et al., 2016.
5 Jouriles et al., 2021.
6 Gqabi & Smit, 2019.
7 Koçtürk & Yüksel, 2023.
8 Tener et al., 2018.
9 Fitzgerald et al., 2008.
10 Kesner & Robinson, 2002.
11 Sinanan, 2011.
12 Toledo & Seymour, 2016.
13 Vilvens, Jones, & Vaughn, 2021.
14 Vladimir & Robertson, 2020.
15 McCarthy et al., 2019.
16 Crabtree, Wilson, & McElvaney, 2021.
17 McElvaney, Murray, & Dunne, 2022.
18 Graham, Rogers, & Davies, 2007.
19 Tener, 2018.
20 Bailey, 2018.
21 Solin, 1986.
22 Levenson & Tewksbury, 2009, pp. 64–65.
23 Bhandari et al., 2011.
24 Bolen & Gergely, 2014; Whiffen & McIntosh, 2005.
25 Rancher et al., 2019.
26 Eisikovits, Tener, & Lev-Wiesel, 2017.
27 Boelen, 2016.
28 Monahan, 2003.
29 Monahan, 2010.
30 Gewirtz-Meydan et al., 2018.
31 Uggen & McElrath, 2014.
32 Aaron & Dallaire, 2010.
33 Turney & Goodsell, 2018.
34 Nichols & Loper, 2012.
35 Reichman et al., 2001.
36 Bruns, 2017.
37 Turney & Halpern-Meekin, 2021.
38 Wildeman, 2010.
39 Aaron & Dallaire, 2010.
40 Emory, 2018.
41 Williams, 2012.
42 Treat et al., 2022.
43 Castaneda, 2021

44 Castaneda, 2021.
45 Fontes, 2005.
46 Cermak & Molidor, 1996.
47 Coburn et al., 2019.
48 Lewis, 2015.
49 Fontes & Plummer, 2010.
50 Leander, Christianson, & Granhag, 2007.
51 Fontes & Plummer, 2010.

8 Don't ask, don't tell
Minor attraction

Many of us can recall the transition from childhood to adolescence, with that first exhilarating and bewildering infatuation with one of our peers. Through an often painful learning curve, the confusion and heartache of young love gave way to what we perceived (at the time) as the seasoned romances of later adolescence and, eventually, adult relationships. But, for a few, the confusion remained. As their friends' romantic attractions kept pace with their developing age cohort, this smaller group found their interests fixed on those just entering the realm of adolescence, or on others still in childhood. As these individuals entered young adulthood and beyond, their interest was not in those considered appropriate for their age. They struggled with the nemesis of a minor attraction.

The *act* of sexual offending is a legally defined behavior, which has been stretched to become a stigmatizing sociocultural category. In contrast, diagnoses of pedophilia and hebephilia—which represent an attraction to prepubescent children and early adolescents, respectively—refer to an *internalized state*. Neither requires that the affected person act on these desires. And only the former is a diagnosis recognized by the American Psychiatric Association.[1]

The terms "pedophile" and "hebephile" are laden with emotional baggage, conjuring not only a disorder, but, for many, an erroneous association with an individual who has already offended. In the late 1860s, "homosexual" was coined as a term for another sexual minority, and it remained the word of choice until well into the twenty-first century.[2] Homosexual is now freighted with sufficient prejudice to be considered an inappropriate locution.[3] In parallel fashion, "minor attracted person" (MAP) is becoming a preferred alternative to pedophile and hebephile. These latter two clinical terms are perceived as demeaning to those who find themselves, through no overt intent, attracted to children and younger adolescents. To counter their shame—experienced not because of their actions, but because of their sexual desires—the phrase "minor attraction" is less clinical.

In a process familiar for other sexual proclivities beyond the mainstream, the assumption that minor attraction must be generated by trauma

DOI: 10.4324/9781003487753-8

or pathology (i.e., a deviation from the normal, giving rise to a social ill) is being challenged. Michael C. Seto, a well-respected psychologist and sexologist, has posited that at least some individuals among this population exhibit a particular sexual orientation.[4] This model, however, has not reduced the spate of studies that correlate minor attraction with pathology. In the same way, early advocacy for sexual minorities did not rein in studies that linked pathology with same-sex interests.[5] This same lens and process has been applied to transgender status.[6] Only the gradual social, cultural, and scientific acceptance of minority sexual orientations and identities as valid alternatives have stemmed the tide of considering same-sex and transgender populations as being pathological.

The paradox between these populations and those who are minor attracted is their choice of sexual objects. A same-sex orientation or identity generally involves same-age peers. A transgender identity is based on self-identification. Advocating for freedom of sexual expression for these groups does not violate age boundaries. Yet if minor attraction *is* a sexual orientation, rather than a pathological response to environmental factors, advocacy for this group stops short of the rallying cry for previously recognized sexual minorities—freedom to engage in sexual activity. Ironically, resistance to the view of minor attraction as a sexual orientation, rather than a paraphilia (an environmentally learned sexual maladaptation), and to freedom for those who are minor attracted, so they can openly share their preferences, is founded on fears similar to those used to challenge other sexual minority movements. People who oppose same-sex behavior assert that such couples are morally reprehensible. Those who oppose transgender options argue that pharmaceutical and surgical modifications to a person's cisgender status are morally reprehensible. And those who oppose greater tolerance or a more open exploration of minor attraction contend that such openness will lead to the morally reprehensible exploitation of children.

This chapter examines the conundrums created by emerging support for MAPs. The opening vignette is one I have heard from multiple clients. It does not explain all aspects of minor attraction, but it does demonstrate doubts that every form of minor attraction can be traced to trauma or a paraphilic response. The avenues through which a sexual orientation toward children manifests itself—nature, nurture, or both—and the issue of whether MAPs who have not acted on their desires can live fulfilling lives despite this abstinence, remain open questions. Those who are minor attracted, their families and supporters, and those who provide mental health services to them all face the difficulties of respecting the rights and dignity of persons who may have violated no law and harmed no individual, yet acknowledge innate desires in conflict with the best interests of their preferred sexual partner groups. And, within the population of those who have sexually offended, there are some who identify as MAPs and make abstinence from their desires a goal.

Does the tail wag the dog? The evolution of social sciences research

Scientific study, in theory, examines evidence and reports its findings without bias. When considered in the context of cultural expectations, social demands, and the limitations of funding, even approaching this ideal is a lofty goal. An example of this struggle is apparent in work completed as sexual minorities were beginning to advocate for a more reasoned perspective. One sexuality theorist argued for the need to maintain an open mind, and to consider both genetic (nature) and environmental (nurture) factors in same-sex orientations.[7] Among other contributing causes, he suggested nutritional insufficiency, sensory deprivation, familial dysfunction, lack of peer interaction, and even congenital hearing loss. Although it is tempting to dismiss this theorizing as aberrant posturing, these hypotheses were expounded in a 1970 article published by John W. Money, a renowned sexologist at Johns Hopkins University. They also appeared in *Psychological Bulletin*, one of the premier psychological journals of the American Psychological Association. While they are viewed as ludicrous now, at the time, those in the social sciences gave these theories serious consideration.

Social science has had a reciprocal impact with social and political practices across the past 160 years.[8] Findings from studies are interdependent and subjective, based on social scientists' spheres of influence.[9] And the ways in which science should engage with social concerns have become a field of study in itself.[10] As a logical outcome of these efforts, there is increasing awareness that scientific practice is influenced by the moral order in which it is embedded.[11] For some, this recognition is a mandate for scientific research to embrace and respond to it.[12] For example, feminists have advocated for research changes that would reduce the social consequences of gender inequality.[13] Others argue that this awareness can be used to increase the impact of research on community-based issues.[14]

These questions are essential in considering minor attraction. Well into the twenty-first century, much of the social science field continues to assure us that minor attraction is a paraphilia—an unnatural aberration. Yet what role have sociocultural norms played in reinforcing that scientific perception? And to what extent should social science research be swayed by postmodern culture, shifting its findings to accommodate a more tolerant view?

The distinction between a paraphilia and a sexual minority is the difference between an *aberration* that can be corrected or suppressed and a *sexual orientation* that can give rise to a sexual identity. It is beyond the scope of this book to discuss the intricate arguments of how and why these divergences arise. But MAPs are becoming a social force, and social scientists will be required to acknowledge their demands for more nuanced research. The impact of this evolution will doubtless be reflected in interventions for those who act out sexually with children.

Toward an understanding of MAPs

A sexual orientation is increasingly recognized as a dynamic and evolving state, rather than a static one. Michael Seto offers a broad definition, seeing it as "a stable tendency to preferentially orient—in terms of attention, interest, attraction, and genital arousal—to particular classes of sexual stimuli."[15] This definition is multidimensional. It encompasses far more than gender, as it reflects the diversity of traits, behaviors, and physical appearances to which an individual may be attracted. It acknowledges the complexity of a sexual orientation.

This nuanced interpretation fits the experience of MAPs. The desired role of a child in their lives varies. Some are drawn to children's playfulness and energy, while others acknowledge having fallen in love.[16] Many embrace their attraction as a sexual orientation, but others continue to adhere to a paraphilia model, describing their preference as the outcome of a sexual addiction or trauma.[17] In partial support of the latter belief, one study found that men with a minor attraction had an increased sexual drive and began masturbating at an earlier age than counterparts who did not fall into this category.[18] Many who identify as MAPs, whether they see their desires as a sexual orientation or a paraphilia, struggle with negative self-perceptions. Self-hatred is common, as are suicidal thoughts.[19] MAPs often experience depression and pessimism about the future.[20] MAPs who choose not to act on their desires are often fearful and avoid situations in which they might feel at risk.[21] The extent to which these beliefs are driven by shame and guilt has not been studied, but the orientation of other sexual minorities was long perceived to be the result of preexisting psychic wounds, rather than recognizing the role of stigma in creating those wounds.

The reality remains bleak for MAPs. They are the modern era's lepers. Their pain is deepened by observing other previously denigrated sexual minorities who are now able to celebrate their status. MAPs must carefully hide their sexual identity from employers, schools, religious groups, and, often, friends and family. Even confidantes who are aware of their secret are often unwilling to discuss it in depth. MAPs are reminded daily that theirs is a shameful secret, even if they take every precaution to ensure the safety of the children with whom they interact.

Minor attraction versus sex with minors: Conflating orientation and behavior?

Consider two scenarios. In one, a man robs a convenience store clerk at gunpoint. In most states, if he is arrested, charged, and convicted, he is a felon and will face the resultant consequences. Despite the straightforwardness of this behavior, the underlying motives for his actions can vary. He may care little about the rights of others and choose to obtain material goods or money in the easiest way possible. He may use drugs and have turned to theft in order to sustain an uncontrollable addiction. Or he may be living in poverty and makes the only choice he believes is open to him to sustain himself and his family.

In the other scenario, a man sexually abuses a child. In most states, if he is arrested, charged, and convicted, he is also a felon and will have to face the consequences. For him, too, the underlying motives for his actions can vary. He may have little or no regard for the rights of others and choose to obtain sexual pleasure from the most accessible source. He may abuse drugs or alcohol and engage in this form of sexual behavior while his judgment is impaired. Or he may be attracted to minors and surrender to the impulse to pruriently engage with a child, either in fantasy (child pornography) or in reality (child sexual abuse).

In instances of either armed robbery or child sexual abuse, the general assumption is a stereotypical view of the offender. As the above scenarios demonstrate, the reality is more complex. Further, among those who are sexual minorities, research has highlighted the potential for dramatic differences in the frequency and intensity of their interests.[22] The same applies to individuals who engaged in sex with minors.

Three illustrative case studies

Case 1

"Alex" was born in California, but his family soon moved to Arizona. He attended college on the East Coast and spent much of his adult life in the West. He had one older brother, and his intact family was close when he was a child.

He first recognized his attraction to early adolescent males when he was about 10 years old. He found himself drawn to a friend's older brothers, ages 13 and 15. At the time, he considered this to be a form of hero worship, admiring them as adolescents whose ages gave them greater freedom. He now acknowledges that what he felt then were deeper romantic stirrings. As Alex matured, his romantic and gender interests remained the same, focusing on males in their early teens. When he was 15 years old, a male neighbor, age 12, would drop by his house to play basketball. Alex eventually asked him to stop doing so, finding the attraction to this youth to be uncomfortable. He struggled with depression during his adolescence, but he also went through periods of happiness and satisfaction. He played sports and mentored and coached younger students.

Alex was never involved with a same-sex partner. As an adolescent, he convinced himself that since he was attracted to same-age peers and older males, he must be gay, but these infatuations were fleeting and lacked substance. He remained primarily interested in early adolescents, so he was increasingly faced with the reality that he was minor attracted. During his junior year of college, he accepted this feeling. At first it was emotional, as he wanted to regress to that younger age. Over time, however, a physical desire manifested itself. Alex now experiences an occasional attraction to older males, but no one over the age of 20. He has found a female life partner who is comfortable with an asexual relationship. She knows about his sexual orientation and accepts it. She understands that he chooses not to act on his inclinations, because of the confusion and pain it would cause for a younger partner.

Case 2

"Rob" was raised in Ohio in an intact family. He was the youngest of three siblings, with an older brother and sister. His father had a professional occupation, and his mother was a homemaker. Both were active in the leadership of a conservative Christian church, and Rob still belongs to this denomination. He studied art and photography in college and has worked in the dramatic arts.

Rob first recognized that he was attracted to males when he was in an early elementary school grade. The feelings were so unsettling that he suppressed them and avoided exploring which males might be attractive. He believed that these feelings were sinful, and his desire to remain in the good graces of his parents and the family's church kept even a remote recognition of his minor attraction at bay. This continued through his early high school years, until he was approached and sexually coerced by an older male friend of the family. At that time, when confronted with his emerging sexuality, Rob chose to consider himself as gay. After engaging sexually with same-age male peers, however, he realized that his primary attraction was to young pubescent males. He continued to suppress his sexual desires until he attended college, where he met his wife. Rob told her he was gay, but he also shared his desire to embrace a heterosexual lifestyle. Their marriage has remained intact for over 40 years, and they have three adult children.

Several years into his marriage, Rob found himself attracted to a young adolescent in the neighborhood. They began to spend time together and rapidly developed what became a mentor/friendship relationship for the child, and a romance/friendship for Rob. He found the playfulness and energy of his young partner rewarding and gradually fell in love with him. The relationship lasted for two years before the boy's parents became suspicious. They questioned their son, who revealed this sexual activity. Rob was arrested, charged, convicted, and spent several years in prison.

Rob continues to grieve over the loss of this relationship, although the two of them have had no contact in over 20 years. He does not believe that their romantic relationship would have survived the boy's maturation into middle adolescence. He recognizes the harm caused by initiating and maintaining a sexual relationship. In addition, he regrets that the potential for a friendship, following the probable decline of his romantic interest when the boy grew older, was lost. Rob would also have liked to have had an opportunity to resolve the pain he caused.

Case 3

"Craig" was raised in an intact family. He had one brother, who was 3 years younger. His father was in the military, and the family moved frequently when he was a child. He had excellent grades and entered college, but he then left to join the military himself. It was during this time that Craig began to abuse alcohol. He was discharged after two years, returned to civilian life, and got a job. He began cohabiting with a woman he met at his place of employment, and she soon became pregnant. They married shortly thereafter, and his wife gave birth to their daughter.

In late adolescence, Craig sexually abused his brother, an early adolescent. As Craig reflected on that behavior, he identified it as a form of acting out and gaining control over someone else. He self-identifies as bisexual, but very few of his partners have been male.

After leaving the military, Craig turned to marijuana as his drug of choice. When his daughter was 3 years old, Craig was smoking marijuana daily. He began fondling her genitals at bath time and then gradually progressed to having her masturbate him until he ejaculated. Each time this occurred, he felt shame and promised his daughter that it would not happen again. Despite his intentions, he repeated the behavior. There finally came a time when he sexually abused her but determined that it would be the last such occurrence. He said, "If daddy does this again, tell mommy." He did, and she did. Craig did nothing to contest his arrest, charges, and conviction. He is now in prison, serving out his sentence.

Craig explains his behavior as a distortion of his love for his daughter. Neither before, during, nor afterward has he experienced being drawn to another child, and his attraction to his daughter occurred during periods in which he was under the influence of marijuana. While Craig has taken full responsibility for what occurred and has explored all aspects of his sexuality, including a sexual compulsion/addiction, he does not consider himself to be minor attracted.

What do they tell us about minor attraction?

These three case studies highlight the different ways in which those who are sexually attracted to or interact with children can experience that inclination. Alex's sexual development extended into an interest in young pubescent males, an attraction he has chosen not to pursue. For Rob, spiritual beliefs created shame and guilt and led him to suppress his feelings, eventually acknowledging a slightly less shameful same-sex orientation. The discovery of an adolescent who could fulfill his romantic ideal led him to act out his desires, with tragic consequences for all involved. Both Alex and Rob would identify themselves as MAPs. In contrast, Craig describes a situational minor attraction. His sexual acting out points to a fluidity in his sexual orientation or a possible paraphilia, but it does not indicate a minor attraction per se.

Development of a minor attraction

The opening paragraphs of this chapter outline what many MAPs experience as this form of attraction emerges.[23] But minor attraction *as a sexual orientation* is still very much a nascent model. To work backward from someone engaging in sexual behavior with a child and assume that the individual who offended was minor attracted is often fallacious. Clinical syndromes, personality disorders, environmental circumstances, and even paraphilias can play a primary role in a decision to engage in such behavior.[24] Still, the concept of minor attraction as a sexual orientation—an impetus for sexual acting out with children—is receiving serious consideration.[25] Of particular relevance, MAPs may demonstrate *diverse* sexual orientations, so an attraction to children may not be an exclusive interest.[26]

Our understanding of a sexual orientation based on age is limited, in part, by the focus of research on child sexual abuse, which centers on the legal system. Such studies target those who have committed criminal acts, as well as the sexual behavior embodied in these acts. The psychological and emotional components of their crimes, including romantic proclivities, are of minimal concern. Instead, the primary goal is to avoid repetition of this sexual behavior. An understanding of its underlying intrapersonal dynamics only becomes a focus of this research if it seems to further that goal.

The link between *having* a minor attraction and *acting* on it may be mediated by a traumatic early childhood experience. Men incarcerated for sexually offending against children are more likely to report a childhood history of physical abuse, emotional abuse, and domestic violence in the home than men who express an interest in children but have not been arrested.[27] A subpopulation of those who sexually offend against children report having been sexually abused as children themselves. Those who are minor attracted but have not acted on their desires still may have experienced childhood maltreatment, but they do not seem to have the level of trauma or the mental or physical chaos to which those who sexually offend have been exposed.[28]

As noted earlier, minor attraction may not be an exclusive behavior. There are MAPs attracted to prepubescent and early pubescent children who are also drawn to adults. The propensity for a romantic attraction to a child, however, increases for those who are exclusively minor attracted.[29] One difficulty writ large in conducting research into these topics is crafting an operational definition of "romantic attraction." What does "falling in love" with a child look like? Some men report an initial stage of infatuation, consistent with romantic love among adults, which evolves into a more enduring bond. Others describe a sense of rapport with a child that is lacking in adult relationships, so this bond is regressive in nature. As with romantic attachments among adults, defining what attracts two individuals becomes a complex and multi-faceted process.

The narrow research focus that exists on minor attraction almost exclusively targets men. Women can also be attracted to minors, but, consistent with a long-standing cultural tendency to dismiss female sexuality, their experiences are largely ignored. Women who do acknowledge a minor attraction often find themselves looked at askance by minor attracted men, so they struggle with feelings of alienation and loneliness in a community they hoped would be understanding.[30] These women remain a minority within a minority, excluded from many of the supports that their male counterparts enjoy.

Barriers to services for MAPs

The stigma that is attached to MAPs leaves them feeling isolated and afraid to seek help.[31] That same stigma can adhere to those who offer services to MAPs, limiting the latter's mental health options.[32] Even if mental health providers are willing to work with MAPs, a primary ethical issue is their duty to report harm to a child.[33] Mandatory reporting of child abuse seems a simple enough requirement in most jurisdictions. If an identifiable child victim is or has been endangered ("abused" is the commonly used term), a mental health provider in possession of that knowledge has a duty to inform the appropriate author-ities of this situation. But reporting laws cannot—and should not—attempt to cover all circumstances, which leaves mental health providers with difficult choices. How far in the past must the endangerment have occurred before a report is no longer required? Even if the endangerment occurred within the past few years, if the victim is now an adult, is a report mandated? Is it ethical to warn a client who is minor attracted that sharing information about victims or potential victims will trigger a report to the appropriate authorities, thereby shutting off an avenue to offer services to those who may be traumatized by abuse? Or is such a warning a means of protecting a client from self-incrimination? Many mental health professionals avoid working with MAPs because of the ethical dilemmas that arise.

There are also those who, being both minor attracted and acting out for other reasons, sexually abuse children with little or no remorse.[34] Their behavior is often symptomatic of a broader failure to empathize with the needs of others (see Chapter 3). MAPs who empathize with the harm that acting on their attraction can create live with uncomfortable emotions.[35] They have internalized the social stigma, prevalent in our culture, which is attached to their inclinations and remain pessimistic about any potential for future happiness. Despite this despondency, shame, and guilt, their fanta-sies are rarely suppressed.[36] Once MAPs have disclosed their orientation, support from family members or friends can mitigate at least some of the stress with which they live, but this admission also risks rejection by these same individuals.[37]

Changing the stigma directed toward those attracted to minors should be aligned with *secondary* prevention efforts that target those at risk for acting on their sexual interests toward children.[38] Present endeavors in this regard are either *primary* or *tertiary*. Primary efforts encourage children to assert themselves as well as admonish parents to be vigilant, in order to avoid the possibility of sexual abuse. Tertiary efforts act to remove and punish those who sexually offend, keeping the community safe from further depredations. Secondary prevention, designed to introduce MAPs to the public and normalize their presence, is more difficult to accomplish. Psychoeducational undertakings have been successful in changing attitudes toward ethnic minorities, but, when applied to minor attraction, they are not as effective.[39] Humanizing approaches may be more efficacious than psychoeducational efforts.[40]

A cultural belief—one not supported by research—is the need for MAPs to avoid all contact with children, in order to minimize the risk of sexual abuse.[41] MAPs, on the other hand, ask to be seen as individuals capable of controlling their sexual desires. Many also look for assistance in managing the stress of accepting their orientation. This latter group are resigned to the fact that theirs *is* an orientation and therefore is immutable.[42] So the availability of helpline services may encourage them to seek mental health treatment.[43]

The elephant in the room for MAPs is the uniqueness of their battle for equality, compared with that of other sexual minorities. They are seeking to be accepted *with* their sexual desires, but their effort is not—and cannot be—a fight for acquiescence in them *acting on* these sexual desires. The difficulty arises in defining "acting on." Between the polar extremes of unrestricted sexual activity with minors and abstinence from all sexual acts and thoughts related to them, there is a middle ground, composed of a wide range of potential behaviors. The risks that such behaviors create in encouraging sexual acting out, however, are unknown.

I have clients who recognize the emotional and psychological damage that a sexual relationship with a child—or even a non-sexual but one-sided romantic relationship—would create, and they abstain from acting on their desires because of it. Likewise, they recognize that child pornography exploits children and refuse to use it. But they fantasize about children they have seen in public places. They masturbate, using videos and photographs culled from online sources that show children in various stages of undress, but who are not nude. At no time is their intent to engage with these children. Just as, in an earlier era, adolescent males were stereotyped as having benefited from the underwear section of the J. C. Penney's catalog, so, too, do these MAPs utilize the images of scantily clad children that are frequently posted online or displayed in public. Do we abhor them for it? Is it repugnant that they find private means with which to act out their fantasies? Should they restrict themselves from even an active fantasy life if it involves children?

The limited amount of research that has been done primarily focuses on those who have been charged with sexual offenses. There is a growing body of studies on MAPs, but it remains a small fraction of the scientific investment in those whose sexual and/or romantic interests focus on children. As clinicians and researchers, we find ourselves in a position similar to the parents of adolescents. These parents may think their children are too young to engage in sexual acts, but—whether they like it or not—it is happening. What they *believe* does not change *reality*. MAPs are speaking out, and they need answers about how to best protect themselves and the children to whom they are attracted. Whether we like it or not, this, too, is happening. And what we believe also does not change reality. We have an ethical responsibility to provide answers.

Notes

  1 American Psychiatric Association, 2022.
  2 Janssen, 2021.
  3 GLAAD Media Reference Guide, n.d.
  4 Seto, 2012.
  5 Cantor, 2012; Rahman & Wilson, 2003.
  6 Ehrbar et al., 2008; Lawrence, 2011; Meyer-Bahlburg, 2010.
  7 Money, 1970, p. 425.
  8 Raphael, 2012
  9 Williamson-Kefu, 2018.
 10 Plaisance & Elliott, 2021.
 11 Caronia & Caron, 2019.
 12 Van Langenhove, 2012.
 13 Kourany, 2006.
 14 Speer & Christens, 2013.
 15 Seto, 2012.
 16 Martjin et al., 2020.
 17 Schaefer et al., 2022.
 18 Wurtele, Simons, & Parker, 2018.
 19 Stevens & Wood, 2019.
 20 Lievesley, Harper, & Elliott, 2020.
 21 Wilpert & Janssen, 2020.
 22 Diamond, 2021.
 23 Lawrence & Willis, 2021.
 24 McPhail, 2018.
 25 Seto, 2017.
 26 Seto, 2017, p. 3.
 27 Wurtele, Simons, & Parker, 2018.
 28 Grady & Levenson, 2021.
 29 Martjin et al., 2020.
 30 Lievesley & Lapworth, 2022.
 31 Levenson, Willis, & Vicencio, 2017.
 32 Parr & Pearson, 2019.
 33 McPhail, Stephens, & Heasman, 2018.
 34 Geiger & Fischer, 2021.

35 Dymond & Duff, 2020; Stevens & Wood, 2019.
36 Lievesley, Harper, & Elliott, 2020.
37 Elchuk, McPhail, & Olver, 2022.
38 Jackson, Ahuja, & Tenbergen, 2022; Lievesley & Harper, 2022.
39 Jara & Jeglic, 2021.
40 Harper et al., 2022.
41 Geradt et al., 2018.
42 Schaefer et al., 2022.
43 Wilpert & Janssen, 2020.

9 Alternatives to the current models

Looking beyond behavior

As I write these chapters, American media is dominated, as it almost always is, by politics and global unrest. But in the background, stories proliferate about scientific discoveries that hold promise for the future of our planet. Many will never come to fruition, being one-off experiments that will show up in a single publication and have their 15 minutes of fame, only to soon disappear from the world stage. Still, a few of these efforts will become breakthroughs, being repeated and refined in a heroic effort to reduce the specter of global warming, replace rapidly diminishing fossil fuel resources, and increase the hope for a sustainable future on this planet.

And in the sphere of treatment for those who sexually offend? Far fewer scientific discoveries offer promises for the future. Research has cautiously expanded the edges of existing models, such as risk–need–response and the good lives model, creating tightly controlled variations on a theme. Successes, when they do appear, are anxiously rated and reported. But there are no daring breakthroughs. No on-the-margins investigator is provided with government funding to explore a radical intervention. Sturdy guardrails hem in the standard routes designed for studies. These roads may be pitted and potholed, but no one dares tempt fate and diverge from the beaten path. The hallmarks of current interventions for those who sexually offend are containment and mandatory inclusion on an offender registry. What has impeded creative problem solving in responding to sexual offending? Chapter 6 argues that social science does not exist in a vacuum. It needs to operate in the broader context of a person's identity, social environment, and culture. But this is still rarely the case. The following are the most salient barriers to advances in treatment for sexual offending.

1 *It is easier to target "child sexual abuse" as the fundamental problem, rather than engage with the possibility that it is symptomatic of a larger social ill.*

The creation of sexual roles and identities is surprisingly recent, as is the impact of this sociocultural shift on our perceptions of sexual behavior.[1] In the evolution of these perceptions, we have reached a point of widespread

DOI: 10.4324/9781003487753-9

agreement—sexual contact between adults and children is unacceptable. Nonetheless, it continues. Studies have examined family dynamics that contribute to poor sexual boundaries, but only a few have considered the social and cultural risks associated with child sexual abuse. More generally, research into social indicators has declined in the United States, a trend continuing from the 1970s through the twenty-first century.[2] For social scientists, the dynamics *underlying* child sexual abuse are of far less concern than the behavior itself. Social science research tends to be influenced by the morality of the culture in which it is embedded,[3] as well as the hyperbole of media reports that showcase the most horrific sexual crimes,[4] so the drive for in-depth studies that address sociocultural accountability has dwindled accordingly.

Instead, the public is left with a caricature of child sexual offenders as monsters who masquerade as normal human beings. Research profiles the types of behavior in which they are likely to engage and characteristics that can delineate a preference for one type of acting out over another. But those studies do little to evaluate the impact of *daily* interpersonal interactions between perpetrator and victim. Most of these encounters are harmless, and many are beneficent, but some are spoiled by discrete acts of sexual abuse. The balance of kindliness versus distrust and its ensuing trauma is largely unstudied, so we have little data from victims to determine the extent to which the sexual act *itself* is traumatic, versus the anguish caused by the betrayal of a relationship supposedly based on fidelity and trust, which still maintains remnants of these elements. The *extent* to which victims perceive other adults or caretakers in their lives as having been complicit, whether these latter individuals were aware of the abuse or not, and the *impact* of such suspicions are also rarely studied. And the paths to recovery and healing that both those who sexually offend and their victims might pursue in their larger interpersonal environment of family and community—as well as which of these avenues might be efficacious—are largely unknown.

2   *The war on drugs campaign taught us that incarceration does not solve social problems. Yet the United States continues to have one of the highest per capita incarceration rates in the world. We have created a broken culture in our single-minded determination to isolate ourselves from those we fear.*

One almost insurmountable difficulty in challenging the current approach to those who sexually offend has been "backlash politics,"[5] defined as (1) a powerful desire to return to a prior social condition, perceived as being more secure than the present one; (2) a strong emphasis on goals and tactics to challenge the current, dominant social scripts, in order to achieve this desired return to the past; and (3) a threshold premise that wends its way into public discourse, so this desire to regress can be incorporated into mainstream thought. The polarization of American culture is symptomatic of fears stemming from a rapidly changing social environment and the goal of much of society—to bring tactics to bear to challenge the dominant, liberalizing script and return to a more conservative social and political cultural view.

Those who sexually offend are not the only minority targeted by those clinging to backlash politics. They are, however, a particularly vulnerable group. The perception that such individuals are reprehensible, and thus undeserving of basic rights, can be maintained with less fear of pushback from those with opposing views. In practical terms, the result is legislation that panders to fears but does little to address the safety of the community, as well as the emotional and psychological well-being of both those who offend and their victims.[6]

3 *Currently employed measures to assess treatment success are politically useful, but their social, cultural, and interpersonal value is questionable.*

Mental health professionals and clergy, particularly those in religious traditions that practice the rite of confession, share one experience in common: we hear life experiences that are confided to few others. While these situations are frequently distressing (e.g., it may be shameful to carry the secret of having had sex with a sister's fiancé before her wedding), they are often not a crime. But sometimes they are. Moreover, they become a crime often enough that we are aware that using a measurement such as recidivism, which is based on rearrests, is a poor indicator of treatment success.[7]

Those convicted of using child pornography have strict prohibitions regarding online access once they are released from incarceration on probation or parole. Yet these restrictions can easily be circumvented, such as by using a disposable cellphone. Routine polygraph examinations monitor proscribed behaviors, but their unreliability is recognized by the judicial system. The data on treatment success, then, most likely are skewed to reflect a more positive outcome than actually exists. Better measurements of recidivism would include detailed information about relapses, both for those found in violation of the conditions imposed upon their release and for those who avoided being caught. For example, how many times, and for how long, did viewing occur? What precipitated this behavior? Which efforts worked when attempting to stop? Which ones did not? Has the number of relapses been increasing or diminishing? Admissions by those who perpetrated physical sexual abuse, however, should be more rigorously pursued, given that their victims need to be protected and offered treatment. But following the rearrest and incarceration of those who *are* recidivists, an honest exploration of their experiences could be a useful tool to better understand the entire process.

4 *There are relatively few studies of the socioeconomic status of those identified as having sexually offended, but more research would doubtless find that lower socioeconomic status groups are overidentified. Sexual offending, like incarceration in general, is a class issue.*

Racial disparity has long been recognized as endemic to incarceration in the United States.[8] It comes as no surprise that socioeconomic status, correlated with race, is also a factor in the sentencing of those who sexually offend with physical victims. Those of lower socioeconomic status receive longer sentences.[9] The stresses confronting families with an incarcerated member are compounded by the stigma of a sexual offense having occurred within the family system (see Chapter 7).

Those prosecuted for child pornography at the federal level are less likely to face such discrimination.[10] Possibly because remote monitoring of computer use initially conceals racial and ethnic disparities, there appears to be a more even socioeconomic distribution of these offenders than is true in the prosecution of those with physical victims. Although no research studies specifically examine child pornography cases, a logical assumption is that the general disparity in sentencing that occurs for those who can afford to retain private legal counsel versus those forced to use public defenders also applies here.[11]

5 *Bias is not overtly acknowledged but remains strong among treatment providers and judicial personnel.*

Legislative bias against those who sexually offend is best understood through the laws that are passed and then supported on judicial appeal.[12] The biases among those within the court system and mental health providers are less glaring, but they are still present. Francis T. Cullen, a criminologist, has given a succinct description of the dilemma: "Conservatives deny the humanity of offenders, whereas liberals deny the pathology of offenders."[13] Whether liberal *or* conservative, those who daily encounter the victims of child sexual abuse face a tough challenge when asked to offer dignity and respect to the individuals responsible for inflicting trauma on these young lives. It can become a difficult effort to experience anything other than repulsion for one human being who can wantonly and callously hurt another by violating them sexually. The vignette opening Chapter 1, however, is a reminder that our emotional responses are created as much by socialization as by innate disgust.

6 *We need only compare the sophistication of the study of attractions between adults with that of attractions between adults and children to realize how cursory the latter field is.*

There is extensive research into the behavioral characteristics, and even the typologies, of those who sexually abuse children.[14] These are the studies that dominate scientific literature. But, compared with studies of adults' attraction to other adults, there is little understanding of *what* attracts adults to children. Research on mutual adult attraction investigates love, passion, intimacy, bonding, and the antitheses of these emotions as relationships break apart— all in exquisite detail. But for those who sexually offend? The assumption underlying any study regarding them is that their primary drive is a patho-logical desire. Tailoring interventions to be based on the premise of a *sexual orientation*, versus a particular form of narcissism or a sociopathic proclivity that sees an easily manipulated sexual partner, could be useful. But even these categorizations seem to be outside the realm of acceptable investiga-tive work. This is probably due to the risk of asking—in a non-judgmental manner—*what* a MAP found fulfilling about either a sexual relationship with a child or, in the case of child pornography, a fantasy about a relationship with a child? Some studies do ask these questions, but they are isolated instances and are rarely replicated.

Eeny, meeny, miny, moe: Determining the risk for reoffending

A male (or, in rare cases, a female or someone who is nonbinary) faces a pre-sentencing investigation after a charge of sexual offending. Or perhaps he (or that rare other) is reaching the end of a sentence. Or his release from prison on parole or probation may be pending. For the person who has sexually offended in each of these scenarios, a looming question must be answered. What option best protects the community?

The community is best protected when pre-sentencing investigators, parole boards, and mental health providers can accurately predict who is at risk to reoffend. One such effort has been the development of actuarial tables, which were a response to the poor predictive ability of clinical judgments. Mental health providers are not very accurate in assessing the risk an individual poses for offending in the future. Their perceptions are clouded by idiosyncratic experiences, emotional investment in a particular client, failure to consider all pertinent data in reaching a conclusion, and a tendency to rely on intuition rather than cold logic. Actuarial tables gather data from empirical studies to examine logical, testable facts that are correlated with recidivism. These types of tables include broad categories, such as age, victim typology (e.g., gender, relationship to the person offending), interpersonal relationships, general criminal behavior, substance abuse, and aggravating or mitigating factors. They have become essential in risk assessments.

The most frequently used actuarial table premiered as Static-99, but more recently it was revised as Static-99R and Static-2000R.[15] These tables function as assessment instruments. Individual items selected from the factors mentioned above receive weighted scores. Based on the total, the risk for reoffending is calculated as a range, going from a low to a high risk for reoffending. Most other actuarial tables function in a similar manner.

An unresolved problem is the question of appropriate categorizations for at least some of the essential items, such as a history of arrests for criminal sexual conduct. For example, a man in his mid-20s was charged with sexual solicita-tion of a minor. He had been arrested at age 17 for similar behavior, and his case was transferred to adult court. At the time, he was able to plead guilty to a non-sexual offense, in order to avoid being placed on a sex offender registry.

His history thus poses an actuarial dilemma. Using the criteria for many of the table's measures, he has no history of a conviction for a *sexual crime*, but that distinction arose through a legal manipulation to avoid such a charge. Based on the actuarial measure being used and the examiner's interpretation of it, the level of risk could change significantly if, instead, he is considered to have *sexually offended* in the past.

In another case, a father was accused of sexual abuse by his daughter, who was living with her mother at the time. Despite her mother's objections, the daughter continued visitation with her father. The mother then reported that her daughter was sexually abused by the father. The appropriate social service agency investigated, substantiated the allegations of abuse, and took steps to protect the child from her father by restricting visitation with him. Despite this decision, the prosecutor's office reviewed the evidence and declined to press charges, disagreeing with the social service agency's contention that sufficient evidence was present to sustain the allegations. If charges of sexual abuse were brought against the father at a future time, the question of *reoffending* would remain open to interpretation, since he was never charged and thus retained his legal innocence, since there was a plausible rationale for doubt.

Despite the intent for such tables to improve clinical judgments, a study of nine of the more popular actuarial instruments found that their predictive ability was consistently at the "low moderate" level.[16] These findings suggest that while actuarial tables are better predictors than chance, their accuracy is far less than desirable when attempting to ascertain risk to the community, or proffering hope for those who have offended but no longer pose a risk. The need for a more comprehensive approach in evaluating the risk for recidivism has long been recognized. A principal drawback in using actuarial tables for risk assessment is their failure to explore underlying dynamics. While these instruments tout evidence that they can predict sexual recidivism—albeit poorly—a meaningful prediction should also be able to offer a *rationale* for what are considered to be risk factors.[17]

Risk factors for reoffending are meta-categorized as either "stable" or "acute."[18] Stable risk factors can be resistant to change and manifest themselves consistently. These include addictions, personality traits, or ingrained maladaptive behaviors. Acute risk factors create stress but are time limited. For example, the death of a significant person in one's life, intoxication, or an unexpected loss of employment are stressors that increase the risk of acting out in maladaptive ways, but they are transient. Overall, the greater the number of maladaptive factors that are present sexually and socially, the greater the risk of recidivism.

Beyond these situational considerations, the criteria used by investigators to evaluate whether someone has reoffended also vary. For some, recidivism means a charge of or rearrest for a sexual offense. For others, it requires a conviction. And, for still others, it may merely be an investigation by law enforcement or a social service agency. These differing expectations for what constitute a reoffense mean that no clear definition exists, so the criteria for maladaptive behaviors can vary dramatically from study to study.

A judicial alternative: The specialized court model

Instead of incarceration, what other options exist to supervise, monitor, and treat those who sexually offend? One available model in the criminal justice system consists of specialized courts—for example, veterans courts, domestic violence courts, and drug courts—that are an alternative for those arrested for specific offenses. Each type of specialized court intervenes by minimizing the need for costly and ineffective incarceration. Two of these courts hold promise as models for people who sexually offend: those designed for defendants charged with drug offenses, and those where the defendants are experiencing a mental disorder.

Drug courts

The first effort to implement what today is considered the drug court model began in Dade County, Florida, in 1989.[19] Over time, the nature and purpose of drug courts in specific jurisdictions has evolved, but their fundamental purpose remains the same as that described in a 1998 article by Steven Belenko.[20] These courts seek to reduce drug use and its associated criminal behaviors. They do so by engaging and retaining defendants involved with drugs in treatment services; concentrating expertise about drug cases in a single courtroom; and incorporating clinical assessments and case management to address defendants' other needs.

Drug courts have evolved to emphasize treatment, and in some jurisdictions they are now conceptualized as "drug treatment courts."[21] Difficulties in implementing such programs continue, including those arising from racial disparities and socioeconomic inequities.[22] But these courts' collaborative approach between the justice system and treatment providers, and their combination of incentives and sanctions, encourages progress and a sense of ownership for defendants that is not matched by more traditional approaches. Ultimately, the drug court model mitigates the onus of drug sentences on a defendant's record. Although most participants initially choose to participate in treatment to avoid incarceration, an attitude of general satisfaction is later expressed by those who complete such programs and, surprisingly, by those who fail to stay the course.[23]

By focusing on defendants charged with criminal drug offenses who are at risk for a reoffense and who demonstrate a substance abuse disorder, drug courts target those most in need of services and most likely to benefit from an intervention, rather than punishment or incarceration. Although drug courts and drug treatment courts differ in the ways in which they approach defendants, there are commonalities toward which all such programs strive.[24]

- In order to be part of a drug court program, participants have to invest a much longer time in treatment than that required by a sentence of incarceration.
- Participants must undergo frequent, random drug screens.
- Treatment by addiction counselors and/or mental health providers is an essential component of the program.
- Defendants are provided with case management services, as appropriate and needed, to address employment, prosocial activities that benefit others or society as a whole, and education, as well as other needs.
- Both rewards and sanctions are in place, offering positive reinforcements for attaining expected goals and handing out negative consequences for failing to do so.

The tenets of this model can easily be generalized to those who sexually offend. Defendants' willingness to invest time and effort by participating in the program, the use of external monitoring (in the case of sexual offending, through polygraphs, rather than drug screens), treatment by appropriate professionals, case management (including necessary supervision), and rewards and sanctions can all be applied to those who sexually offend. For those who would pose a risk to the community, incarceration remains a necessary alternative. But for those who have sexually offended against convenient (i.e., easily accessible) victims and have a limited history of sexual acting out, the potential to remain in the community and continue to provide emotional and monetary support for their families is a far better option than incarceration—with its resultant financial burden to the state and trauma to families—and the inefficacious treatment approaches currently being pursued.

Mental health courts

The causes behind the flood of individuals with mental illness who are brought before the criminal justice system are beyond the scope of this book. Suffice it to say that the deinstitutionalization movement of the 1950s and 1960s, as well as a lack of adequate community mental health care, were significant contributing factors.[25] Mental health courts, like drug courts, recognize that defendants with a mental illness are better served through treatment than by incarceration. Using an interdisciplinary approach, mental health courts encourage defendants to (1) complete a program that requires mental health services, (2) demonstrate dedicated participation in the program, and (3) refrain from criminal behavior.[26] Mental health courts face difficulties in serving those with co-occurring disorders, and they run up against the racial and ethnic disparities that exist within the entire judicial system.[27] Despite these problems, mental health courts have proven to be efficacious in significantly reducing recidivism.[28]

For those who have sexually offended and suffer from a mental illness or a co-occurring mental disorder, a variation on the mental health court model serves a more useful purpose than incarceration. For these defendants, although their salient *crime* is a sexual offense, its *motivation* is frequently a psychosis, a delusion, or severely impaired judgment that is manifested by a more general failure to act in rational and socially acceptable ways. Again, services such as external monitoring, treatment by appropriate professionals, and case management offer a hopeful outcome, which incarceration does not.

A sociocultural alternative: The Amish model

Postmodern Americans rely on a process of incarceration and offender registration to protect children from sexual abuse. The mental health needs of those who sexually offend are addressed in isolation *from* the community. There exists a culture, however, that chooses to integrate those who offend *into* the community. The model they have developed cannot be fully incorporated into the mainstream, but it does offer an intriguing window into the possibilities of reintegration for those who offend.

The Amish are most frequently recognized for their simple, unadorned clothing and their use of horse-drawn buggies for transportation. These obvious but superficial symbols often represent all that is known about their culture. But in recent years, the struggle to find a way to significantly have an impact on sexual abuse has led to a creative collaboration between civil authorities and some Amish communities.

The Amish are the largest among several groups described as Plain people.[29] These groups are collective cultures, where individual autonomy gives way to a dependency on the larger group. Their loyalty is to the Amish church—consisting of their family, neighbors, and the community. They live in settlements peopled by other Amish, and their reliance on each other for spiritual, emotional, and psychological support effectively excludes the world that surrounds them. They are willing to negotiate with non-Amish people for business purposes and even maintain friendships with them. But there is a strong and distinct psychological barrier between the Amish and those outside that society.

In recent years, negotiations have increased between the criminal justice system, mental health providers, and the Amish church to offer services to those who sexually offend. Following exposés of abuse by Catholic priests, the media began its search for the next big story.[30] That story became, among others, sexual exploitation by the Boy Scouts of America, Protestant denominations, and the Amish. When the Amish thus became heightened targets for arrest and criminal adjudication, they found themselves in an untenable position. Child sexual abuse was traditionally handled within the church, through internal judicial decisions. Still, they grappled with their perception of an omniscient and omnipresent God, whose plan deputizes responsible parties. The Amish remain subject to God's will, including as it is manifested by the state.[31]

By enlisting the aid of Amish leaders, a novel program was initiated in Lancaster County, Pennsylvania. The negotiations addressed the greatest drawback in responding to child sexual abuse in Plain communities: the lack of reliable reporters when abuse occurred. If mandatory reporting statutes, which include members of the clergy in Pennsylvania, were to be effective, a majority of the Amish ministry must also abide by them. To do so, the consequences for those Amish who sexually offended and were reported to outside authorities would need to meet with approval from constituent Amish settlements. (As history demonstrates, laws that are out of favor with the public—in this case, the Amish—rarely serve their intended purpose.)

In many cases, the acceptable compromise was determined to be minimal or no incarceration. Instead, the person identified as a sexual offender would serve an extended period of supervision within the Amish community. The injustice in such an arrangement, some argued, was a lack of incarceration for an Amish person who sexually offended and was charged with a crime, compared with prison sentences for non-Amish individuals who were convicted for the same crimes. Others pointed out that this distinction was moot, since our justice system had already demonstrated an inherent inequity in sentencing, predicated on financial resources, education, and socioeconomic status.[32]

Under this program, those Amish who sexually offend may be allowed to receive residential treatment in facilities that cater to the Amish. Once they are returned to the community, local committees, composed of Amish peers, monitor their supervision and well-being. *State supervision*, via probation and parole, relies on external monitoring, such as registration as a sex offender, sessions with a probation or parole officer, unannounced visits to the home, cellphone monitoring, and screenings for drugs and alcohol. *Amish supervision plans* involve members of the community, who are part of the collective culture in which the person who offended lives, and usually include the creation of an accountability committee. Their monitoring is more comprehensive, intense, and prolonged than any the state can offer.

It is possible, then, to supervise those who sexually offend in their homes and within their community, as is being done by the Amish. The culture in which this can successfully occur is unusual in postmodern America, but its emphasis on *community accountability* is intriguing. Are there applicable models in which families and community groups or resources could take greater responsibility for the supervision and well-being of those who sexually offend and thus allow them to remain in place? Such plans would be less intrusive, much cheaper than incarceration, and less traumatic for families.

Overcoming obstacles to change

Legislators, the justice system, and social science researchers all face the same dilemma. One has only to think back to the Edsel automobile to understand the problem.[33] The Ford Motor Company researched and planned at great length for the Edsel, only to pull it from their line of cars within two years, due to plummeting sales. All their research and all of their marketing efforts could not overcome a major hurdle—the public did not want it.

Models are available for legislation, judicial programs, and avenues of research that could rewrite the current narrow formulas for how best to handle those who sexually offend. But such alterations are useless if the public cannot be sold on them. The necessary, *fundamental* change is a better understanding of a person who sexually offends. And that requires an effort to educate the public and revise their perceptions.

The principal revision needs to be a realization that, under our current system, the premise of increased safety for the community is an illusion. The frequency of recidivism is low for sexual offenders who are incarcerated and released, but some studies use the criterion of *any* subsequent arrest for criminal behavior, while others use the criterion of an arrest for a sexual offense. The potential for recidivism *without being caught* is much greater for those who view child pornography. Online means are monitored by probation and parole officers, but alternative devices are easily obtained, and mandatory polygraphs are not foolproof. Therefore, the principal measure of success in reducing this type of recidivism is illusory and most likely underestimates how often it occurs. Nor does the very measure itself offer much in the way of providing an understanding of the behaviors engaged in by those who sexually offend (in any of its aspects), reform, and then relapse. Recidivism will probably still remain low, but we have no clear understanding of *what* recidivism actually involves.

Likewise, various predictors of risk are ineffective. Actuarial tables fare better than clinical judgments, but they are still inaccurate. Previous chapters in this book have cited the ineffectiveness of mandatory registration for those who have offended, either as a safety measure or a deterrent. Incarceration removes those who have sexually offended from the community for a time; creates a hardship for their family; and, if they have received treatment, returns them with potential marginal improvements (due to mental health interventions), but primarily with a sense of having been punished to satisfy the community.

Can genuine change occur? The following chapter discusses ways in which this can happen.

Notes

1 Angelides, 2005.
2 Aria, Misuraca, & Spano, 2020.
3 Caronia & Caron, 2019.
4 Cucolo & Perlin, 2013.
5 Alter & Zürn, 2020.
6 Calkins et al., 2014.
7 Some people may assume that mental health professionals are required by law to immediately report any abuse confessed by a client, but this is not necessarily the

case. Many clients (1) report abuse that is in the distant past, (2) do not disclose the names of victims or geographic locations, or (3) otherwise are sufficiently vague, so there is no identifiable victim to report, and/or no clear governmental agency that has jurisdiction if a report were to be filed.

 8 Nellis, 2021.
 9 D'Alessio & Stolzenberg, 1993.
10 Wolak, Finkelhor, & Mitchell, 2011.
11 Ovalle, 2021.
12 Adelman, 2022.
13 Cullen, 2012, p. 102.
14 Lim et al., 2021.
15 Phenix, Helmus, & Hansen, 2015.
16 Tully, Chou, & Browne, 2013.
17 Mann, Hanson, & Thornton, 2010.
18 Hanson & Harris, 2000.
19 Belenko, 1990.
20 Belenko, 2021.
21 Lurigio, 2008.
22 Gordon, 2018.
23 Carey, Mackin, & Finigan, 2020.
24 National Drug Court Resource Center [NDCRC], n.d.
25 Torrey et al., 2010.
26 Edwards et al., 2020.
27 Gaba et al., 2022.
28 Fox et al., 2021.
29 Nolt & Meyers, 2007.
30 Weaver, 1998.
31 Estep, 1996.
32 Western & Pettit, 2010.
33 Marshall, 2021.

10 Distant horizons

Implementing change

As a psychologist with many years of experience, I am still prone to thera-peutic blunders. One such gaffe occurred in a session with an older man who, as a young adult, had been charged and convicted of a sexual offense. His wife remained at his side, and he turned his incarceration into an opportunity, becoming a zealous advocate for those who, like him, are stigmatized by the daunting forces of the legal system. Nevertheless, he remains a convicted felon, and a lifetime registrant as a sex offender.

During one of our sessions, he summarized the bleak reality of his situation with brutal clarity. In a misguided attempt at support, I said, "I'm thankful that you have a home." "I have a 'place,'" he retorted, "but not a 'home.'" A place, but not a home. That statement has stayed with me. It is a powerful reminder of the status of those who sexually offend. The preceding chapters have examined how we respond to these pariahs of the postmodern age, and how the ripple effect of that attitude bodes poorly, not just for people who offend, but also for their families and their victims.

Previous chapters have also outlined the dilemma of addressing sexual offending, and the impasse in finding an approach that better serves everyone involved. After challenges to the present situation have been aired and the dust has settled, the fundamental problem still remains. In our collective con-sciousness, those who sexually offend are (as the title of Chapter 1 suggests) monsters—fiendish caricatures of human beings. This book joins the thin ranks who characterize those who offend in the context of relationships: his-torical, cultural, social, and familial. Having done so, how can the risk—the *real* risk, which cannot be ignored, of further sexual acting out that harms children—be tempered by responses that respect the needs and rights of those who commit these acts and avoid further victimization of the very children meant to be protected?

Before summarizing the status quo and recommending changes, it is important to recall that our present beliefs, practices, and policies did not emerge without precedent. While some of them are the products of measured social change, more are the result of irrational anxiety. Social groups are extremely susceptible to the contagion of fear.[1] For instance, cellphones are

DOI: 10.4324/9781003487753-10

now ubiquitous, but in the early twentieth century, the introduction of the first quaint form of telephones met with a phobic response.[2] And for some, the revelation in 1980 that serial killer John Wayne Gacy performed as Pogo the Clown at children's parties spiked a fear of clowns.[3] Social attitudes toward those who sexually offend have followed a slower trajectory and are more sustained, but they demonstrate the same unreasoning fear.

What arguments can be made, then, for maintaining the status quo? And what arguments can be proffered in favor of change? There are persuasive elements to each approach.

Arguments for continuing present policies and practices

If it works, don't fix it

An adversarial approach toward those who sexually offend has a logical history behind it. There are rational arguments for perceiving those who offend as the nemesis of order and safety, who therefore must be isolated, punished, treated, and supervised—all in the name of protection and risk management.[4] Proactive and reactive concerns are intertwined. Everyone in the locale where they have chosen to make their home deserves to feel secure, so assurances of safety and security that have been made to community members should remain intact. Those who violate that security should be placed in check. Using this argument, our present system is viable. It is the *severity* of consequences that are meted out, and the *application* of these consequences, which are questionable. Incarceration, offender registration, and monitoring, although ineffective at present, continue to be the "go to" responses for almost all sexual offenses against children, regardless of the nature of the offense. The potential for effectively reintegrating those who offend into the community is lost, not because the current system declines to offer these opportunities, but because they are ineffectively applied. Research into a more efficacious use of incarceration, as well as better treatment and monitoring within the community, will fine-tune the approaches now in place and improve the existing system.

The heightened risk to children

Some acknowledge that community protection and risk management efforts may be overzealous, and they struggle with a need to balance the civil and moral rights of individuals who sexually offend with the rights of those who have been victimized. Laws passed to offer protection from such offenses are usually named after victims of brutal crimes, but such legislation is crafted to also guard those who face sexual assaults that are less heinous, but potentially no less psychologically traumatizing. From this perspective, *any* sexual abuse of a child is traumatic, so the most severe consequences must be employed.

As a comparable argument, consider a parent who repeatedly physically abuses a child. Many who commit physical abuse have no deep-seated intention of doing so the first time, much less a desire to do so again. But the child is still there, tensions remain, similar circumstances arise, and the behavior repeats itself. That parent may feel guilt and remorse and develop a shameful self-perception, but these overwhelmingly negative attributes are not enough to stop the cycle of abuse. Some form of external monitoring and deterrence will be necessary to protect the child's well-being, not only when exposed to violence, but afterward, as an assurance that their abusive parent will not harm them again.

Yet the trajectory so often followed by interventions after such situations arise differs between instances of physical and sexual abuse. Children in physically abusive or neglectful homes are removed and placed with relatives or, if necessary, in foster care. Contact with the abusive or neglectful parent or caretaker is restricted. The safety of any abused child is paramount. But the harshness of the physical abuse or neglect is also evaluated. If sufficiently severe, a parent or caretaker may be incarcerated. In many cases, however, the perpetrator becomes part of a treatment plan to reunite the family. Reunification may be slow and cautious, but phone calls, online contact, and visits (initially supervised and eventually unsupervised) may all be part of a process of returning children to their homes.

A much slower procedure, if it occurs at all, will reunify a person who has sexually offended and their victim. The urge to sexually abuse someone is treated as a more difficult impulse to manage than outbursts of anger. Perhaps because this urge is insidious and can so easily be hidden, while anger is more often expressed by a loud and obvious confrontation, the drive to reunite those who have sexually offended with their victims is less intense. Regardless of the reason, sexual abuse continues to be seen as a more serious violation of a child's rights than physical abuse or neglect, requiring more stringent physical and emotional distance from the perpetrator, and long-term incarceration as a consequence of perpetrating that abuse.

The potential for restorative justice

Another argument for maintaining the present system regarding those who sexually offend is the expansion of the restorative justice model. Traditional paradigms rely heavily on punishment. Punishment is assumed to result in future deterrence, rehabilitation, and accountability, processes believed to reduce recidivism.[5] The argument for incarceration assumes that those who offend pose a risk to the community and need to be removed from it. Paradoxically, defendants are often charged but released on bond until sentencing, which can occur many months after their arrest. This practice sends an implicit but powerful message—the purpose of our judicial system is less about safety for the community and more about punishment.

In contrast, restorative justice attempts to align the efforts toward those who offended, their victims, and the community. While accountability— holding those who offend responsible for their actions—remains a primary goal, this purpose is achieved by repairing harm, rather than through retribution or punishment.[6] Restorative justice invokes shame, but its focus is on the *behavior*, and not on the offending individual per se, thus reducing the risk for stigmatization.[7] It offers an interdependent relationship, emphasizing dialogue and support, in addition to criticism. Shaming the behavior rather than the person is an effort to retain positive bonds within a relationship. Although the ultimate responsibility for managing the offending behavior is legally mandated, there is movement toward a reconciliation with the community.[8]

Restorative justice has met with a mixed reception. Some states embrace it, while others resist the model.[9] The criminal justice curriculum in higher education has been slow to incorporate its principles.[10] As a new model, restorative justice continues to evolve, moving from being narrowly tied to the criminal aspects of those who offend to a broader-based intervention, encompassing complex issues of social justice.[11] While restorative justice has long-term potential, its efficacy is dependent on its reception.

Arguments for changing the present system

The potential to tailor treatment to the offense

Those who sexually offend may (1) be antisocial or sociopathic (lacking the ability to experience guilt or remorse for their behavior); (2) exhibit a severe mental illness; or (3) use sex with children to create an interpersonal relationship or for related reasons. At present, there is little distinction among the treatments offered to those who are predatory, those who are disorganized and mentally ill, and those who struggle to meet an interpersonal need through their offending behavior. To some extent, this necessary separation can be achieved through the restorative justice model, but even then, change only goes so far. Our justice system has done too little to incorporate mental health services into the earliest phases of assessing and processing those who sexually offend. This lack of ability to successfully categorize the behavior— as a form of mental disorder, a personality type, the development of certain traits, or a motivation—has led to resignation and an attitude that no categorization is needed.

There are those who sexually offend against children and have little or no remorse for their behavior. For them, children, as well as most other people within their sphere of influence, are objects. They lack an ability to empathize with others. Therefore, given the right circumstances, they pose a danger not only to children, but also to any other person with whom they interact. The degree of risk to others falls on a continuum, based on the severity of their inability to empathize. But we err in assuming that their predatory nature is confined to the sexual assault of children. In most cases, such individuals pose a much broader predatory risk, but they have been flagged because they were caught with a child.

Those with a serious mental illness have difficulty managing in the real world. They are plagued by hallucinations (sounds, voices, and images that are not real), delusions (magical beliefs that they insist are true), and other forms of distorted thinking. At times, their moods move from extreme elation to the depths of depression. Amid this ever-shifting chaos, they may act out and sexually offend against a child. Their reasons for doing so are often complex, and they may also be minor attracted. At other times, these individuals respond to distorted beliefs. It becomes essential to evaluate the underlying reasons for their behavior, in order to determine whether treatment is warranted for a sexual offense or for an underlying psychosis. This is a step too often missing in our current system.

Lastly, there are those who are minor attracted and act on their desire to be involved with children by engaging in sexual acts. They are probably exhibiting a sexual orientation. There are also those who, for other reasons, act out sexually with children. These individuals are probably showing evidence of a paraphilia, or fetish behavior. At present, we have little understanding of what constitutes a sexual orientation versus a paraphilia, or, if a paraphilia is present, of knowing what the differing ways in which it may play out are. We are now becoming aware that these distinctions do exist and need to be addressed. Those who are sexually and romantically attracted to children, thus manifesting a probable sexual orientation, and those who are acting out in response to trauma, doubtless need different treatment approaches to support future abstinence from these behaviors. Current research, however, offers little understanding of what these treatments might be.

Alternatives to incarceration and offender registration that can reduce the damage inflicted on victims and families

Victims of sexual crimes often desire acknowledgments of remorse from those who have offended against them. Our current judicial system offers little to encourage the expression of such remorse.[12] In exchange for a plea bargain that avoids a trial, a defendant may be able to plead guilty to a charge that carries a lesser penalty, but that bargain also disguises the offense that was committed, such as by shifting a more severe charge of sexual assault to a lesser one, or dismissing accompanying charges. In this legal conundrum, few perpetrators assert a desire to slice through the Gordian knot and speak with genuine remorse to their victims, discussing the details of behaviors that have been ignored legally. Until and unless those who have perpetrated an offense can speak out with the knowledge that their honesty will not trigger new charges or further consequences, silence is the better choice.

Incarceration enhances self-perceptions of social inadequacy and increases alienation.[13] Its negative impact on work-related, romantic, and social relationships is inevitable. Those who sexually offend are often individuals who demonstrate poor interpersonal boundaries, even before being incarcerated. Prison does nothing to rehabilitate their social skills or prepare them for reentry into their community. Research also suggests that stigmatization aggravates the affected person's potential for aggression and their defiance of norms and rules.[14]

There are both primary and secondary consequences of legislative efforts to manage those who sexually offend.[15] Primary consequences are those that reduce opportunities for reintegration in direct proportion to the degree of the offense. These include restrictions on housing, employment, and potential future activities. Secondary consequences include negative public reactions toward those who have sexually offended. These can become generalized into a "courtesy stigma"—the tendency for negative attitudes to expand from being directed at an initial target and include those who appear to be supportive of that targeted individual, including family, friends, and employers.[16]

Both types of consequences can be reduced if the neighbors of those who have sexually offended receive education about the nature of sexual offending and thus are provided with a realistic understanding of the minimal risks created by living near those who have offended.[17] Nonetheless, education is not a panacea. There inevitably are those who still remain cautious, distrustful, and resentful. But when dialogue and education are available, fear and mistrust are markedly reduced.

Willingness to demonize a minority has been a sociocultural pattern throughout history

Coercion through the application of stigma is an ancient practice. Across millennia, those in power have employed shame and stigma to persuade citizens to adhere to expectations.[18] In the same way, religious institutions and the media have used these mechanisms to maintain standards of behavior. The presence of online social media adds another layer to the pressures that can be brought to bear to ensure compliance. All of these practices are highly effective in highlighting a group of individuals or certain group behaviors, effectively demonizing and ostracizing their members. This has certainly been the process used toward those who sexually offend.

As long as sexual offending was simply seen as a severe stigma, those who were targeted could remain partially hidden, at least until the 1990s. At that point, the federal government required each state to publish a registry of those who had sexually offended, so anonymity became more difficult.[19] The social momentum that gave rise to the formation of these registries is far from over, despite widespread recognition of their ineffectiveness.[20]

In part, the general public may fail to recognize the consequences of mandatory registration as a sexual offender. Social psychological research demonstrates that people underestimate the severity of social pain.[21] Feelings of ostracism or shame are underrated by those observing the impact of social stigma, and empathy is only induced through experiencing it oneself. There is also evidence that cultures emphasizing independence find stigma and ostracism to be more painful than cultures based on interdependence.[22] This finding seems counterintuitive, but it reflects the greater isolation of those ostracized in independent cultures. A public focus on the perceived reduction in risk provided by offender registration fails to consider the emotional consequences for those whose names appear on it.

The typology of "sex offender"—despite no evidence to suggest a certain personality type, specific traits, or particular characteristics that consistently identify such a category—creates a demonized minority, based on its members' behavior. Sadly, the impetus behind these efforts often has a genuine, if misplaced, intent to be helpful. Other factors in our cultural attitudes also continue to be problematic, such as the overrepresentation of males who sexually offend against female children, which means that feminist advocacy logically incorporates efforts to protect the well-being of females of all ages. A major problem arises when there is no effort to balance this draconian legislation of mandatory registration, which was influenced by a misguided attempt to protect children, with less stringent responses.[23] Some see this focus on a registry for offenders as reflective of a more generalized tendency in society: a belief that future harm (of any sort) is imminent, so there is a need for greater security. Sociologists have coined the term "risk society" to explain this fear-based phenomenon.[24]

The impact of stigma is socially crippling

A sociological model applicable to those who have sexually offended is known as labeling theory. Public shaming attached to the term "sex offender" is internalized by those to whom the label is applied, thus changing their identity.[25] This new identity becomes central to their sense of self as they pursue social interactions.[26] Self-perceptions of those who have sexually offended irrevocably change once they are listed on a register.[27] Some cite the existence of a hierarchy among those who have offended, with persons who are minor attracted or who have sexually abused children placed in the lowest echelons of the community so labeled. Nonetheless, there is camaraderie and a sense of place among those convicted of sexual crimes that is lacking elsewhere, whereas full socialization is often difficult to achieve. Such attitudes dampen the efforts of those who have sexually offended to desist from such behaviors in the future.[28]

If those who sexually offend are to leave behind both a social and a self-identity based on offending, how are they best able to do so? Any such effort is hampered by a generalized stigma of dishonesty and unreliability that follows anyone who has been incarcerated,[29] and disclosure to a potential employer is a source of shame and disgrace.[30] A study completed in the United Kingdom, where registration of those who offend is not as transparent as in the United States, found that distancing oneself from an identity associated with sexual offending is an integral part of developing a positive social self, one that includes a future self-identity that reduces the risk of reoffending.[31] Without this possibility, chronic ostracism can lead to feelings of resignation and hopelessness.[32] Therefore, elimination of public sex offender registries appears to be a compelling need in efforts to reduce recidivism and strengthen the self-worth of those who sexually offend.

Minor attraction can be addressed more easily than it now is

The stigma of minor attraction—seen as dark, shameful, and furtive—takes its toll. And if other adverse experiences in childhood exist, they compound resistance to revealing such a secret in counseling.[33] Too often, it comes to light only after a report of sexual abuse of a child or the use of child pornography. Abstinence without support is a lonely vigil. Nonetheless, shame, fear, and stigma contribute to avoiding sharing one's status as a MAP with confidantes or family members, as well as counselors.

Currently, the very concept of minor attraction is questioned as being valid. Instead, three other schools of thought regarding sexual acting out with children remain firmly entrenched.[34] *Feminist theory* conceptualizes a sexual attraction to children as a precursor to sexual acting out, and it sees violence as a social problem that is rooted in gender issues, since heterosexual offending predominates. The appropriate intervention for an attraction to children addresses it as a destructive force. *Psychology* continues to perceive minor attraction as an individual pathology—a paraphilia or a sexual disorder. As with any sexual disorder, it can be treated if it is addressed through scientific study and effective interventions. And for those who study *history*, particularly post-colonial scholars, sexual acting out with minors falls under the broad scope of power inequities in all human interactions, which demonstrate a way for one entity to dominate another. Culturally, then, sexual offending is a historically sanctioned means of demonstrating power.

None of these perspectives offer the alternative of addressing this sexual orientation as a sexual and romantic longing. Nor do they take into account a full understanding of an individual who struggles with an attraction to minors, a propensity that cannot be met without emotional injury to at least one party. At best, these three positions are explanatory, but they offer no effective answers (despite psychology's belief in treatment). At worst, they are dismissive. A model where minor attraction is seen as a sexual orientation, however, respects those who struggle to manage desires that otherwise cannot be expressed. It deserves further scientific research and exploration.

Organizations working toward change

Several national and international organizations offer support for those who are minor attracted and challenge legislation that restricts the civil rights of those who have sexually offended. They have websites, which include links to information; videos that explain the phenomenon of attraction to children and illustrate ways to manage these sexual feelings; and referrals to potential treatment sources. These organizations advocate for changes in legislation, and some encourage the prevention of child abuse.

The Prostasia Foundation advocates for the well-being of children but remains aware that the rights of those perceived as being a danger to children are often violated.[35] The foundation's focus centers on the protection of children, advocacy for human and civil rights, and positivity in educational messages about sexual behavior. It also invests in ongoing research designed to better understand and support MAPs. The foundation also partners with the MAP Support Club.[36] Membership is vetted, and the club's purpose is to provide a positive community experience for MAPs who are committed to the safety and well-being of children and, therefore, choose not to act on their desires. The club also has dedicated channels to the services of mental health professionals trained to work with those who are minor attracted.

B4U-ACT, organized in 2003, notes on its website that "as an alliance of therapists, researchers, and MAPS, B4U-ACT's mission is to promote a science-informed understanding about people in our communities with an attraction to children or adolescents, and to support them living in truth and dignity."[37] The program offers peer support for those who are minor attracted, as well as support for their families and friends. It remains committed to the safety of children. B4U-ACT maintains a therapist referral program. Whenever possible, MAPs are matched with a therapist trained in their needs. The program also offers workshops and research consultation.

Virtuous Pedophiles was founded in 2012 as a peer-support organization for MAPs. "Our mission is to improve the lives of pedophiles, but never at the expense of the welfare of children."[38] Its website includes numerous resources, with "Find Out More" tabs to writings by those integrally involved with the group, and encouragement for anyone seeking answers in their struggle. The group advocates for the well-being and safety of children and believes that this can occur, in part, through a better understanding of those attracted to them.

The National Association for Rational Sexual Offense Laws (NARSOL) is a grassroots advocacy organization that "envisions a society free from public shaming, dehumanizing registries, discrimination, and unconstitutional laws."[39] Its website offers information on federal and state legislation, research, and media reports pertinent to the legal status of those who sexually offend.

Sex Addicts Anonymous (SAA), "a fellowship of individuals who share their experience, strength, and hope with each other so they may overcome their sexual addiction and help others recover from sexual addiction or dependency," employs a 12-step recovery model addressing those who perceive their sexual desires as being beyond their control.[40] As with other 12-step programs (e.g., Alcoholics Anonymous, Narcotics Anonymous), groups are formed through community organizations, created either locally or online. Some of these groups are composed entirely of MAPs.

The distant horizon: A more tolerant society

Return for a moment to the scenario in Chapter 1, about a severely disturbed man who gunned down three people in a convenience store. With the easy access to and portability of firearms in the United States, homicide is prolific. But a question rarely asked is, how many times would someone kill? While multiple homicides and serial killers make the headlines, most murders committed in this country are more mundane. A bar fight. A domestic quarrel. An alcohol- or drug-infused argument taken too far. In most of these cases, the person who is convicted and incarcerated will not have an opportunity to kill again for many years, if at all. But how often *would* a person kill again? Or, using another perspective, how many times is homicide the result of a perfect storm of events that lead to an isolated, tragic outcome? Most people do not spend their days murdering others.

We know that the recidivism rate among those who sexually offend, at least as far as can be determined, is quite low. Do we believe that incarceration, probation or parole, and sex offender registries are such effective deterrents that, contrary to every other form of criminal behavior, those who sexually offend are "scared straight" by these draconian measures? Or, like murder, are there relatively few individuals who pose a significant risk of repetitive acting out against multiple victims? If the latter proposition is true, then the majority of efforts we make vis-à-vis sexual offending constitute a fool's errand.

But as tragically misplaced as our steps may be, we journey on that fool's errand for a reason. We do so because a father looks into the eyes of his little girl, wide with fear, as she recounts what her much-loved uncle made her do. Because a mother holds her little boy as he cries and says he is sorry for doing what he did to his older cousin, when, in fact, he was the victim—coerced and manipulated—and did nothing wrong. There is an emotional debt that accrues when children are molested, and someone must pay the price. Who better than the person at fault?

But how should that price be paid? We create a system that too often revictimizes the victim yet maintain that we are satisfied with it. We formulate mechanisms that purport to create change, but, when they fail, we justify their continued use. We do all this because we are determined that these people— these *sex offenders*—are the monsters under the bed.

Everyone has the potential to become a monster. We ignore the times when we risked the lives of ourselves, our children, and others as we slid into the driver's seat, far too exhausted to take the wheel, but determined to make the trip. Thankfully, we arrived safely, with no one in our vehicle or anyone else dead or seriously maimed because of our actions. We dismiss the emotionally neglectful or abusive moments of anger that we focus, with laser precision, on our own children, because, after all, we love them, we didn't hit them, and they know our frustration will pass. We explain away our own harmful behaviors, based on past injustices and trauma. But when we apply these rationalizations and excuses to those who sexually offend, our argument is, *we* would never hurt a child that way.

We prefer not to recognize that the steady increase in individuals on the sex offender registries means that the number of family trees with someone who sexually offended grows larger *every day*. These registries have not been in existence long enough for a significant quantity of lifetime registrants to drop off, due to death, so children will grow up with their fathers, uncles, grandfathers, cousins, and even brothers prominently displayed on these lists. It remains to be seen whether these numbers will stabilize or decrease, due to changes in our attitudes toward and treatment of those who sexually offend, or whether the registries will continue to become the outsized twenty-first-century version of a scarlet letter.

Hitler fomented a despised class of people, based on their ethnicity. Early America also did so, founded on race—a blot on our culture that still resonates today. Stigmatization based on a common behavior carries a unique power, affecting too many people, across too many categories. From rich to poor, from powerful to powerless, and from high to low socioeconomic status, the stigma of sexual offending knows no social boundaries. Like the witch hunts of earlier societies, anyone can stand accused of this behavior. That potential exacerbates our fears and reduces our tolerance.

But there are noble reasons to confront these fears and increase our tolerance. Not the least of these is the principle of dignity and respect accorded to citizens under our Constitution. The legal rights of those who have sexually offended have been eroded and need to be returned. Moreover, the moral rights of dignity and respect supersede these legal rights. Every major religion contains a version of the Golden Rule. We seem to have ignored that tenet in our misguided effort to protect the victims of sexual offenses. We have lost the vision of what it means to *truly* protect our children. And we have forgotten the worth of those who struggle, as do we all, with unwelcome desires.

Notes

 1 Summerscale, 2023.
 2 Day, 1933.
 3 Female First, 2021.
 4 Petrunik, 2002.
 5 Zehr, 2015.
 6 Crocker, 2016.
 7 McAlinden, 2005.
 8 Sheuerman, 2018.
 9 Sliva, 2017.
10 Stroup, 2019.
11 Winslade, 2019.
12 Hamilton-Smith, 2019.
13 Rokeach, 2000.
14 Poon & Teng, 2017.

15 Burchfield & Mingus, 2014.
16 Goffman, 1963.
17 Burchfield, 2012.
18 Trottier, 2018.
19 Evans & Cubellis, 2015.
20 Hamilton-Smith, 2019, p. 95.
21 Nordgren, Banas, & McDonald, 2011.
22 Over & Uskul, 2016.
23 Ilea, 2018.
24 Lacombe, 2008.
25 Becker, 1963; Lemert, 1972.
26 Uggen, Manza, & Behrens, 2004.
27 Evans & Cubellis, 2015.
28 Willis, Levenson, & Ward, 2010.
29 Moran, 2012.
30 Tovey, Winder, & Blagden, 2023.
31 Hulley, 2016.
32 Williams, Eckhardt, & Maloney, 2021.
33 Levenson, Willis, & Vicencio, 2017.
34 Small, 2015.
35 Prostasia Foundation, n.d.
36 Prostasia Foundation, n.d.
37 B4U-ACT, n.d.
38 Virtuous Pedophiles, n.d.
39 National Association for Rational Sexual Offense Laws [NARSOL], n.d.
40 Sex Addicts Anonymous [SAA], n.d.

References

Aaron, Lauren, and Danielle H. Dallaire. 2010. Parental Incarceration and Multiple Risk Experiences: Effects on Family Dynamics and Children's Delinquency. *Journal of Youth and Adolescence, 39*, 1471–1484. https://doi.org/10.1007/s10 964-009-9458-0

Abracen, Jeffrey, Jan Looman, and Meaghan Ferguson. 2017. Substance Abuse among Sexual Offenders: Review of Research and Clinical Implications. *Journal of Sexual Aggression, 23*, 235–250. https://doi.org/10.1080/13552600.2017.1334967

Adelman, Lynn. 2022. The Harm in Making Outcasts of Sexual Offenders. *Raritan, 42*(1), 128–144, 174. www.proquest.com/openview/2875dd875ef98029d9b2b 9bd7da60fcc/1?pq-origsite=gscholar&cbl=30927

Akhtar, Leena Mehreen. 2010. Intangible Casualties: The Evacuation of British Children during World War II. *The Journal of British History, 37*(3), 224–254. PMID: 20481138.

Allely, Clare Sara. 2020. Contributor Role of Autism Spectrum Disorder Symptomatology to the Viewing of Innocent Images of Children (IIOC) and the Experience of the Criminal Justice System. *Journal of Intellectual Disabilities and Offending Behaviour, 11*(3), 171–189. https://doi.org/10.1108/J1DOB-11-2019-0026

Alter, Karen J., and Michael Zürn. 2020. Conceptualizing Backlash Politics: Introduction to a Special Issue on Backlash Politics in Comparison. *The British Journal of Politics and International Relations, 22*(4), 563–584. https://doi.org/10/1177/136914812 0947958

American Psychiatric Association. 2022. *Diagnostic and Statistical Manual of Mental Disorders, 5th Edition – Text Revision*. Washington, DC: American Psychiatric Association.

American Psychological Association. 2009. Report of the American Psychological Association Task Force on Appropriate Therapeutic Responses to Sexual Orientation. www.apa.org/pi//gbt/resources/sexual-orientation.aspx

Anagol, Padma. 2020. Historicising Child Sexual Abuse in Early Modern and Modern India: Patriarchal Norms, Violence, and Agency of Child-Wives and Young Women in the Institution of Child Marriage. *South Asian Studies, 36*(2), 177–189. https://doi. org/10.1080/02666030.2020.1821 515

Anderson, Jane. 2015. Comprehending and Rehabilitating Roman Catholic Clergy Offenders of Child Sexual Abuse. *Journal of Child Sexual Abuse, 24*, 772–795. https://doi.org/10.1080/1053871.2015.1077367

Anderson, Joel, and Elise Holland. 2015. The Legacy of Medicalizing "homosexuality": A Discussion on the Historical Effects of Non-Heterosexual Diagnostic Classifications. *Sensoria: A Journal of Mind, Brain, and Culture, 11*(1), 4–15.

Andrews, D. A., James Bonta, and R. D. Hoge. 1990. Classification for Effective Rehabilitation: Rediscovering Psychology. *Criminal Justice and Behavior, 17*(1), 19–52. https://doi.org/10.1177/0093854890017001004

Andrews, D. A., and Stephen J. Wormith. 1989. Personality and Crime: Knowledge Destruction and Construction in Criminology. *Justice Quarterly, 6*(3), 289–309. https://doi.org/10/1080/07418828900090221

Andrews, D. A., Ivan Zinger, Robert D. Hoge, James Bonta, Paul Genateau, and Francis T. Cullen. 1990. Does Correctional Treatment Work? A Clinically Relevant and Psychologically Informed Meta-Analysis. *Criminology, 28*(3), 369–404. https://doi.org/10.1111/j.1745-9125.1990.tb01330.x

Andrews, Don, James Bonta, and Stephen Wormith. 2011. The Risk-Need-Responsivity (RNR) Model: Does Adding the Good Lives Model Contribute to Effective Crime Prevention? *Criminal Justice and Behavior, 38*, 735–755. https://doi.org/10.1177/0093854811406356

Angelides, Steven. 2005. The Emergence of the Paedophile in the Late Twentieth Century. *Australian Historical Studies, 126*, 272–295.

Aria, Messimo, Michaelangelo Misuraca, and Maria Spano. 2020. Mapping the Evolution of Social Research and Data Science on 30 Years of Social Indicators Research. *Social Indicators Research, 149*, 803–831. https://doi.org/10/1007/s11205-020-02281-3

Ashley, Florence. 2019. Homophobia, Conversion Therapy, and Care Models for Trans Youth: Defending the Gender-Affirmative Approach. *Journal of LGBT Youth, 17*(4), 361–383. https://doi.org/10.108019361653.2019.1665610

B4U-ACT. n.d. B4U-ACT. Accessed January 5, 2024. www.b4uact.org/

Bailey, Beth. 1989. *From Front Porch to Back Seat: Courtship in Twentieth-Century America*. Baltimore, MD: Johns Hopkins University Press.

Bailey, Danielle J. S. 2018. A Life of Grief: An Exploration of Disenfranchisement and Grief in Sex Offender Significant Others. *American Journal of Criminal Justice, 43*, 641–667. https://doi.org/10.1007/s12103.017.9416-4

Baptist, Edward E. 2001. "Cuffy," "Fancy Maids," and "One-Eyed Men." Rape, Commodification, and the Domestic Slave Trade in the United States. *The American Historical Review, 106*(5), 1619–1650. https://doi.org/10.2307/2692741

Baril, Karine, Marc Tourigny, Pierre Paillé, and Robert Pauzé. 2016. Characteristics of Sexually Abused Children and Their Nonoffending Mothers Followed by Child Welfare Services: The Role of a Maternal History of Child Sexual Abuse. *Journal of Child Sexual Abuse, 25*(5), 504–523. https://doi:org//10.1080/10538712.2016.1176096

Barlow, David H., Harold Leitenberg, and Stewart W. Agras. 1969. Experimental Control of Sexual Deviation through Manipulation of the Noxious Scene in Covert Sensitization. *Journal of Abnormal Psychology, 74*(5), 596–601. https://doi.org/10.1016/B978-0-08-023346-8.50008-4

Barnett, Georgia D., Rebecca Manderville-Norden, and Janine Rakestrow. 2014. The Good Lives Model or Relapse Prevention: What Works Better in Facilitating Change? *Sexual Abuse: A Journal of Research and Treatment, 26*(1), 3–33. https://doi.org/10.1177/1079063212474473

Becker, Howard S. 1963. *Outsiders: Studies in the Sociology of Deviance.* New York: Free Press.

Belenko, Stephen. 1990. The Impact of Drug Offenders on the Criminal Justice System. In *Drugs, Crime, and the Criminal Justice System*, Ralph Weisheit (Ed.). Cincinnati, OH: Anderson Publishing. www.ojp.gov/ncjrs/virtual-library/abstracts/impact-drug-offenders-criminal-justice-system-drugs-crime-and

Belenko, Stephen. 2021. Research on Drug Courts: A Critical Review. *Drug Court Review, 1*(1). https://ntcrc.org/wp-content/uploads/2021/08/DCRVolume1.pdf

Bhandari, Suchitra, David Winter, David Messer, and Chris Metcalfe. 2011. Family Characteristics and Long-Term Effects of Childhood Sexual Abuse. *British Journal of Clinical Psychology, 50*, 435–451. https://doi.org/10.1111/j.2044-8260.2010.02006.x

Bierie, David M., and Kristen M. Budd. 2018. Romeo, Juliet, and Statutory Rape. *Sexual Abuse, 30*(3), 296–321. https://doi.org/10.1177/1079063216658451

Bikers Against Predators. n.d. Bikers against Predators. Accessed January 5, 2024. www.bikersagainstpredators.com

Bingham, Adrian. 2019. "It Would Be Better for the Newspapers to Call a Spade a Spade": The British Press and Child Sexual Abuse, c. 1918–90. *History Workshop Journal, 88*, 99–110. https://doi.org/10.1093/hwj/dbz006

Bingham, Adrian, Lucy Delap, Louise Jackson, and Louise Settle. October, 2015. Sexual Abuse: A Hidden History. *Today's History.* www.historytoday.com/archive/sexual-abuse-hidden-history

Birgden, Astrid, and Heather Cucolo. 2011. The Treatment of Sex Offenders: Evidence, Ethics, and Human Rights. *Sexual Abuse: A Journal of Research and Treatment, 23*(3), 295–313. https://doi.org/10.1177/1079063210381412

Blewer, Robyn. 2020. Testing the Law and Testing a Child's Evidence: Nineteenth-Century Corroboration Reforms and Child Witness Testimony. *Australian Historical Studies, 51*, 266–281. https://doi.org/10.1080/1031461X.2019.1697304

Boelen, Paul A. 2016. Improving the Understanding and Treatment of Complex Grief: An Important Issue for Psychotraumatology. *European Journal of Psychotraumatology, 7*(1), 32609. https://doi.org/10.3402/ejpt.v7.32609

Bolen, Rebecca A., and Kellie B. Gergely. 2014. A Meta-Analytic Review of the Relationship between Nonoffending Caregiver Support and Postdisclosure Functioning in Sexually Abused Children. *Trauma, Violence, & Abuse*, 16(3), 258–279. https://doi.org/10.1177/1524838014526307.

Bonnar-Kidd, Kelly. 2010. Sexual Offender Laws and Prevention of Sexual Violence or Recidivism. *American Journal of Public Health, 100*(3), 412–419. https://doi.org/10.2105/AJPH.2008.153254

Bonta, James, and D. A. Andrews. 2017. *The Psychology of Criminal Conduct* (6th Edition). New York: Routledge. https://doi.org/10.4324/9781315677187

Borzecki, Mark, and J. Stephen Wormith. 1987. A Survey of Treatment Programmes for Sex Offenders in North America. *Canadian Psychology, 28*(1), 30–44. https://psycnet.apa.org/doi/10.1037/h0079881

Bradford, John McD. W. 1983. Research on Sex Offenders: Recent Trends. *Psychiatric Clinics, 6*(4), 715–731. https://doi.org/10.1016/S0193-953X(18)30806-2

Bradford, John McD. W. 1990. The Antiandrogen and Hormonal Treatment of Sex Offenders. In *Handbook of Sexual Assault: Issues, Theories, and Treatment of the Offender*, William. L. Marshall, D. R. Laws, and Howard. E. Barbaree (Eds.).

New York: Springer. www.ojp.gov/ncjrs/virtual-library/abstracts/antiandrogen-and-hormonal-treatment-sex-offenders-handbook-sexual

Bruns, Angela. 2017. Consequences of Partner Incarceration for Women's Employment. *Journal of Marriage and Family*, *79*, 1331–1352. https://doi.org/10.1111/jomf.12412

Bulfin, Ailise. 2021. "Monster, Give Me My Child": How the Myth of the Paedophile as a Monstrous Stranger Took Shape in Emerging Discourses on Child Sexual Abuse in Late Nineteenth-Century Britain. *Nineteenth-Century Contexts: An Interdisciplinary Journal*, *43*(2), 221–245. https://doi.org/10.1080/08905495.2021.1897373

Burchfield, Keri B. 2012. Assessing Community Residents' Perceptions of Local Registered Sex Offenders: Results from a Pilot Survey. *Deviant Behavior*, *33*(4), 241–259. https://doi.org/10.1080/01639625.2011.573396

Burchfield, Keri B., and William Mingus. 2014. Sex Offender Reintegration: Consequences of the Local Neighborhood Context. *American Journal of Criminal Justice*, *39*, 109–124. https://doi.org/10.1007/s12103-012-9195-x

Byrne, James M., Arthur J. Lurigio, and Roger Pimentel. September, 2009. New Defendants, New Responsibilities: Preventing Suicide among Alleged Sex Offenders in the Federal Pretrial System. *Federal Probation*, *73*(2), 40–44. www.ojp.gov/ncjrs/virtual-library/abstracts/new-defendants-new-responsibilities-preventing-suicide-among

Cage, Claire E. 2019. Child Sexual Abuse and Medical Expertise in Nineteenth-Century France. *French Historical Studies*, *42*(3), 391–421. https://doi.org/10.1215/00161071-7558315

Caldwell, Michael F., and Brenda M. Caldwell. 2022. The Age of Redemption for Adolescents Who Were Adjudicated for Sexual Misconduct. *Psychology, Public Policy, and the Law*, *28*(2), 167–178. http://dx.doi.org/10.1037/law0000343

Calkins, Cynthia, Elizabeth Jeglic, Robert A. Beatty, Steve Zeidman, and Anthony D. Perillo. 2014. Sexual Violence Legislation: A Review of Case Law and Empirical Research. *Psychology, Public Policy, and the Law*, *20*(4), 443–462. http://dx.doi.org/10.1037/law0000027

Calleja, Nancy G. 2016. Deconstructing a Puzzling Relationship: Sex Offender Legislation, Crimes that Inspired It, and Sustained Moral Panic. *Justice Policy Journal*, *13*(1). www.cjcj.org/media/import/documents/jpj_sex_offender_legislation.pdf

Cantor, James A. 2012. Is Homosexuality a Paraphilia? The Evidence for and against. *Archives of Sexual Behavior*, *41*, 237–247. http://dx.doi.org/10.1007/s10508-012-9900-3

Caputo, Alicia A., and Stanley L. Brodsky. 2004. Citizen Coping with Community Notification of Released Sex Offenders. *Behavioral Sciences and the Law*, *22*, 239–252. https://doi.org/10.1002/bsl.566

Carey, Shannon M., Juliette R. Mackin, and Michael W. Finigan. 2020. What Works Best? The Ten Key Components of Drug Court: Research-Based Best Practices. *Drug Court Review*, *8*(1), 16–42. https://ntcrc.org/wp-content/uploads/2021/08/DCR_Best-Practices-In-Drug-Courts.pdf

Caronia, Letizia, and André H. Caron. 2019. Morality in Scientific Practice: The Relevance and Risks of Situated Scientific Knowledge in Application-Oriented Scientific Research. *Human Studies*, *42*, 451–481. https://doi.org/10.1007/s10746-018-09491-2

Carr, David. 1987. Freud and Sexual Ethics. *Philosophy*, *62*(241), 361–373. https://doi.org/10.1017/S0031819100038845

Castaneda, Nivea. 2021. "It's In Our Nature as Daughters to Protect Our Families… You Know?" The Privacy Rules of Concealing and Revealing Latina Child Sexual Abuse Experiences. *Journal of Family Communication, 21*(1), 3–16. https://doi.org/10.1080/15267431.2020/1856851

Centers for Disease Control and Prevention. n.d. Youth Online. Accessed November 8, 2023. http://nccd.cdc.gov/youthonline/

Cermak, Pamela, and Christian Molidor. 1996. Male Victims of Child Sexual Abuse. *Child and Adolescent Social Work Journal, 13*, 385–400. https://doi.org/10.1007/BF01875856

Chassiakos, Yolanda (Linda) Reid, Jenny Radesky, Dimitri Christakis, Megan Morano, and Corinn Cross. 2016. Children and Adolescents and Digital Media. *Pediatrics, 138*(5). https://doi.org/10.1542/peds.2016-2593

Chatzitoffis, Andreas, Adrian Desai E. Boström, Josephine Savard, Katarina Görts Öberg, Stefan Arver, and Jussi Jokinen. 2022. Neurochemical and Hormonal Contributors to Compulsive Sexual Behavior Disorder. *Current Addiction Reports, 9*, 23–31. https://doi.org/10.1007/s40429-021-00403-6

Chenier, Elise. 2012. The Natural Order of Disorder: Pedophilia, Stranger Danger and the Normalising Family. *Sexuality and Culture, 16*, 172–186. https://psycnet.apa.org/doi/10.1007/s12119-011-9116-z

Choi, Charles. 2002. Brain Tumour Causes Uncontrollable Pedophilia. www.newscientist.com/article/dn2943-brain-tumour-causes-uncontrollable-paedophilia/

Christensen, Larissa S. 2018. The New Portrayal of Female Child Sexual Offenders in the Print Media: A Qualitative Content Analysis. *Sexuality & Culture, 22*, 176–189. https://doi.org/10.1007/s12119-017-9459-1

Clarke, Martin, Susan Brown, and Birgit Völlm. 2017. Circles of Support and Accountability for Sex Offenders: A Systematic Review of Outcomes. *Sexual Abuse, 29*(5), 446–478. https://doi.org/10.1177/1079063215603691

Cleves, Rachel Hope. 2020. *Unspeakable: A Life beyond Sexual Morality*. Chicago, IL: The University of Chicago Press. https://doi.org/10.7208/chicago/9780226733678.001.0001

Clucas, Rob. 2017. Sexual Orientation Change Efforts, Conservative Christianity, and Resistance to Sexual Justice. *Social Sciences, 6*(2), 54. https://doi.org/10.3390/socsci6020054

Coburn, Patricia Z., Madison B. Harvey, Shelbi F. Anderson, Heather L. Price, Kristin Chong, and Deborah Connolly. 2019. Boys Abused in a Community Setting: An Analysis of Gender, Relationship, and Delayed Prosecutions in Cases of Child Sexual Abuse. *Journal of Child Sexual Abuse, 28*(5), 586–607. https://doi.org/10.1080/10538712.2019.1580329

Coviello, Peter. 2008. The Sexual Child: Or, This American Life. *Raritan, 21*(4), 134–160. www.academia.edu/20362460/The_Sexual_Child_or_This_American_Life

Crabtree, Elaine, Charlotte Wilson, and Rosaleen McElvaney. 2021. Childhood Sexual Abuse: Sibling Perspectives. *Journal of Interpersonal Violence, 36*(5–6), NP3304–NP3325. http://dx.doi.org/10.1177/0886260518769356

Craisatti, Jackie, and Phil Hodes. 1992. Mentally Ill Sex Offenders: The Experience of a Secure Unit. *British Journal of Psychiatry, 161*, 846–849. https://doi.org/10.1192/bjp.161.6.846

Crocker, Diane. 2016. Balancing Justice Goals: Restorative Justice Practitioner's Views. *Contemporary Justice Review, 19*(4), 462–478. https://doi.org/10.1080/10282580.2016.1226815

Cucolo, Heather Ellis, and Michael L. Perlin. 2013. They're Planting Stories in the Press: The Impact of Media Distortions on Sex Offender Law and Policy. *Articles & Chapters, 715.* http://dx.doi.org/10.2139/ssrn.2221462

Cullen, Francis T. 2012. Taking Rehabilitation Seriously: Creativity, Science, and the Challenge of Offender Change. *Punishment and Society, 14*(1), 94–114. https://doi.org/10.1177/1462474510385973

Cullen, Francis T., John B. Cullen, and John F. Wozniak. 1988. Is Rehabilitation Dead? The Myth of the Punitive Public. *Journal of Criminal Justice, 16*(4), 303–317. https://doi.org/10.1016/0047-2352(88)90018-9

Cullen, Francis T., and Paul Gendreau. 2000. Assessing Correctional Rehabilitation Policy, Practice, and Prospects. *Criminal Justice, 3,* 109–175. www.ojp.gov/ncjrs/virtual-library/abstracts/assessing-correctional-rehabilitation-policy-practice-and-prospects

Dagmang, Ferdinand D. 2012. Ecological Way of Understanding and Explaining Clergy Sexual Misconduct. *Sexuality & Culture, 16,* 287–305. https://doi.org/10.1007/s12119-011-9124-z

D'Alessio, Stewart J., and Lisa Stolzenberg. 1993. Socioeconomic Status and the Sentencing of the Traditional Offender. *Journal of Criminal Justice, 21*(1), 61–77. https://doi.org/10.1016/0047-2352(93)90006-9

Davidson, Roger. 2001. "This Pernicious Delusion": Law, Medicine, and Child Sexual Abuse in Early Twentieth-Century Scotland. *Journal of the History of Sexuality, 10*(1), 62–76. https://doi.org/10.1353/sex.2001.0006

Day, Clarence. May 13, 1933. Father Lets in the Telephone. *The New Yorker,* 17–20. www.newyorker.com/magazine/1933/05/13/father-lets-in-the-telephone

Deer, Sarah. 2009. Decolonizing Rape Law: A Native Feminist Synthesis of Safety and Sovereignty. *Wicazo Sa Review, 24*(2), 149–167. https://doi.org/10.1353/wic.0.0037

DeLisi, Matt, Alan J. Drury, and Michael J. Elbert. 2019. The Etiology of Antisocial Personality Disorder: The Differential Roles of Adverse Childhood Experiences and Childhood Psychopathology. *Comprehensive Psychiatry, 92,* 1–6. https://psycnet.apa.org/doi/10.1016/j.comppsych.2019.04.001

deMause, Lloyd. 1998. The History of Child Abuse. *The Journal of Psychohistory, 25*(3), 216–236. https://psychohistory.com/articles/the-history-of-child-abuse/

Deming, Adam, and Jerry L. Jennings. 2020. The Absence of Evidence-Based Practices (EBPs) in the Treatment of Sexual Abusers: Recommendations for Moving toward the Use of a True EBP Model. *Sexual Abuse, 32*(6), 679–705. https://doi.org/10.1177/1079063219843897

Denney, Andrew S., Kent R. Kerley, and Nickolas G. Gross. 2018. Child Sexual Abuse in Protestant Christian Congregations: A Descriptive Analysis of Offence and Offender Characteristics. *Religions, 9*(1), 27. https://doi.org/10.3390/rel9010027

Denno, Deborah W. 1998. Life before the Modern Sex Offender Statutes. *Northwestern University Law, 92,* 1317. http://ir.lawnet.fordham.edu/faculty_scholarship/113

Devlin, Rachel. 2005. "Acting Out the Oedipal Wish": Father-Daughter Incest and the Sexuality of Adolescent Girls in the United States, 1941–1965. *Journal of Social History, 38*(3), 609–633. https://doi.org/10.1353/jsh.2005.0027

Diamond, Lisa M. 2021. The New Genetic Evidence on Same-Sex Gender Sexuality: Implications for Gender Fluidity and Multiple Forms of Sexual Diversity. *The Journal of Sex Research, 58*(7), 818–837. https://doi.org/10.1080/00224499.2021.1879721

Dockterman, Eliana. 2020. Sex Abuse Claims Against Boy Scouts Now Surpass 82,000. *New York Times*. www.nytimes.com/2020/11/15/us/boy-scouts-abuse-cla ims-bankruptcy.html

Doyle, Caoimhe, Elle Douglas, and Gary O'Reilly. 2021. The Outcomes of Sexting for Children and Adolescents: A Systematic Review of the Literature. *Journal of Adolescence*, *29*, 86–113. https://doi.org/10.1016/j.adolescence.2021.08.009

Drescher, Jack, et al. 2016. The Growing Regulation of Conversion Therapy. *Journal of Medical Regulation*, *102*(2), 7–12. http://dx.doi.org/10.30770/2572-1852-102.2.7

Dymond, Harriet, and Simon Duff. 2020. Understanding the Lived Experience of British Nonoffending Paedophiles. *The Journal of Forensic Practice*, *22*(2), 71–81. http://dx.doi.org/10.1108/JFP-10-2019-0046

Earls, Christopher M., and Vernon L. Quinsey. 1985. What Is to Be Done? Future Research on the Assessment and Treatment of Sex Offenders. *Behavioral Sciences and the Law*, *3*(4), 377–390. https://doi.org/10.1002/bsl.2370030405

Edwards, Emily R., Gina Sissoko, Dylan Abrams, Daniel Samost, Stephanie LaGamma, and Joseph Geraci. 2020. Connecting Mental Health Court Participants with Services: Process, Challenges, and Recommendations. *Psychology, Public Policy, and the Law*, *26*(4), 463–475. https://psycnet.apa.org/doi/10.1037/law0000236

Ehrbar, Randall H., Marjorie C. Witty, Hans G. Ehrbar, and Walter O. Bockting. 2008. Clinician Judgment in the Diagnosis of Gender Identity Disorder in Children. *Journal of Sex & Marital Therapy*, *34*, 385–412. https://doi.org/10.1080/009262 30802219398

Eisikovits, Zvi, Dafna Tener, and Rachel Lev-Wiesel. 2017. Adult Women Survivors of Intrafamilial Child Sexual Abuse and Their Current Relationship with the Abuser. *American Journal of Orthopsychiatry*, *87*(3), 216–225. https://doi.org/10.1037/ort 0000185

Elbert, Michael J., Alan J. Drury, and Matt DeLisi. 2022. Child Pornography Possession/ Receipt Offenders: Developing a Forensic Profile. *Psychiatry, Psychology, and the Law*, *29*(1), 93–106. https://doi.org/10.1080/13218719.2021.1904447

Elchuck, Desiree L., Ian V. McPhail, and Mark E. Olver. 2022. Stigma-Related Stress, Complex Correlates of Disclosure, Mental Health, and Loneliness in Minor-Attracted People. *Stigma and Health*, *7*(1), 100–112. https://psycnet.apa.org/doi/10.1037/sah 0000317

Emory, Allison Dwyer. 2018. Explaining the Consequences of Paternal Incarceration for Children's Behavioral Problems. *Family Relations*, *67*, 302–319. https://doi.org/ 10.1111/fare.12301

Estep, William R. 1996. *The Anabaptist Story: An Introduction to Sixteenth-Century Anabaptism*. Third Edition, Chapter 1: "The Birth of Anabaptism." Grand Rapids, MI: William B. Eerdmans Publishing Co. www.eerdmans.com/9781467420907/ the-anabaptist-story/

Evans, Douglas N., and Michelle A. Cubellis. 2015. Coping with Stigma: How Registered Sex Offenders Manage Their Public Identities. *American Journal of Criminal Justice*, *40*, 593–619. https://psycnet.apa.org/doi/10.1007/s12103-014-9277-z

Federal Research Division, Library of Congress. 2022. Sex Offender Registration and Notification Act – Summary and Assessment of Research. https://smart.ojp.gov/doc/ SORNA-Summary-Assessment-Research.pdf

Feimster, Crystal N. 2009. General Benjamin Butler and the Threat of Sexual Violence during the American Civil War. *Daedalus*, *138*(2), 126–134. www.amacad.org/publ ication/threat-sexual-violence-during-american-civil-war

Feldman, M. P. 1966. Aversion Therapy for Sexual Deviations: A Critical Review. *Psychological Bulletin, 65*(2), 65–79. https://psycnet.apa.org/doi/10.1037/h0022913

Female First. 2021. Sinister Saturday: The man that sparked a fear f clowns: John Wayne Gacy. www.femalefirst.co.uk/features/john-wayne-gacy-killer-clown-pogo-true-crime-story-sinister-saturday-1275680.html

Field, L. H., and Mark Williams. 1970. The Hormonal Treatment of Sexual Offenders. *Medicine, Science, and the Law, 10*(1), 27–34. https://doi.org/10.1177/0025802 47001000105

Field, Leopold. 1973. Benperidol in the Treatment of Sexual Offenders. *Medicine, Science, and the Law, 13*(3), 195–196. https://doi.org/10.1177/00258024730 1300306

Fitzgerald, Monica M., Renee A. Schneider, Seoka Salstrom, Heidi M. Zinzow, Joan Jackson, and Rebecca Fossel. 2008. Child Sexual Abuse, Early Family Risk, and Childhood Parentification: Pathways to Current Psychosocial Adjustment. *Journal of Family Psychology, 22*(2), 320–324. https://psycnet.apa.org/doi/10.1037/0893-3200.22.2.320

Fontes, Lisa Aronson. 2005. *Child Abuse and Culture: Working with Diverse Families*. New York: Guilford.

Fontes, Lisa Aronson, and Carol Plummer. 2010. Cultural Issues in Disclosure of Child Sexual Abuse. *Journal of Child Sexual Abuse, 19*, 491–518. https://doi.org/10.1080/10538712.2010.512520

Ford, Jeffrey G. 2001. Healing Homosexuals: A Psychologist's Journey through the Ex-Gay Movement and the Science of Reparation Therapy. *Journal of Gay and Lesbian Psychotherapy, 5*(3/4), 69–86. https://doi.org/10.1300/J236v05n03_06

Formicola, Jo Renee. 2020a. The Global Consequences of Catholic Clerical Sexual Abuse. *Journal of Church and State, 62*(1), 1–4. https://doi.org/10.1093/jcs/csz087

Formicola, Jo Renee. 2020b. Clerical Sexual Abuse: Popes and the Policy of Sin. *Journal of Church and State, 62*(1), 135–157. https://doi.org/10.1093/jcs/csz093

Foucault, Michel. 1990. *The History of Sexuality, Volume 1: An Introduction*. New York: Vintage Books.

Fox, Bryanna, Lauren N. Miley, Kelly G. Kortright, and Rachelle J. Wetsman. 2021. Assessing the Effect of Mental Health Courts on Adult and Juvenile Recidivism: A Meta-Analysis. *American Journal of Criminal Justice, 46*, 644–664. https://doi.org/10.1007/s12103-021-09629-6

Fox, Kathryn J. 2013. Incurable Sex Offenders, Lousy Judges, and the Media: Moral Panic Sustenance in the Age of New Media. *American Journal of Criminal Justice, 13*(1), 160–181. https://doi.org/10.1007/s12103-012-9154-6

Fox, Kathryn J. 2017. Contextualizing the Policy and Pragmatics of Reintegrating Sex Offenders. *Sexual Abuse: A Journal of Research and Treatment, 27*(1), 38–50. https://doi.org/10.1177/1079063215574711

Frank, David John, Bayliss J. Camp, and Steven A. Boutcher. 2010. Worldwide Trends in the Criminal Regulation of Sex, 1945 to 2005. *American Sociological Review, 75*(6), 867–893. https://doi.org/10.1177/0003122410388493

Freeman-Coppage, Darren J., and Sharon G. Home. 2019. "What Happens if the Cross Falls and Crushes Me?" Psychology and Spiritual Promises and Perils of Lesbian and Gay Christian Celibacy. *Psychology of Sexual Orientation and Gender Diversity, 6*(4), 486–497. https://psycnet.apa.org/doi/10.1037/sgd0000341

Freud, Sigmund. 2016. *Three Essays on the Theory of Sexuality: The 1905 Edition*. Edited by Philippe Van Haute and Herman Westerink. New York: Verso.

Furby, Lita, Mark R. Weinrott, and Lyn Blackshaw. 1989. Sex Offender Recidivism: A Review. *Psychological Bulletin, 105*(1), 3–30. https://psycnet.apa.org/doi/10.1037/0033-2909.105.1.3

Gaba, Ayorkar, Paige M. Shaffer, Michael Andre, Debra A. Pinals, Dara Drawbridge, and David Smelson. 2022. Racial and Ethnic Differences in Behavioral Health, Criminal Legal System Involvement, and Service Needs among Mental Health Court Participants: Implications for Services Delivery. *Psychological Services, 19*(4), 636–647. https://psycnet.apa.org/doi/10.1037/ser0000669

Gaca, Kathy L. 2014. Marital Rape, Pulsating Fear, and the Sexual Maltreatment of Girls, Virgins, and Women in Antiquity. *The American Journal of Philology, 135*(3), 303–357. https://doi.org/10.1353/ajp.2014.0025

Gallagher, Bernard, Michael Bradford, and Ken Pease. 2008. Attempted and Completed Incidents of Stranger-Perpetrated Child Sexual Abuse and Abduction. *Child Abuse & Neglect, 32*(5), 517–528. http://dx.doi.org/10.1016/j.chiabu.2008.02.002

Geiger, Brenda, and Michael Fischer. 2021. One-Time Spinners and Spin-Thrill Seekers in Sex Offenses Against Minors: Is Situational Prevention Possible? *Journal of Child Sexual Abuse, 30*(5), 597–615. https://doi.org/10.1080/10538712.2021.1938772

Gendreau, Paul, and Robert R. Ross. 1987. Revivification of Rehabilitation: Evidence from the 1980s. *Justice Quarterly, 4*(3), 349–407. https://doi.org/10.1080/07418828700089411

Geradt, Max, Sara Janhnke, Julia Heinz, and Jürgen Hoyer. 2018. Is Contact with Children Related to Legitimizing Beliefs toward Sex with Children among Men with Pedophilia? *Archives of Sexual Behavior, 47*, 375–387. https://link.springer.com/article/10.1007/s10508-017-1042-1

Gesser, Nili. 2021. What You Expect Is Not What You Get: The Antitherapeutic Impact of Sex Offender Community Notification Meetings on Community Members. *Psychology, Public Policy, and the Law, 27*(3), 432–447. https://doi.org/10.1037/law0000303.

Gewirtz-Meydan, Ateret, Wendy Walsh, Janis Wolak, and David Finkelhor. 2018. The Complex Experience of Child Pornography Survivors. *Child Abuse & Neglect, 80*, 238–248. https://doi.org/10.1016/j.chiabu.2018.03.031

Giuliani, Fabianne. 2009. Monsters in the Village? Incest in Nineteenth Century France. *Journal of Social History, 42*(4), 919–932. https://doi.org/10.1353/jsh.0.0180

GLAAD Media Reference Guide. n.d. 11th Edition. Accessed February 13, 2024. https://glaad.org/reference/?gad_source=1&gclid=EAIaIQobChMIofrC357UhgMVpUb_AR3KHA2TEAAYASAAEgIWq_D_BwE

Glaser, Bill. 2011. Paternalism and the Good Lives Model of Sex Offender Rehabilitation. *Sexual Abuse: A Journal of Research and Treatment, 23*(3), 329–345. https://doi.org/10.1177/1079063210382044

Glaser, Daniel. 1974. Remedies for the Key Deficiencies in Criminal Justice Evaluation and Research. *Journal of Research in Crime and Delinquency, 11*(2), 144–154. https://doi.org/10.1177/002242787401100205

Gleason, Mona. 2017. "Knowing Something I Was Not Meant to Know": Exploring Vulnerabilities, Sexuality, and Childhood, 1900–1950. *The Canadian Historical Review, 98*(1), 35–59. https://doi.org/10.3138/chr.3564

Goffman, Irving. 1963. *Stigma: Notes on the Management of Spoiled Identity.* New York: Simon and Schuster, Inc.

Gordon, Deanika. 2018. The Family Framework in a Drug Treatment Court. *Socius: Sociological Research for a Dynamic World, 4*, 1–11. https://doi.org/10.1177/2378023118761462

Gqgabi, Rosemary Boitumelo, and Elizabeth Ivy Smit. 2019. Psycho-Social Effects of Father-Daughter Incest: Views of South African Social Workers. *Journal of Child Sexual Abuse, 28*(7), 840–859. https://doi.org/10.1080/10538712.2019.1581870

Grady, Melissa D., and Jill S. Levenson. 2021. Prevalence Rates of Adverse Childhood Experiences in a Sample of Minor-Attracted Persons: A Comparison Study. *Traumatology, 27*(2), 227–235. https://psycnet.apa.org/doi/10.1037/trm0000273

Graham, Lisa, Paul Rogers, and Michelle Davies. 2007. Attributions in a Hypothetical Child Sexual Abuse Case: Roles of Abuse Type, Family Response, and Respondent Gender. *Journal of Family Violence, 22*, 733–745. https://doi.org/10.1007/s10896-007-9121-z

Graveris, Dainis. 2024. How Many People REALLY Watch Porn? *Sexual Alpha.* https://sexualalpha.com/how-many-people-watch-porn-statistics/

Green, Amy E., Myeshia Price-Feeney, Samuel Dorison, and Casey J. Pick. June 18, 2020. Self-Reported Conversion Efforts and Suicidality among US LGBTQ Youths and Young Adults, 2018. *American Journal of Public Health, 110*(8), 1221–1227. http://dx.doi.org/10.2105/AJPH.2020.305701

Grønnerød, Cato, Jarna Soilevuo Grønnerød, and Pål Grøndahl. 2015. Psychological Treatment of Sexual Offenders against Children: A Meta-Analytic Review of Treatment Outcome Studies. *Trauma, Violence, & Abuse, 16*(3), 280–290. https://doi.org/10.1177/1524838014526043

Groth, Nicholas A., and H. Jean Birnbaum. 1978. Adult Sexual Orientation and Attraction to Underage Persons. *Archives of Sexual Behavior, 7*, 175–181. https://doi.org/10.1007/BF01542377

Gullace, Nicolette F. 1997. Sexual Violence and Family Honor: British Propaganda and International Law during the First World War. *The American Historical Review, 102*(3), 714–747. https://doi.org/10.2307/2171507

Gully, Kevin, Christine Mitchell, Clifford Butter, and Richard Harwood. 1990. Sex Offenders: Identifying Who Can Complete a Residential Treatment Program. *Behavioral Sciences and the Law, 8*, 465–471. https://psycnet.apa.org/doi/10.1002/bsl.2370080412

Hamilton-Smith, Guy. 2019. The Agony and the Ecstasy of #MeToo: The Hidden Costs of Reliance on Carceral Politics. *Southwestern Law Review, 49*, 93–121. https://rss.swlaw.edu/sites/default/files/2020-01/3%20Hamilton-Smith_Finalv2.pdf

Haney, Craig. 2009. Media, Criminology, and the Death Penalty. *58, DePaul Law Review, 689*, 692. https://via.library.depaul.edu/law-review/vol58/iss3/7

Hanson, Karl R., Guy Bourgon, Leslie Helmus, and Shannon Hodgson. 2009. The Principles of Effective Correctional Treatment Also Apply to Sexual Offenders: A Meta-Analysis. *Criminal Justice and Behavior, 36*(9), 865–891. https://doi.org/10.1177/0093854809338545

Hanson, Karl R., Arthur Gordon, Andrew J. R. Harris, Janice K. Marques, William Murphy, Vernon L. Quincey, and Michael C. Seto. 2002. First Report of the Collaborative Outcome Data Project on the Effective of Psychological Treatment for Sex Offenders. *Sexual Abuse, 14*(2), 169–194. https://doi.org/10.1177/107906320201400207

Hanson, Karl R., and Andrew J. R. Harris. 2000. Where Should We Intervene? Dynamic Predictors of Sex Offense Recidivism. *Criminal Justice and Behavior, 27*, 6–35. https://psycnet.apa.org/doi/10.1177/0093854800027001002

Hanson, Karl R., Seung C. Lee, and David Thornton. 2022. Long-Term Recidivism Rates among Individuals at High Risk to Sexually Reoffend. *Sexual Abuse, 36*(11). https://doi.org/10.1177/10790632221139166

Harkins, Leigh, Vanja E. Flak, Anthony R. Beech, and Jessica Woodhams. 2012. Evaluation of a Community-Based Sex Offender Treatment Program Using a Good Lives Model Approach. *Sexual Abuse: A Journal of Research and Treatment, 24*(6), 519–543. https://doi.org/10.1177/1079063211429469

Harper, Craig A., Rebecca Lievesley, Nicholas J. Blagden, and Kerensa Hocken. 2022. Humanizing Pedophilia as Stigma Reduction: A Large-Scale Intervention Study. *Archives of Sexual Behavior, 51*, 945–960. https://doi.org/10.1007/s10 508-021-02057-x

Harris, Danielle Arlanda, Amelie Pedneault, and Gwenda Willis. 2019. The Pursuit of Primary Human Goods in Men Desisting from Sexual Offending. *Sexual Abuse, 31*(2), 197–219. https://doi.org/10.1177/1079063217729155

Heineman, Elizabeth. 2008. The History of Sexual Violence in Conflict Zones; Conference Report. *Radical History Review, 101*, 5–21. https://doi.org/10.1215/01636545-2007-035

Hodes, Rebecca. 2015. Kink and the Colony: Sexual Deviance in the Medical History of South Africa, c. 1893–1939. *Journal of South African Studies, 41*(4), 1–19. https://doi.org/10.1080/03057070.2015.1049486

Hoffer, Tia A., Joy Lynn E. Shelton, Stephen Behnke, and Philip Erdberg. 2010. Exploring the Impact of Child Sex Offender Suicide. *Journal of Family Violence, 25*, 777–786. https://doi.org/1007/s10896-010-9335-3

Holmen, Nicole. 2010. Examining Greek Pederastic Relationships. *Inquiries, 2*(2). www.inquiriesjournal.com/a?id=175

Hoppe, Trevor, Ilan Meyer, Scott De Orio, Stefan Vogler, and Megan Armstrong. 2020. Civil Commitment of People Convicted of Sexual Offenses in the United States. UCLA School of Law, Williams Institute. https://williamsinstitute.law.ucla.edu/publi cations/civil-commitment-us/

Horowitz, Emily. 2015. *Protecting Our Kids? How Sex Offender Laws Are Failing Us.* Santa Barbara, CA: Praeger Publishing.

Horowitz, Emily. 2023. *From Rage to Reason: Why We Need Sex Crime Laws Based on Facts, Not Fear.* New York: Bloomsbury Publishing.

Howell, Elizabeth F. 2014. Ferenczi's Concept of Identification with the Aggressor: Understanding Dissociative Structure with Interacting Victim and Abuser Self-States. *The American Journal of Psychoanalysis, 74*, 48–59. http://doi.org/10.1057.ajp.2013.40

Howey, Whitney, Brad Lundahl, and Andrea Assadollahi. 2022. Effectiveness of Residential Treatment for Juveniles with Problematic Sexual Behavior: A Systematic Review. *International Journal of Environmental Research and Public Health, 19*, 15625. http://dx.doi.org/10.3390/ijerph192315625

Hulley, Joanne L. 2016. "While This Does Not in Any Way Excuse My Conduct…": The Role of Treatment and Neutralizations in Desistance from Sexual Offending. *International Journal of Offender Therapy and Comparative Criminology, 60*(15), 1776–1790. https://doi.org/10.1177/0306624X16668177

Hunter, John A., Aurelia J. Figueredo, Neil M. Malamuth, and Judith V. Becker. 2003. Juvenile Sex Offenders: Toward the Development of a Typology. *Sexual Abuse: A Journal of Research and Treatment, 15*, 27–48. https://doi.org/10.1023/A:102066 3723593

Ilea, Adine. 2018. What about 'the Sex Offenders'? Addressing Sexual Harm from an Abolitionist Perspective. *Critical Criminology, 26*, 357–372. https://doi.org/10.1007/s10612-018-9406-y

Jackson, Louise A. 2000. 'Singing Birds as Well as Soap Suds': The Salvation Army's Work with Sexually Abused Girls in Edwardian England. *Gender & History*, *12*(1), 107–126. https://doi.org/10.1111/1468-0424.00173

Jackson, Theodore, Koushank Ahuja, and Gilian Tenbergen. 2022. Challenges and Solutions to Implementing a Community-Based Wellness Program for Non-Offending Minor-Attracted Persons. *Journal of Child Sexual Abuse*, *31*(3), 316–332. https://doi.org/10.1080/10538712.2022.2056103

Jackson, Stevi, and Sue Scott. 2015. Conceptualizing Sexuality. In *Sexualities: Identities, Behaviors, and Society*, 2nd Ed., pp. 9–21, edited by Michael Kimmel and the Stony Brook Sexualities Research Group. New York: Oxford University Press.

Janssen, Diederik F. 2021. Homosexual/Heterosexual: First Print Uses of the Terms by Daniel von Kászony (1868–1871). *Journal of Homosexuality*, *68*(14), 2574–2579. https://doi.org/10.1080/00918369.2021.1933777

Jara, Giovanna A., and Elizabeth Jeglic. 2021. Changing Public Attitudes toward Minor Attracted Persons: An Evaluation of an Anti-Stigma Intervention. *Journal of Sexual Aggression*, *27*(3), 299–312. https://doi.org/10.1080/13552600.2020.1863486

Jones, Stanton L., and Mark A. Yarhouse. 2011. A Longitudinal Study of Attempted Religiously Mediated Sexual Orientation Change. *Journal of Sex & Marital Therapy*, *37*, 404–427. https://doi.org/10.1080/0092623X.2011.607052

Jordan, Kirsten, Tamara Sheila Nadine Wild, Peter Fromberger, Isabel Müller, and Jürgen Leo Müller. 2020. Are There Any Biomarkers for Pedophilia and Sexual Child Abuse? A Review. *Frontiers in Psychiatry*, *10*, Article, 940. https://doi.org/10.3389/fpsyt.2019.00940

Jouriles, Ernest N., Tricia Gower, Caitlin Rancher, Emily Johnson, Mindy L. Jackson, and Renee McDonald. 2021. Families Seeking Services for Sexual Abuse: Intimate Partner Violence, Mothers' Psychological Distress, and Mother-Adolescent Conflict. *Journal of Family Psychology*, *35*(1), 103–111. https://psycnet.apa.org/doi/10.1037/fam0000798

Kahn, Rachel E., Gina Ambroziak, R. Karl Hanson, and David Thornton. 2017. Release from the Sex Offender Label. *Archives of Sexual Behavior*, *46*, 861–864. http://doi.org/10.1007/s10508-017-0972-y

Katz-Wise, Sabra L. 2015. Sexual Fluidity in Young Adult Women and Men: Associations with Sexual Orientation and Sexual Identity Development. *Psychology and Sexuality*, *6*(2), 189–208. https://doi.org/10.1080/19419899.2013.876445

Katz-Wise, Sabra L., Lynsie R. Ranker, Allegra R. Gordon, Ziming Xuan, and Kimberly Nelson. 2023. Sociodemographic Patterns in Retrospective Sexual Orientation Identity and Attraction Change in the Sexual Orientation Fluidity in Youth Study. *Journal of Adolescent Health*, *72*, 437–443. http://doi.org/10.1016/j.jadohealth.2022.10.015

Katz-Wise, Sabra L., Sari L. Reisner, Jaclyn White Hughto, and Colton L. Keo-Meier. 2016. Differences in Sexual Orientation Diversity and Sexual Fluidity in Attractions among Gender Minority Adults in Massachusetts. *Journal of Sex Research*, *53*(1), 74–84. http://dx.doi.org/10.1080/00224499.2014.1003028

Katz-Wise, Sabra L., and Keran P. Todd. 2022. The Current State of Sexual Fluidity Research. *Current Opinions in Psychology*, *48*, 101497. http://dx.doi.org/10.1016/j.copsyc.2022.101497

Kesner, John E., and Margaret Robinson. 2002. Teachers as Mandated Reporters of Child Maltreatment: Comparisons with Legal, Medical, and Social Services

Reporters. *Children and Schools*, *24*(4), 222–231. http://dx.doi.org/10.1093/cs/24.4.222

Kincaid, James R. 1992. *Child-Loving: The Erotic Child and Victorian Culture.* New York: Routledge.

Kinsey, Alfred C., Wardell B. Pomeroy, and Clyde E. Martin. 1948. *Sexual Behavior in the Human Male*. Bloomington, IN: Indiana University Press.

Kinsey, Alfred C., Wardell B. Pomeroy, Clyde E. Martin, and Paul H. Gebhard. 1953. *Sexual Behavior in the Human Female*. Philadelphia, PA: W. B. Saunders Co.

Knack, Natasha, Dave Holmes, and Paul Fedoroff. 2020. Motivational Pathways Underlying the Onset and Maintenance of Viewing Child Pornography on the Internet. *Behavioral Science and the Law*, *38*, 100–116. https://doi.org/10.1002/bsl.2450

Koçtürk, Nilüfer, and Fadime Yüksel. 2023. Individual and Familial Characteristics of Sexual Abuse Victims with Intellectual Disability. *Current Psychology*, *42*, 2006–2013. https://doi.org/10.1007/s12144-021-01604-y

Kourany, Janet A. 2006. Getting Philosophy of Science Socially Connected. *Philosophy of Science*, *73*, 991–1002. https://doi.org/10.1086/518804

Kraanen, Fleur L., and Paul M. G. Emmelkamp. 2011. Substance Misuse and Substance Use Disorders in Sex Offenders: A Review. *Clinical Psychology Review*, *31*, 478–489. https://doi.org/10.1016/j.cpr.2010.11.006

Kuhle, L. F., E. Schlinzig, G. Kaiser, T. Amelung, A. Konrad, R. Röhle, and K. M. Beier. 2017. The Association of Sexual Preference and Dynamic Risk Factors with Undetected Child Pornography Offending. *Journal of Sexual Aggression*, *23*(1), 3–18. https://doi.org/10.1080/13552600.2016.1201157

Lacombe, Dany. 2008. Consumed with Sex: The Treatment of Sex Offenders in Risk Society. *British Journal of Criminology*, *48*, 55–74. https://doi.org/10.1093/bjc/azm051

Lam, Austin A., Stephanie R. Penney, and Alexander J. F. Simpson. 2022. Serious Mental Illness and Sexual Offending in Forensic Psychiatric Patients. *Sexual Abuse*, *35*(1), 1–24. https://doi.org/10.1177/10790632221088012

Langevin, Ron, and Reuben Lang. 1990. Substance Abuse among Sex Offenders. *Annals of Sex Research*, *3*, 392–424. https://doi.org/10.1007/BF00850442

Langevin, Ron, Mara Langevin, Suzanne Curnoe, and Jerald Bain. 2008. The Prevalence of Diabetes among Sexual and Violent Offenders and Its Co-Occurrence with Cognitive Impairment, Mania, Psychotic Symptoms, and Aggressive Behavior. *International Journal of Prisoner Health*, *4*(2), 83–95. http://dx.doi.org/10.1080/17449200802038215

Lanning, Kenneth V. 2010. *Child Molesters: A Behavioral Analysis For Professionals Investigating the Sexual Exploitation of Children*, Fifth Edition. National Center for Missing and Exploited Children. www.missingkids.org/content/dam/missingkids/pdfs/publications/nc70.pdf

Larsen, Rasmus Rosenberg, Jarkko Jalava, and Stephanie Griffiths. 2020. Are Psychopathy Checklist (PCL) Psychopaths Dangerous, Untreatable, and Without Conscience? A Systematic Review of the Empirical Evidence. *Psychology, Public Policy, and the Law*, *26*(3), 297–311. https://doi.org/10.1037/law0000239.

Latessa, Edward J., Shelley L. Johnson, and Deborah Koetzle. 2020. *What Works (and Doesn't) in Reducing Recidivism*. New York: Routledge.

Lawrence, Amy L., and Gwenda M. Willis. 2021. Understanding and Challenging Stigma Associated with Sexual Interest in Children: A Systematic Review.

International Journal of Sexual Health, 33(2), 144–162. https://doi.org/10.1080/19317611.2020.1865498

Lawrence, Anne A. 2011. Do Some Men Who Desire Sex Reassignment Have a Mental Disorder? Comment on Meyer-Bahlburg (2010). *Archives of Sexual Behavior, 40,* 651–654. https://doi.org/10.1007/s10508-010-9720-2

Levenson, Jill S., and Richard Tewksbury. 2009. Collateral Damage: Family Members of Registered Sex Offenders. *American Journal of Criminal Justice, 34,* 54–68. https://doi.org/10.1007/s12103-008-9055-x

Levenson, Jill S., Gwenda M. Willis, and Claudia Vicencio. 2017. Obstacles to Help-Seeking for Sexual Offenders: Implications for Prevention of Sexual Abuse. *Journal of Child Sexual Abuse, 26*(2), 99–120. http://dx.doi.org/10.1080/10538712.2016.1276116

Levenson, Jill S., Kristen Zgoba, and Richard Tewksbury. 2007. Sex Offender Residence Restrictions: Sensible Crime Policy or Flawed Logic? *Probation: A Journal of Correctional Philosophy and Practice, 7*(3). www.uscourts.gov/federal-probation-journal/2007/12/sex-offender-residence-restrictions-sensible-policy-or-flawed

Lewin, Linda, and Christi Ann Bergen. 2001. Attachment Behaviors, Depression, and Anxiety in Nonoffending Mothers of Child Sexual Abuse Victims. *Child Maltreatment, 6*(4), 365–375. http://dx.doi.org/10.1177/1077559501006004009

Lewis, Michael. 2015. The Origins of Lying and Deception in Everyday Life. *American Scientist, 103,* 128–135. http://dx.doi.org/10.1511/2015.113.128

Lievesley, Rebecca, Craig A. Harper, and Helen Elliott. 2020. The Internalization of Social Stigma among Minor-Attracted Persons: Implications for Treatment. *Archives of Sexual Behavior, 49,* 1291–1304. https://doi.org/10.1007/s10508-019-01569-x

Lievesley, Rebecca, Craig A. Harper, Helen Swaby, and Ellie Woodward. 2022. Identifying and Working with Appropriate Treatment Targets with People Who Are Sexually Attracted to Children. *Journal of Sex and Marital Therapy, 49*(5), 497–516. https://doi.org/10.1080/0092623X.2022.2149437

Lievesley, Rebecca, and Rhia Lapworth. 2022. "We Do Exist:" The Experience of Women Living with a Sexual Interest in Minors. *Archives of Sexual Behavior, 51,* 879–896. https://doi.org/10.1007/s10508-021-02160-z

Lim, Yeong Yeon, Suzaily Wahab, Jay Kumari, Fauziah Ibrahim, and Mohammad Rahim Kamaluddin. 2021. Typologies and Psychological Profiles of Child Sexual Abusers: An Extensive Review. *Children, 8,* 333. http://dx.doi.org/10.3390/children8050333

Lipton, Douglas S., Robert Martinson, and Judith Wilks. 1975. *The Effectiveness of Correctional Treatment: A Survey of Treatment Evaluation Studies.* Praeger. https://books.google.com/books/about/The_Effectiveness_of_Correctional_Treatm.html?id=m7EYAAAAIAAJ

Lollar, Courtney E. 2013. Child Pornography and the Restitution Revolution. *Journal of Criminal Law and Criminology, 103*(2), 343–306. https://scholarlycommons.law.northwestern.edu/jclc/vol103/iss2/1

Looman, Jan, Jeffrey Abracen, Roberto DiFazio, and Greg Maillet. 2004. Alcohol and Drug Abuse among Sexual and Nonsexual Offenders: Relationship to Intimacy Deficits and Coping Strategy. *Sexual Abuse: A Journal of Research and Treatment, 16*(3), 177–189. https://doi.org/10.1023/B:SEBU.0000029131.67660.ae

López-Romero, Laura, Cutrin Olalla, Lorena Maneiro, and Randall T. Salekin. 2022. Proposed Specifiers for Conduct Disorder – Short Version (PSCD-SV): Psychometric Properties, Concurrent Correlates and Parenting Predictions. *Child Psychiatry and Human Development*, *54*(5), 1258–1273. http://dx.doi.org/10.1007/s10 578-022-01335-6

Lösel, Friedrich, and Martin Schmucker. 2005. The Effectiveness of Treatment for Sexual Offenders: A Comprehensive Meta-Analysis. *Journal of Experimental Criminology*, *1*(1), 117–146. https://doi.org/10.1007/s11292-004-6466-7

Lurigio, Arthur J. 2008. The First 20 Years of Drug Treatment Courts: A Brief Description of Their History and Impact. *Federal Probation*, *72*(1), www.uscourts.gov/sites/defa ult/files/72_1_2_0.pdf

Ly, Than, R. Gregg Dwyer, and J. Paul Federoff. 2018. Characteristics and Treatment of Internet Child Pornography Offenders. *Behavioral Science and the Law*, *36*(2), 216–234. https://doi.org/10.1002/bsl.2340

Malinen, Sanna, Gwenda M. Willis, and Lucy Johnston. 2014. Might Informative Media Reporting of Sexual Offending Influence Community Members' Attitudes toward Sex Offenders? *Psychology, Crime, & Law*, *20*(6), 535–552. https://doi.org/ 10.1080/1068316X.2013.793770

Mallory, Christy, Taylor N. T. Brown, and Kerith J. Conron. 2018. Conversion Therapy and LGBTQ Youth. *UCLA School of Law: The Williams Institute*. https://williamsinstit ute.law.ucla.edu/publications/conversion-therapy-and-lgbt-youth/

Mann, Ruth E., R. Karl Hanson, and David Thornton. 2010. Assessing Risk for Sexual Recidivism: Some Proposals on the Nature of Psychologically Meaningful Risk Factors. *Sexual Abuse: A Journal of Research and Treatment*, *22*(2), 191–217. https:// doi.org/10.1177/1079063210366039

Marotta, Phillip L. 2017. A Systematic Review of Behavioral Health Interventions for Sex Offenders with Intellectual Disabilities. *Sexual Abuse: A Journal of Research and Treatment*, *29*(2), 148–185. https://doi.org/10.1177/1079063215569546

Marshall, Colin. 2021. *The Story of the Edsel, Ford's Infamously Failed Car Brand of the 1950s*. www.openculture.com/2021/10/the-story-of-the-edsel-fords-infamou sly-failed-car-brand-of-the-1950s.html#google_vignette

Marshall, W. L., and W. D. Pithers. 1994. A Reconsideration of Treatment Outcome with Sex Offenders. *Criminal Justice and Behavior*, *21*(1), 10–27. https://doi.org/ 10.1177/0093854894021001003

Martinello, Emily. 2015. Reviewing Risk Factors of Individuals with Intellectual Disabilities as Perpetrators of Sexually Abusive Behaviors. *Sexuality and Disability*, *33*(2), 269–278. https://doi.org/10.1007/s11195-014-9365-5

Martinson, Robert. 1979. New Findings, New Views: A Note of Caution Regarding Sentencing Reform. *Hofstra Law Review*, *7*(2), 243–258. https://fbaum.unc.edu/ teaching/articles/Martinson1979.pdf

Martjin, Frederica M., Kelly M. Babchishin, Lesleigh E. Pullman, and Michael Seto. 2020. Sexual Attraction and Falling in Love in Persons with Pedohebephilia. *Archives of Sexual Behavior*, *49*, 1305–1318. http://doi.org/10.1007/s10508-019-10579-9

Massey, Kristina, Jan Burns, and Anke Franz. 2021. Young People, Sexuality, and the Age of Pornography. *Sexuality and Culture*, *25*, 318–316. https://doi.org/10.1007/ s2119-020-09771-z

Maxwell, Caitlin. 2009. Moving beyond Rape as a "Weapon of War": An Exploration of Militarized Masculinity and Its Consequences. *Canadian Woman Studies*, *28*(1), 108–120. https://cws.journals.yorku.ca/index.php/cws/article/view/30786

McAlinden, Anne-Marie. 2005. The Use of 'Shame' with Sexual Offenders. *British Journal of Criminology*, *45*, 373–394. https://doi.org/10.1093/bjc/azh095

McCarthy, Andrea, Mireille Cyr, Mylène Fernet, and Martine Hebert. 2019. Maternal Emotional Support Following the Disclosure of Child Sexual Abuse: A Qualitative Study. *Journal of Child Sexual Abuse*, *28*(3), 257–279. https://doi.org/10.1080/10538712.2018.1534919

McCloskey, Laura, and Jennifer A. Bailey. 2000. The Intergenerational Transmission of Risk for Child Sexual Abuse. *Journal of Interpersonal Violence*, *15*(10), 1019–1035. https://doi.org/10.1177/088626000015010001

McElvaney, Rosaleen, Rachael McDonnell Murray, and Simon Dunne. 2022. Siblings' Perspectives of the Impact of Child Sexual Abuse Disclosure on Sibling and Family Relationships. *Family Process*, *61*(2), 858–872. https://doi.org/10.1111/famp.12681

McKenna, Neil. 2005. *The Secret Life of Oscar Wilde*. New York: Basic Books.

McMurtrie, Jacqueline. 2011. The Criminal Justice System's Disparate Treatment of Individuals with Fetal Alcohol Spectrum Disorders in Cases Involving Sexual Activity. *Journal of Psychiatry and the Law*, *39*(1), 159–177. https://doi.org/10.1177/009318531103900106

McPhail, Ian V. 2018. Age of Onset in Pedohebephilic Interests. *Archives of Sexual Behavior*, *47*, 1313–1317. https://doi.org/10.1007/s10508-018-1198-3

McPhail, Ian V., Skye Stephens, and Ainslie Heasman. 2018. Legal and Ethical Issues in Treating Clients with Pedohebephilic Interests. *Canadian Psychology*, *59*(4), 369–381. http://dx.doi.org/10.1037/cap0000157

Meloy, Michelle, Jessica Boatwright, and Kristin Curtis. 2013. Views from the Top and Bottom: Lawmakers and Practitioners Discuss Sex Offender Laws. *American Journal of Criminal Justice*, *38*, 616–638. https://doi.org/10.1007/s12103-012-9189-8

Meloy, Michelle, Kristin Curtis and Jessica Boatwright. 2013. Policymakers' Perceptions on Their Sex Offender Laws: The Good, the Bad, and the Ugly. *Criminal Justice Studies*, *26*(3), 273–288. https://doi.org/10.1080/1478601X.2012.744307

Meloy, Michelle, Yustina Saleh, and Nancy Wolff. 2007. Sex Offender Laws in America: Can Panic-Driven Legislation Ever Create Safer Societies? *Criminal Justice Studies*, *20*(4), 423–443. https://doi.org/10.1080/14786010701758211

Meyer-Bahlburg, Heino F. L. 2010. From Mental Disorder to Iatrogenic Hypogonadism: Dilemmas in Conceptualizing Gender Identity Variants as Psychiatric Conditions. *Archives of Sexual Behavior*, *39*, 461–476. http://dx.doi.org/10.1007/s10508-009-9532-4

Miller v. California, 413 US 15 (1973). https://supreme.justia.com/cases/federal/us/413/15/.

Million, Diane. 2009. Felt Theory: An Indigenous Feminist Approach to Affect and History. *Wicazo Sa Review*, *24*(2), 53–76. https://doi.org/10.1353/wic.0.0043

Miyaguchi, Koji, and Sadaaki Shirataki. 2014. Executive Functioning Problems of Juvenile Sex Offenders with Low Levels of Measured Intelligence. *Journal of Intellectual and Developmental Disability*, *39*(3), 253–260. https://doi.org/10.3109/13668250.2014.925103

Mock, Steven E., and Richard P. Eibach. 2012. Stability and Change in Sexual Orientation Identity over a 10-Year Period in Adulthood. *Archives of Sexual Behavior*, *41*, 641–648. http://dx.doi.org/10.1007/s10508-011-9761-1

Mogavero, Melanie C. 2016. Autism, Sexual Offending, and the Criminal Justice System. *Journal of Intellectual Disabilities and Offending Behaviour*, *1*(3), 116–126. http://dx.doi.org/10.1108/JIDOB-02-2016-0004

Monahan, Kathleen. 2003. Death of an Abuser: Does the Memory Linger On? *Death Studies*, *27*, 641–651. https://doi.org/10.1080/07481180302899

Monahan, Kathleen. 2010. Themes of Adult Sibling Sex Abuse Survivors in Later Life: An Initial Exploration. *Clinical Social Work Journal*, *38*, 361–369. https://doi.org/10.1007/s10615-010-0286-1

Money, John. 1970. Sexual Dimorphism and Homosexual Gender Identity. *Psychological Bulletin*, *74*(6), 425–440. https://psycnet.apa.org/doi/10.1037/h0033067

Monson, Candice M., Lisa M. Jones, P. Clayton Rivers, and Steven B. Blum. 1998. Alcohol and Sex Offending: What Do Child Sex Offenders Think About Drinking? *Journal of Addictions and Offender Counseling*, *19*, 15–27. https://doi.org/10.1002/j.2161-1874.1998.tb00132.x

Moran, Dominique. 2012. Prisoner Reintegration and the Stigma of Prison Time Inscribed on the Body. *Punishment and Society*, *14*(5), 564–583. https://doi.org/10.1177/1462474512464008

Moser, Charles. 2001. Paraphilia: A Critique of a Confused Concept. In *Sex Therapy: Innovations and Alterations*, 91–108.Edited by Peggy J. Kleinplatz. New York: Routledge.

Movement Advancement Project. 2023. Equality Maps Snapshot: LGBTQ Equality by State. www.lgbtmap.org/equality-maps

Najdowski, Cynthia J., M. D. Hayley, M. D. Cleary, and Margaret Stevenson. 2016. Adolescent Sex Offender Registration Policy: Perspectives on General Deterrence Potential from Criminology and Developmental Psychology. *Psychology, Public Policy, and the Law*, *22*(1), 114–125. http://dx.doi.org/10.1037/law0000059

National Association for Rational Sex Offender Laws [NARSOL]. Vision, Mission, and Goals. n.d. Accessed January 5, 2024. www.narsol.org/about/vision-mission-and-goals/

National Children's Advocacy Center. n.d. Child Sexual Abuse: Perpetrators Manipulatin – Disclosure – Prevention. Accessed January 5, 2024. www.nationalcac.org/wp-content/uploads/2018/02/CSA-Perpetrators.pdf

National Drug Court Resource Center [NDCRC]. n.d. What Are Drug Courts? National Treatment Court Resource Center. Accessed October 8, 2023. https://ntcrc.org/what-are-drug-courts/

Nellis, Ashley. 2021. The Color of Justice: Racial and Ethnic Disparity in State Prisons. www.sentencingproject.org/reports/the-color-of-justice-racial-and-ethnic-disparity-in-state-prisons-the-sentencing-project/

Nichols, Emily Bover, and Ann Booker Loper. 2012. Incarceration in the Household: Academic Outcomes of Adolescents with an Incarcerated Household Member. *Journal of Youth and Adolescence*, *41*, 1455–1471. https://doi.org/10.1007/s10964-012-9780-9

Nicolosi, Joseph, A. Dean Byrd, and Richard W. Potts. 2000. Retrospective Self-Reports of Changes in Homosexual Orientation: A Consumer Survey of Conversion Therapy Clients. *Psychological Reports*, *86*(3), 1071–1088. https://doi.org/10.2466/pr0.2000.86.3c.1071

Nitescu, Vasile, Doina Rambo, and Valentin Nitescu. 2020. Neurotransmitters in the Sexuality of the Pedophile and the Pedophile Killer. *Journal of Clinical Sexology*, *3*(1), 1–18. www.journalofclinicalsexology.com/wp-content/uploads/2020/05/NEUROTRANSMITTERS-IN-SEXUALITY.pdf

Nolt, Steven M., and Thomas J. Meyers, 2007. *Plain Diversity: Amish Cultures and Identifies*. Baltimore, MD: Johns Hopkins University Press.

Nordgren, Loren F., Kasia Banas, and Geoff McDonald. 2011. Empathy Gaps for Social Pain: Why People Underestimate the Pain of Social Suffering. *Journal of Personality and Social Psychology, 100*(1), 120–128. http://dx.doi.org/10.1037/a0020938

North American Man/Boy Love Association [NAMBLA]. n.d. Accessed September 8, 2023. www.nambla.org

Office of Sex Offender Sentencing, Monitoring, Apprehending, Registering, and Tracking [SMART]. Legislative History of Federal Sex Offender Registration and Notification. n.d. Accessed October 8, 2023. https://smart.ojp.gov/sorna/current-law/legislative-history

Olver, M. E., C. E. Marshall, W. L. Marshall, and T. P. Nicholaichuk. 2018. A Long-Term Outcome Assessment of the Effects on Subsequent Reoffense Rates of a Prison-Based CBT/RNR Sex Offender Treatment Program with Strength-Based Elements. *Sexual Abuse, 32*(2), 1–27. https://doi.org/10.1177/1079063218807486

Orlov, Alexander. 2005. The Price of Victory, the Cost of Aggression. *History Today, 55*(4), 24. www.historytoday.com/archive/price-victory-cost-aggression

Ovalle, Brianna M. 2021. Examining the Quality of Representation by Public Defenders Compared to Private Attorneys. *The Mid-Southern Journal of Criminal Justice,* 20, Article 5. https://mds.marshall.edu/cgi/viewcontent.cgi?article=1010&context=msjcj

Over, Harriet, and Ayse K. Uskul. 2016. Culture Moderates Children's Responses to Ostracism Situations. *Journal of Personality and Social Psychology, 110*(5), 710–724. https://psycnet.apa.org/doi/10.1037/pspi0000050

Pande, Ishita. 2012. Coming of Age: Law, Sex, and Childhood in Late Colonial India. *Gender and History, 24*(1), 205–230. https://doi.org/10.1111/j.1468-0424.2011.01676.x

Parker, Richard J. 2022. *The Correctional Helicopter: How and Why Correctional Agencies Fail to Rehabilitate Offenders.* https://thecorrectionalhelicopter.com/

Parr, Jennifer, and Dominic Pearson. 2019. Non-Offending Minor-Attracted Persons: Professional Practitioners' Views on the Barriers to Seeking and Receiving Their Help. *Journal of Child Sexual Abuse, 28*(8), 945–967. https://doi.org/10.1080/10538712.2019.1663970

Perverted Justice. n.d. Accessed December 12, 2023. www.perverted-jusice.com

Petrunik, Michael G. 2002. Managing Unacceptable Risk: Sex Offenders, Community Response, and Social Policy in the United States and Canada. *International Journal of Offender Therapy and Comparative Criminology, 46*(4), 483–511. https://doi.org/10.1177/0306624X02464009

Peugh, Jordan, and Steven Belenko. 2001. Examining the Substance Use Patterns and Treatment Needs of Incarcerated Sex Offenders. *Sexual Abuse: A Journal of Research and Treatment, 13*(3), 179–195. https://doi.org/10.1177/107906320101300303

Phenix, Amy, Leslie-Maaike Helmus, and R. Karl Hansen. 2015. Static 99R & Static 2002R Evaluators' Workbook. https://psychologyinterns.org/wp-content/uploads/Static-99RandStatic-2002R_EvaluatorsWorkbook-Jan2015.pdf

Plaisance, Kathryn S., and Kevin C. Elliott. 2021. A Framework for Analyzing Broadly Engaged Philosophy of Science. *Philosophy of Science, 88*(4), 594–615. https://doi.org/10.1086/713891

Poon, Kai-Tak, and Fei Teng. 2017. Feeling Unrestricted by Rules: Ostracism Promotes Aggressive Responses. *Aggressive Behavior, 43,* 558–567. https://doi.org/10.1002/ab.21714

Prescott, David S., Gwenda Willis, and Tony Ward. 2022. Monitoring Therapist Fidelity to the Good Lives Model (GLM). *International Journal of Offender Therapy and Comparative Criminology, 68*(1), 131–147. https://doi.org/10.1177/0306624X22 1086572

Pritchard, Colin, and Elizabeth King. 2005. Differential Suicide Rates in Typologies of Child Sex Offenders in a 6-Year Consecutive Cohort of Male Suicides. *Archives of Suicide Research, 9*, 35–43. https://doi.org/10.1080/13811110590512903

Prostasia Foundation. n.d.a. Prostasia Foundation. Accessed January 5, 2024. https://prostasia.org/

Prostasia Foundation. n.d.b. Map Support Club. Accessed January 5, 2024. https://prostasia.org/project/map-support-club/

Przybylski, Roger. 2015. Recidivism of Adult Sex Offenders. *National Criminal Justice Association.* https://smart.ojp.gov/sites/g/files/xyckuh231/files/media/document/recidivismofadultsexualoffenders.pdf

Rahman, Qazi, and Glenn D. Wilson. 2003. Born Gay? The Psychobiology of Human Sexual Orientation. *Personality and Individual Differences, 34*(8), 1337–1382. https://doi.org/10.1016/S0191-8869(02)00140-X

Rancher, Caitlin, Ernest N. Jouriles, Emily Johnson, Katrina Cook, and Renee McDonald. 2019. Self-Blame for Interpersonal Conflict Among Female Adolescents Who Have Been Sexually Abused. *Journal of Family Psychology, 33*(8), 982–987. http://dx.doi.org/10.1037/fam0000539.

Raphael, Lutz. 2012. Embedding the Human and Social Sciences in Western Societies, 1880–1980: Reflections on Trends and Methods of Current Research. In *Engineering Society: The Role of Human and Social Sciences in Modern Societies, 1880–1980,* Edited by Kerstin Brückweh, Dirk Schumann, Richard F. Wetzell, and Benjamin Zieman. Basingstroke, UK: Palgrave McMillan. https://doi.org/10.1057/9781137284501_2

Reichman, Nancy E., Julian O. Teitler, Irwin Garfinkel, and Sara S. McLanahan. 2001. Fragile Families: Sample and Design. *Children and Youth Services Review, 23*(4/5), 303–326. https://doi.org/10.1016/S0190-7409(01)00141-4

Rice, Marnie E., Grant T. Harris, Carol Lang, and Catherine Cormier. 2006. Violent Sex Offenses: How Are They Best Measured from Official Records? *Law and Human Behavior, 30*(4), 525–541. https://doi.org/10.1007/s10979-006-9022-3

Richardson, R. C. February, 2020. A Maidservant's Lot. www.historytoday.com/archive/maidservants-lot

Righthand, Sue, and Carlann Welch. 2004. Characteristics of Youth Who Sexually Offend. *Journal of Child Sexual Abuse, 3*(3/4), 15–32. https://doi.org/10.1300/J070v13n03_02

Rimer, Jonah R., and Karen Holt. 2023. "It Was in Control of Me": Notions of Addiction and Online Child Sexual Exploitation Material Offending. *Sexual Abuse, 35*(1), 3–30. https://doi.org/10.1177/10790632211070797

Rind, Bruca, Philip Tromovitch, and Robert Bauserman. 1998. A Meta-Analytic Examination of Assumed Properties of Child Sexual Abuse Using College Samples. *Psychological Bulletin, 124*(1), 22–53. http://dx.doi.org/10.1037/0033-2909.124.1.22

Risto, Inka, et al. 2018. Pedophilic Sex Offenders Are Characterized by Reduced GABA Concentration in the Dorsal Anterior Cingulate Gyrex. *Neuroimage: Clinical, 18*, 335–341. http://dx.doi.org/10.1016/j.nicl.2018.01.018

Robertson, Stephen. 2002. Age of Consent Law and the Making of Modern Childhood in New York City, 1886–1921. *Journal of Social History*, *35*(4), 781–798. http://dx.doi.org/10.1353/jsh.2002.0059

Rokeach, Ami. 2000. Offence Type and the Experience of Loneliness. *International Journal of Offender Therapy and Comparative Criminology*, *44*(5), 549–563. https://doi.org/10.1177/0306624X00445003

Rosik, Christopher H., and Paul Popper. 2014. Clinical Approaches to Conflicts Between Religious Values and Same-Sex Attractions: Contrasting Gay-Affirmative, Sexual Identity, and Change-Oriented Models of Therapy. *Counseling and Values*, *59*, 222–237. https://doi.org/10.1002/j.2161-007X.2014.00053.x

Ross, Robert R., and James Hilborn. 2008. *Rehabilitating Rehabilitation: Neurocriminology for Treatment of Antisocial Behavior*. Ottawa: Cognitive Centers of Canada.

Ryan, Caitlin, Russell B. Toomey, Rafael M. Diaz, and Stephen T. Russell. 2020. Parent-Initiated Sexual Orientation Change Efforts with LGBT Adolescents: Implications for Young Adult Mental Health and Adjustment. *Journal of Homosexuality*, *67*(2), 159–173. https://doi.org/10.1080/00918369.2018.1538407

Ryan, Miriam, Mathew McCauley, and Davine Walsh. 2019. The Virtuous Circle: A Grounded Theory Exploration of the Good Lives Model. *Sexual Abuse*, *31*(8), 908–929. https://doi.org/10.1177/1079063218780730

Schaefer, Adelle, Alexander Wittenberg, Igor Galynker, and Lisa J. Cohen. 2022. Qualitative Analysis of Minor-Attracted Persons' Subjective Experience: Implications for Treatment. *Journal of Sex & Marital Therapy*, *49*(4), 391–411. https://doi.org/10.1080/0092623X.2022.2126808

Schalkwijk, Frans, Patrick Luyten, Theo Ingenhoven, and Jack Dekker. 2021. Narcissistic Personality Disorder: Are Psychodynamic Theories and the Alternative DSM-5 Model for Personality Disorders Finally Going to Meet? *Frontiers in Psychology*, *12*, Article, 676733. https://psycnet.apa.org/doi/10.3389/fpsyg.2021.676733

Scheuerman, Heather L. 2018. Understanding Shame: Examining How Justice and Emotions Operate in the Context of Restorative Justice. *Sociology Compass*, *12*, e12561. https://doi.org/10.1111/soc4.12561

Serovich, Julianne M., Shannon M. Craft, Paula Toviessi, Rashmi Gangamma, Tiffany McDowell, and Erika L. Grafsky. 2008. A Systematic Review of the Research Base on Sexual Orientation Therapies. *Journal of Marital and Family Therapy*, *34*, 227–238. https://doi.org/10.1111/j.1752-0606.2008.00065.x

Seto, Michael. 2012. Is Pedophilia a Sexual Orientation? *Archives of Sexual Behavior*, *41*, 231–236. https://doi.org/10.1007/s10508-011-9882-6

Seto, Michael. 2017. The Puzzle of Male Chronophilias. *Archives of Sexual Behavior*, *46*, 3–22. https://doi.org/10.1007/s10508-016-0799-y

Sex Addicts Anonymous [SAA]. n.d. Sex Addicts Anonymous. Accessed January 5, 2024. https://saa-recovery.org/our-program/

Shaffer, Howard J. 2012. *APA Addiction Syndrome Handbook* (Editor). Washington, DC: American Psychological Association.

Shedler, Jonathan. 2018. Where Is the Evidence for "Evidence-Based" Therapy? *Psychiatric Clinics of North America*, *41*, 319–329. http://dx.doi.org/10.1016/j.psc.2018.02.001

Simeone, Stephanie. 2018. *The Effects of Media Exposure on Perceptions of Residence Restrictions*. CUNY Academic Works. https://academicworks.cuny.edu/jj_etds/60/

Sinanan, Allison N. 2011. The Impact of Child, Family, and Child Protective Services Factors on Reports of Child Sexual Abuse Recurrence. *Journal of Child Sexual Abuse*, *20*, 657–673. http://dx.doi.org/10.1080/10538712.2011.622354

Skinner, Burhus E. 1953. *Science and Human Behavior*. New York: McMillan.

Sliva, Shannon M. 2017. A Tale of Two States: How U.S. State Legislatures Consider Restorative Justice Policies. *Contemporary Justice Review, 20*(2), 255–273. https://doi.org/10.1080/10282580.2017.1307111

Smaal, Yorick. 2013a. Historical Perspectives on Child Sexual Abuse, Part 1. *History Compass, 11*(9), 702–714. https://doi.org/10.1111/hic3.12083

Smaal, Yorick. 2013b. Historical Perspectives on Child Sexual Abuse, Part 2. *History Compass, 11*(9), 715–726. https://doi.org/10.1111/hic3.12073

Small, Jamie L. 2015. Classing Sex Offenders: How Prosecutors and Defense Attorneys Differentiate Men Accused of Sexual Assault. *Law & Society Review, 49*(1), 109–141. https://doi.org/10.1111/lasr.12126

Smethurst, Alex J., Jennifer Bamford, and Ruth J. Tully. 2021. A Systematic Review of Recidivism Rates of Older Adult Male Sex Offenders. *Applied Psychology in Criminal Justice, 16*(1), 23–51. https://apcj.shsu.edu/journal/index.php?mode=view&item=159

Socia, Kelly M. Jr., and Janet P. Stamatel. 2010. Assumptions and Evidence behind Sex Offender Laws: Registration, Community Notification, and Residence Restrictions. *Sociology Compass, 4*(1), 1–20. https://doi.org/10.1111/j.1751-9020.2009.00251.x

Solin, Cynthia A. 1986. Displacement of Affect in Families Following Incest Disclosure. *American Journal of Orthopsychiatry, 56*(40), 570–576. https://doi.org/10.1111/j.1939-0025.1986.tb03489.x

Speer, Paul W., and Brian D. Christens. 2013. An Approach to Scholarly Impact through Strategic Engagement in Community-Based Research. *Journal of Social Issues, 69*(4), 734–753. https://doi.org/10.1111/josi.12039

Spitzer, Robert L. 2003. Can Some Gay Men and Lesbians Change Their Sexual Orientation? 200 Participants Reporting a Change from Homosexual to Heterosexual Orientation. *Archives of Sexual Behavior, 32*(5), 403–417. https://doi.org/10.1023/A:1025647527010

Spitzer, Robert L. 2012. Spitzer Reassesses His 2003 Study of Reparative Therapy of Homosexuality. *Archives of Sexual Behavior, 41*, 757. https://doi.org/10.1007/s10508-012-9966-y

Sproul, Jana. 2021. The Sun Only Sets on Their Dreams: Tracing the Origins and Impacts of Child Sexual Exploitation and Tourism in the Caribbean. *Caribbean Quarterly: A Journal of Caribbean Culture, 67*(4), 427–452. https://doi.org/10.1080/00086495.2021.1996013

Steans, Jennifer, and Simon Duff. Perceptions of Sex Offenders with Intellectual Disabilities: A Comparison of Forensic Staff and the General Public. *Journal of Applied Research in Intellectual Disabilities, 33*(4), 711–719. https://doi.org/10.1111/jar.12467

Steely, Molly, Tusty Ten Bensel, Tabrina Bratton, and Robert Lytle. 2018. All Part of the Process? A Qualitative Examination of Change in Online Child Pornography Behaviors. *Criminal Justice Studies, 31*(3), 279–296. https://doi.org/10.1080/1478601X.2018.1492389

Stevens, Eleanor, and Jane Wood. 2019. "I Despise Myself for Thinking About Them": A Thematic Analysis of the Mental Health Implications and Employed Coping Mechanisms of Self-Reported Non-Offending Minor Attracted Persons. *Journal of Child Sexual Abuse, 28*(8), 968–989. https://doi.org/10.1080/10538712.2019.1657539

Stevens, Richard. 2008. *Sigmund Freud: Examining the Essence of His Contribution*. New York: MacMillan.

Stevenson, Kim. 2017. 'Not Just the Ideas of a Few Enthusiasts': Early Twentieth Century Legal Activism and Reformation of the Age of Sexual Consent. *Cultural and Social History*, *14*(2), 219–236. https://doi.org/10.1080/14780038.2017.1290999

Stinson, Jill D., Bruce D. Sales, and Judith V. Becker. 2008. *Sex Offending: Causal Theories to Inform Research, Prevention, and Treatment*. Washington, DC: American Psychological Association.

Stroup, Brandon. 2019. Conceptualizing and Implementing a Restorative Justice Concentration: Transforming the Criminal Justice Curriculum. *Contemporary Justice Review*, *22*(4), 334–350. https://doi.org/10.1080/10282580.2019.1672046

Sullins, D. Paul, Christopher H. Rosik, and Paul Santero. 2021. Efficacy and Risk of Sexual Orientation Change Efforts: A Retrospective Analysis of 125 Exposed Men. *PubMed*. https://doi.org/10.12688/f1000research.51209.2

Summerscale, Kate. 2023. From Clowns to Kayaks: A History of Fear and Loathing. *BBC History Magazine*, *24*(2), 29–32. https://pocketmags.com/bbc-history-magaz ine/february-2023/articles/1258653/from-clowns-to-kayaks-a-history-of-fear-and-loathing#exitplusarticle

Suprina, Jeffrey S., et al. 2019. Best Practices in Cross-Cultural Counseling: The Intersection of Spiritual/Religious Identity and Affectional/Sexual Identity. *Journal of LGBT Issues in Counseling*, *13*(4), 293–325. https://doi.org/10.1080/15538 605.2019.1662360

Tambe, Ashwini. 2020. The Moral Standards of Age Hierarchies: The UN Debates a Common Minimum Marriage Age, 1951–1962. *The American Historical Review*, *125*(2), 451–459. https://doi.org/10.1093/ahr/rhaa191

Tan, Erica S. N., and Mark A. Yarhouse. 2010. Facilitating Congruence between Religious Beliefs and Sexual Identity with Mindfulness. *Psychotherapy: Theory, Research, Practice, Training*, *47*(4), 500–511. http://dx.doi.org/10.1037/a0022081

Tener, Dafna. 2018. The Secret of Intrafamilial Child Sexual Abuse: Who Keeps It and How? *Journal of Child Sexual Abuse*, *27*(1), 1–21. https://doi.org/10.1080/10538 712.2017.1390715

Tener, Dafna, Efrat Lusky, Noam Tarshish, and Shosh Turjeman. 2018. Parental Attitudes Following Disclosure of Sibling Sexual Abuse: A Child Advocacy Intervention Center Study. *American Journal of Orthopsychiatry*, *88*(6), 661–669. http://dx.doi. org/10.1037/ort0000311

Testa, Megan, and Sara G. West. 2010. Civil Commitment in the United States. *Psychiatry (Edgemont)*, *7*(10), 30–40. https://doi.org/10(2010):30-40

Thomas, Calvin. 2009. On Being Post-Normal: Heterosexuality after Queer Theory. In *The Ashgate Research Companion to Queer Theory*, Noreen Giffney and Michael O'Rourke (Eds.). New York: Routledge. www.researchgate.net/publication/2924 75858_On_being_post-normal_Heterosexuality_after_queer_theory

Thomas, Sandra P. 2014. The Deepest, Darkest Secret. *Issues in Mental Health Nursing*, *35*, 321–322. https://doi.org/10.3109/01612840.2014.899303

Thompson, Cheryl W. August 25, 2020. Sex Offender Registries Often Fail Those They Are Designed to Protect. *NPR*. All Things Considered. https://one.npr.org/?shared MediaId=808229392:905927007

Thompson, Sarah. 2014. Sexting Prosecutions: Minors as a Protected Class from Child Pornography Charges. *University of Michigan Journal of Law Reform Caveat*, *48*(1). https://repository.law.umich.edu/mjlr_caveat/vol48/iss1/2/

Thorstad, David. 1991. Man/Boy Love and the American Gay Movement. *Journal of Homosexuality*, *20*(1/2), 251–274. https://doi.org/10.1300/J082v20n01_15

Toledo, Annikvan, and Fred Seymour. 2016. Caregiver Needs Following Disclosure of Child Sexual Abuse. *Journal of Child Sexual Abuse*, 25(4), 403–414. https://doi.org/10.1080/10538712.2016.1156206

Torrey, E. Fuller, Aaron D. Kennard, Don Eslinger, Richard Lamb, and James Pavie. 2010. *More Mentally Ill Persons Are in Jails and Prisons Than Hospitals: A Survey of the States*. Arlington, VA: Treatment Advocacy Center and National Sheriff's Association. www.sheriffs.org/sites/default/files/uploads/Final%20Jails%20v%Hospitals%20Study.pdf

Toulalan, Sarah. 2014. "Is He a Licentious Lewd Sort of Person?": Constructing the Child Rapist in Early Modern England. *Journal of the History of Sexuality*, 23(1), 21–52. https://doi.org/10.7560/JHS23102

Tovey, Laura, Belinda Winder, and Nicholas Blagden. 2023. "It's OK if You were In for Robbery or Murder, but Sex Offending, That's a No-No": A Qualitative Analysis of the Experiences of 12 Men with Sexual Convictions Seeking Employment. *Psychology, Crime, & Law*, 29(6), 653–673. https://doi.org/10.1080/1068316X.2022.2030736

Trammel, Rebecca, and Scott Chenault. 2009. "We Have to Take These Guys Out." Motivations for Assaulting Incarcerated Child Molesters. *Symbolic Interactions*, 32(4), 334–350. https://doi.org/10.1525/si.2009.32.4.334

Treat, Sarah, Patricia Vanhook, Lenee Hendrix, Kelsey Wallace, and Judy McCook. 2022. Responding to the Challenges and Barriers Unique to Rural Appalachian Sexual Assault Nurse Examiner Programs. *Journal of Forensic Nursing*, 18(3), 139–145. https://doi.org/10.1097/jfn.0000000000000388

Trottier, Daniel. 2018. Coming to Terms with Shame: Exploring Mediated Visibility Against Transgressions. *Surveillance & Society*, 16(2), 170–182. https://doi.org/10.24908/ss.v16i2.6811

Tully, Ruth J., Shihning Chou, and Kevin D. Browne. 2013. A Systematic Review on the Effectiveness of Sex Offender Risk Assessment Tools in Predicting Sexual Recidivism in Adult Male Sex Offenders. *Clinical Psychology Review*, 33, 287–316. https://doi.org/10.1016/j.cpr.2012.12.002

Turner, Heather A., David Finkelhor, Sherry L. Hamby, and Anne Shattuck. 2013. Family Structure, Victimization, and Child Mental Health in a Nationally Representative Sample. *Social Science and Medicine*, 87, 39–51. https://doi.org/10.1016/j.socscimed.2013.02.034

Turney, Kristin, and Rebecca Goodsell. 2018. Parental Incarceration and Children's Wellbeing: Findings from the Fragile Families and Child Well-being Study. *The Future of Children*, 28, 147–164. https://psycnet.apa.org/doi/10.1007/978-3-030-16707-3_5

Turney, Kristin, and Sarah Halpern-Meekin. 2021. Incarceration and Family Instability: Considering Relationship Churning. *Journal of Marriage and the Family*, 83, 1287–1309. https://doi.org/10.1111/jomf.12794

Uggen, Christopher, Jeff Manza, and Angela Behrens. 2004. 'Less Than Average Citizen': Stigma, Role Transition, and the Civic Reintegration of Clandestine Felons. In *After Crime and Punishment: Pathways to Offender Reintegration*, Shadd Marune and Russell Immarigeon (Eds.). Portland, OR: Willan Publishing. http://dx.doi.org/10.4324/9781843924203

Uggen, Christopher, and Suzy McElrath. 2014. Parental Incarceration: What We Know and Where We Need to Go. *The Journal of Law and Criminology*, 104(3), 597–604. https://scholarlycommons.law.northwestern.edu/jclc/vol104/iss3/3/

U.S. Department of Justice, Bureau of Justice Statistics. 2003. Recidivism of Sex Offenders Released from Prison in 1994. https://bjs.ojp.gov/content/pub/pdf/rsorp94.pdf

Van Langenhove, Luke. 2012. Global Issues: Make Social Sciences Relevant. *Nature, 484,* 442. http://dx.doi.org/10.1038/484442a

Vandiver, Donna, Jeremy Braithwaite, and Mark Stafford. 2017. *Sex Crimes and Sex Offenders.* New York: Routledge.

Venables, Noah C., Jens Foell, James R. Yancey, Kevin M. Beaver, William G. Iacono, and Christopher G. Patrick. 2018. Integrating Criminological and Mental Health Perspectives on Low Self-Control: A Multi-Domain Analysis. *Journal of Criminal Justice, 56,* 2–10. https://doi.org/10.1016/j.jcrimjus.2017.10.004

Vilvens, Heather L., David E. Jones, and Lisa M. Vaughn. 2021. Exploring the Recovery of Non-Offending Parents after a Child's Sexual Abuse Event. *Journal of Child and Family Studies, 30,* 2690–2704. https://doi.org/10.1007/s10826-021-02082-3

Virtuous Pedophiles. n.d. About Us / Mission Statement. Accessed January 5, 2024. https://virped.org/aboutvp/ and https://virped.org/mission/

Vladimir, Marina, and Derek Robertson, 2020. The Lived Experiences of Non-Offending Fathers with Children Who Survived Sexual Abuse. *Journal of Child Sexual Abuse, 29*(3), 312–332. https://doi.org/10.1080/10538712.2019.1620396

von Krafft-Ebing, Richard. 2011. *Psychopathia Sexualis: The Classic Study of Deviant Sex.* Translated by Franklin S. Klaf. New York: Skyhorse Publishing.

Waldram, James B. 2009. "It's You and Satan, Hanging Out at a Pre-School": Notions of Evil and the Rehabilitation of Sexual Offenders. *Anthropology and Humanism, 34*(2), 219–234. http://dx.doi.org/10.1111/j.1548-1409.2009.01039.x

Walgrave, Lode, Tony Ward, and Estelle Zinsstag. 2021. When Restorative Justice Meets the Good Lives Model: Contributing to a Criminology of Trust. *European Journal of Criminology, 18*(3), 444–460. https://doi.org/10.1177/1477370819854174

Walker, Allyn, Robert P. Butters, and Erin Nichols. 2022. "I Would Report It Even If They Have Not Committed Anything": Social Service Students' Attitudes toward Minor-Attracted People. *Sexual Abuse, 34*(1), 52–77. https://doi.org/10.1177/1079063221993480

Walsh, Anthony. 1984. Differential Sentencing Patterns among Felony Offenders and Non-Sex Offenders. *The Journal of Criminal Law and Criminology, 75*(2), 443–458. https://doi.org/10.2307/1143162

Ward, Tony. 2002. Good Lives and the Rehabilitation of Offenders: Promises and Problems. *Aggression and Violent Behavior, 7*(5), 513–528. http://dx.doi.org/10.1016/S1359-1789(01)00076-3

Ward, Tony, and Karen Salmon. 2011. The Ethics of Care and Treatment of Sex Offenders. *Sexual Abuse: A Journal of Research and Treatment, 23*(3), 379–413. https://doi.org/10.1177/1079063210382049

Ward, Tony, and Claire Stewart. 2003. The Treatment of Sex Offenders: Risk Management and Good Lives. *Professional Psychology: Research and Practice, 34*(4), 353–360. http://dx.doi.org/10.1037/0735-7028.34.4.353

Ware, Jason, Andrew Frost, and Anna Hay. 2010. A Review of the Use of Therapeutic Communities with Sexual Offenders. *International Journal of Offender Therapy and Comparative Criminology, 54*(5), 721–742. https://doi.org/10.1177/0306624X09343169

Weaver, Paul. 1998. *News and the Culture of Lying: How Journalism Really Works.* New York: The Free Press.

Weir, John. August 23, 1994. Mad About the Boys. *The Advocate, 34–37*, 661–662. http://advocate.com

Western, Bruce, and Becky Pettit. 2010. Incarceration and Social Inequality. *Daedalus: Journal of the American Academy of Arts and Sciences, 139*(3). www.amacad.org/publication/incarceration-social-inequality

Whiffen, Valerie E., and Heather Beth McIntosh. 2005. Mediators of the Link Between Childhood Sexual Abuse and Emotional Distress: A Critical Review. *Trauma, Violence, & Abuse, 6*(1), 24–39. http://doi.org/10.1177/1524838004272543.

Wikipedia. n.d. Airplane!. Accessed September 4, 2023. https://en.wikipedia.org/wiki/Airplane!/

Wikipedia. n.d.b. Chester the Molester. Accessed September 4, 2023. https://en.wikipedia.org/wiki/Chester_the_Molester/

Wikipedia. n.d.c. To Catch A Predator. Accessed October 30, 2023. https://en.wikipedia.org/wiki/To_Catch_a_Predator/

Wildeman, Christopher. 2010. Paternal Incarceration and Children's Physically Aggressive Behaviors: Evidence from the Fragile Families and Child Wellbeing Study. *Social Forces, 81*(1), 285–310. http://dx.doi.org/10.2307/40927563

Wilkinson, Deave J., and Amy Johnson. 2020. A Systematic Review of Qualitative Studies Capturing the Subjective Experiences of Gay and Lesbian Individuals of Faith or Religious Affiliation. *Mental Health, Religion, and Culture, 23*(1), 80–95. https://doi.org/10.1080/13674676.2020.1724919

Williams, Kipling D., Christopher I. Ekchardt, and Molly A. Maloney. 2021. Attending to the Ignored: Clinical Implications of Social Psychological Research on Ostracism. *Zeitschrift für Psychologie, 228*(3), 148–153. http://dx.doi.org/10.1027/2151-2604/a000446

Williams, Timothy. 2012. A Tribe's Epidemic of Child Sexual Abuse, Minimized for Years. www.nytimes.com/2012/09/20/us/us-steps-in-as-child-sex-abuse-pervades-sioux-tribe.html

Williamson-Kefu, Majon. 2018. Writing from Somewhere: Reflections on Positioning Research. *Journal of Intercultural Studies, 40*(1), 5–15. https://doi.org/10.1080/07256868.2018.1552570

Willis, Gwenda M., and Randolph C. Grace. 2008. The Quality of Community Reintegration Planning for Child Molesters: Effects on Sexual Recidivism. *Sexual Abuse: A Journal of Research and Treatment, 20*(2), 218–240. https://doi.org/10.1177/1079063208318005

Willis, Gwenda M., Jill S. Levenson, and Tony Ward. 2010. Desistance and Attitudes toward Sex Offenders: Facilitation or Hindrance? *Journal of Family Violence, 25*, 545–556. https://doi.org/10.1007/s10896-010-9314-8

Willis, Gwenda M., Tony Ward, and Jill S. Levenson. 2014. The Good Lives Model (GLM): An Evaluation of GLM Operationalization in North American Treatment Programs. *Sexual Abuse: A Journal of Research and Treatment, 26*(1), 58–81. https://doi.org/10.1177/1079063213478202

Willis, Gwenda M., Pamela M. Yates, Theresa A. Gannon, and Tony Ward. 2012. How to Integrate the Good Lives Model into Treatment Programs for Sexual Offending: An Introduction and Overview. *Sexual Abuse: A Journal of Research and Treatment, 25*(2), 123–142. https://doi.org/10.1177/1079063212452618

Wilpert, Julia, and Ellen Janssen. 2020. Characteristics of Offending and Non-Offending CSA Helpline Users Explored. *Journal of Forensic Practice, 22*(3), 173–183. http://dx.doi.org/10.1108/JFP-03-2020-0011

Winslade, John. 2019. Can Restorative Justice Promote Social Justice? *Contemporary Justice Review, 22*(3), 280–289. https://doi.org/10.1080/10282580.2019.1644173

Wolak, Janis, David Finkelhor, and Kimberly Mitchell. 2011. Child Pornography Possessors: Trends in Offending Case Characteristics. *Sexual Abuse: A Journal of Research and Treatment, 23*(1), 22–42. https://doi.org/10.1177/1079063210372143

Wolpe, Joseph. 1958. *Psychotherapy by Reciprocal Inhibition*. Stanford, CA: Stanford University Press.

Wormith, J. Stephen, and Alexandra M. Zidenberg. 2018. The Historical Roots, Current Status, and Future Applications of the Risk-Need-Responsivity Model (RNR). In *New Frontiers in Offender Treatment*, Elizabeth L. Jeglic and Cynthia Caulkins (Eds.). Springer, 11–41. https://doi.org/10.1007/978-3-030-01030-0_2

Wurtele, Sandy K., Dominique A. Simons, and Leah J. Parker. 2018. Understanding Men's Self-Reported Sexual Interest in Children. *Archives of Sexual Behavior, 47*, 2255–2264. https://doi.org/10.1007/s10508-018-1173-z

Yarhouse, Mark A. 2001. Sexual Identity Development: The Influence of Valuative Frameworks on Identity Synthesis. *Psychotherapy, 38*(3), 331–341. http://dx.doi.org/10.1037/0033-3204.38.3.331

Yarhouse, Mark A. 2008. Narrative Sexual Identity Therapy. *The American Journal of Family Therapy, 36*, 196–210. https://doi.org/10.1080/01926180701236498

Yarhouse, Mark A., and Erica S.-N. Tan. 2005. Addressing Religious Conflicts in Adolescents Who Experience Sexual Identity Confusion. *Professional Psychology: Research and Practice, 36*(5), 530–536. http://dx.doi.org/10.1037/0735-7028.36.5.530

Zatkin, Judith, Miranda Sitney, and Keith Kaufman. 2022. The Relationship between Policy, Media, and Perceptions of Sexual Offenders between 2007 and 2017: A Review of the Literature. *Trauma, Violence, & Abuse, 23*(3), 953–968. https://doi.org/10.1177/1524838020985568

Zehr, Howard. 2015. *The Little Book of Restorative Justice: Revised and Updated (Justice and Peacebuilding)*. https://livingjusticepress.org/product/little-book-of-restorative-justice/

Zezina, Mariie R. 2010. Without a Family: Orphans of the Postwar Period. *Russian Studies in History, 48*(4), 59–73. https://doi.org/10.2753/RSH1061-1983480404

Index

For Product Safety Concerns and Information please contact our EU
representative GPSR@taylorandfrancis.com
Taylor & Francis Verlag GmbH, Kaufingerstraße 24, 80331 München, Germany

www.ingramcontent.com/pod-product-compliance
Lightning Source LLC
Chambersburg PA
CBHW061254220326
41599CB00028B/5646